Recent Researches in Epigraphy and Numismatics

Recent Researches in Epigraphy and Numismatics

Edited by

Dr. Mahesh Kalra
Dr. Suraj A. Pandit

Kaveri Books
New Delhi-110002

First Published in 2018
ISBN 978-81-7479-218-1

Published by
Kaveri Books
4832/24, Ansari Road
New Delhi - 110 002 (India)
Tel.: 011-2328 8140, 4707 2321
E-mail: info@kaveribooks.com,
kaveribooks@gmail.com
Website: www.kaveribooks.com

Laser Typesetting by : Tamalika Computers, Delhi

PRINTED IN INDIA

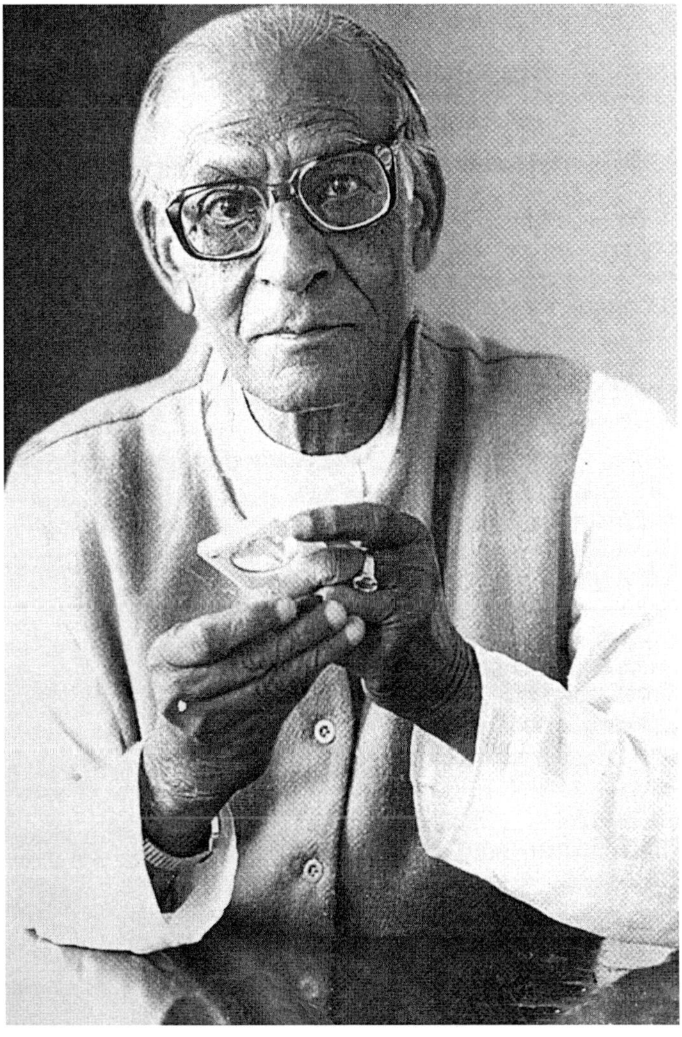

Dedicated to the revered memory

of

Dr. Parmeshwari Lal Gupta

(24 December 1914 - 29 July 2001)

Doyen of Indian Numismatics

Preface

This book is dedicated to the revered memory of Dr. Parmeshwari Lal Gupta (1914-2001), the doyen of Indian Numismatics who pioneered the study of Indian Numismatics in independent India with his book, 'COINS' published for the first time in 1969 by the National Book Trust of India as a befitting tribute to the two-and-half millennia of Indian Coinage from 6th century B.C.E. till modern period with unbroken continuity.

Dr. P. L. Gupta's unique contribution to Indian Numismatics was to string various coin series together for the first time since the study of Indian Numismatics began in the colonial period by the great orientalists from British civil and military cadre beginning with James Prinsep, Alexander Cunningham and in succession by numerous other Indian and British orientalists till India's independence in the middle of the twentieth century. However, most numismatists studied Indian numismatics as a set of series classified as local or imperial series, ancient, medieval or modern or based on dynasties of various periods of India's long history. It was Dr. P. L. Gupta's unique contribution of connecting these heterogenous series as pearls with a string to form the necklace of Indian Numismatics. Another major contribution of Dr. P. L. Gupta was to mentor a whole generation of numismatic researchers with focus on only academic study of Indian coinages with a firm emphasis on mastering scripts, coin types and various other features of Indian coin series.

Dr. P. L. Gupta's book 'COINS' has been a beacon of light to many generations of students of History and Numismatics, usually serving a first work of introduction to a subject of gigantic proportions related to India's tradition of continuous issuing of coins of different types for over two-and-half-millennia. Though termed as 'outdated' in some quarters, the book is yet to be replaced by another standard work of reference despite almost five decades since it first appeared. Its continued publication and popularity remains undented and yet it is a very simplistic work on a subject easily understood by the uninitiated. Thus, in 2015, a group of interested numismatic researchers came together to honour Dr. P. L. Gupta's unique legacy of academic numismatics and commemorate his 101st Birth

Anniversary as the National Numismatic Day in India on 24 December 2015. A small function was organized at the Centre for Extra-Mural Studies (CEMS), University of Mumbai where a 'Silver Coin' was released on the occasion minted with Dr. P. L. Gupta's portrait and inscription in Persian to honour the great personality.

The first National Numismatic Conference (NAT NUM CONF 2016) was held after gauging the fantastic response to the first National Numismatic Day held in 2015. The Nat Num Conf' 2016 was a reasonable success with 35 paper presentations (of which 23 papers are published in this volume) during the Conference held with Dr. Sanjay Garg as the President of Nat Num Conf. Nat Num Conf 2016 had three Numismatic Sections with the Ancient Section headed by Dr. Susmita Basu-Majumdar, Kolkata University; Dr. Garg helming the Medieval India Section and Mr. Bazil Shaikh, Ex-Reserve Bank of India heading the Modern Numismatics Section. The Epigraphy Section had Dr. Anuradha Ranade as Section President. Though Nat Num Conf 2016 did not have a formal Archaeology and History Sessions, the conference had a paper on Archaeology and Numismatics by Dr. Kurush F. Dalal and History-based articles in all sections.

Nat Num Conf 2016's success was possible due to the fantastic support, we received from Dr. Kavita Rege, Principal of Sathaye College. The team of CHAEN consisting of Mr. Venkitachalam Iyer (Venki), Chaitanya Bhide, Mohit Kapoor and Milind Vora was the biggest support in planning and executing the Conference to the minutest detail. The other biggest support was the team of volunteers from the Ancient Indian Culture Department at Sathaye College led by Prof. Radha Sabnis, Dr. Milind Paradkar, Ms. Shamika Sarvankar and Ms. Nishigandha Usapkar. A special thanks to Dr. Sanjay Garg and Mrs. Nurussaba Garg, Dr. Dilip Balsekar, Executive Editor, Maharashtra State Gazetteer and Dr. Arvind Jamkhedkar, ex-Director, Maharashtra State Department of Museums and Archaeology for guiding the Nat Num Conf 2016 to its successful conclusion.

Last but not the least, we thank Dr. P. L. Gupta's family consisting of his sons, Shri Santosh Kumar and Shri Ashok Kumar Gupta and his grandsons, Shri Punit Kumar Gupta and Shri Sunit Kumar Gupta for their unstinted support and sage advice at all stages of the conference. We also thank the Board and Trustees of Gopaldas Guldavadi Devi Memorial Trust (created by Dr. P. L. Gupta in the memory of his parents) for sponsoring three Cash Prizes, each of 5000 INR in the memory of Dr. P. L. Gupta with the name 'Dr. P. L. Gupta Best Paper in Ancient Numismatics' (awarded to Mr. Sandip Pan), 'Dr. P. L. Gupta Best Paper in Modern Numismatics' (awarded to Mr. Raamesh Gowri Raghavan) and 'Dr. P. L. Gupta Best Paper in Epigraphy' (awarded to Dr. Ambarish Khare).

– Editors

Contents

List of Contributors

Abhick Sarkar, M.Phil. (Ancient Indian History and Culture), University of Calcutta; abhick.babai@gmail.com

Dr. Ambarish V. Khare, Asst. Professor of Sanskrit, SBL Centre of Sanskrit and Indological Studies, Tilak Maharashtra Vidyapeeth, 1242 Sadashiv Peth, Pune- 411 030; avkhare@gmail.com

Anand Kanitkar, M. A. Indology, Master of Cultural Landscapes, C1/401, Shivasagar City, Phase I, Suncity Road, Off Sinhgad Road, Pune - 411 051; Email: kanitkaranand@gmail.com

Dr. Anuradha K. Ranade, Principal, DSPM's K. V. Pendharkar College, Dombivali (E), Dist. Thane, Maharashtra; anuradharanade17@gmail.com

Adv. Ashok Shahani, M.A. M.Com. L.L.B., 1-A, Shiv Ratan, Road No. 2, 45, Sion (East), Mumbai - 400022; sagsim@rediffmail.com

Chaitanya Bhide, Dept. of Extra-Mural Studies, University of Mumbai, Kalina Mumbai 400097; chaitu.bhide@gmail.com

Harshada Wirkud, Research Scholar, Deccan College, Post Graduate and Research Institute, Deemed University, Pune - 411 006; Email: harshsaaz7@gmail.com

Dr. Kurush F. Dalal, Asst. Prof. (Archaeology) & Director (Field Archaeology), Dept. of Extra-Mural Studies, University of Mumbai, Kalina, Mumbai 400 097; kurushdalal@gmail.com

Dr. Mahesh A. Kalra, Director, Centre for Numismatic Information & Studies (CENNUMIS), C/1804, Lake Pleasant, Phase 2, Chandivali Farm Road, Powai, Mumbai - 400 076; drkalra1@gmail.com

Dr. Manjiri Bhalerao, Associate Professor, SBL Centre of Sanskrit and Indological Studies, Tilak Maharashtra Vidyapeeth, 1242 Sadashiv Peth, Pune- 411 030; manjiri24@gmail.com

Dr. Milind Paradkar, Director, Horizon, 702, Alaknanda, Plot No. 66, Sector 17, Kalamboli, Navi Mumbai 410218; discover.horizon@gmail.com.

Mukesh Sharma, Research Assistant, The Indian Institute of Research in Numismatic Studies, Anjaneri, Nasik, Maharashtra; mukesh.kmc@gmail.com

Dr. Prachi Moghe, Asst. Director (Post-Graduate & Research Department), Bharatiya Vidya Bhavan, Mumbai - 400 007; prachiamoghe@gmail.com

Raamesh Gowri Raghavan, 2/23, Vijay Enclave, Waghbil Naka, Ghodbunder Road, Thane 400615 INDIA; iambecomedeath@gmail.com

Sandip Pan, Research Assistant, The Indian Institute of Research in Numismatic Studies, Anjaneri, Nasik, Maharashtra; sandippan90@gmail.com

Dr. Sanjay Garg, Deputy Director, National Archives of India, New Delhi - 110001; sgarg30@hotmail.com

Shamika Sarvankar, Deccan College, Post Graduate and Research Institute, Deemed University, Pune - 411 006; shamikasarvankar27@gmail.com

Soumya Ghosh, M. Phil Student, Dept. of Ancient Indian History and Culture, University of Calcutta; soumya.hist@gmail.com

Sreemanti Laha, M.Phil. Research Fellows, Department of Ancient Indian History & Culture, University of Calcutta; twinka180292@gmail.com

Dr. Suraj A. Pandit, Head of Department, Ancient Indian Culture, Buddhist Studies, Sathaye College, Dixit Road, Vile Parle (East), Mumbai 400 057; surajpanditkanheri@gmail.com

Suvasree Chatterjee, M.Phil. Research Fellows, Department of Ancient Indian History & Culture, University of Calcutta; suvasree.chatt9@gmail.com

Venkichatalam Iyer, Dept. of Extra-Mural Studies, University of Mumbai, Kalina, Mumbai 400097; vinuiyer84@gmail.com

Presidential Address

Dr. Sanjay Garg

Dear Friends,

It is indeed a privilege for me to join you all in this unique numismatic Conference – which presents a distinctive blend of young and senior academics together with a diverse group of people who are passionate about coins, and about history in general, who have assembled here from far and wide. At the outset I would like to thank the organizers – Dr. Mahesh Kalra, Director, Centre for Numismatic Information & Studies (CENNUMIS) and Convenor, Centre for History, Archaeology, Epigraphy & Numismatics (CHAEN), together with Dr. Suraj Pandit, and all other members of the Organising Committee for choosing me to preside over the First National Numismatic Conference being held here at Mumbai.

In the beginning I said that this is a unique Conference. What is so unique about this conference? Many conferences and symposia are being held in various parts of India and around the world, practically on each day of the year. What makes this Conference unique is that this is the first ever Conference that is dedicated to the memory of the man who has contributed so much to the field of Indian numismatic studies. Dr. Parmeshwari Lal Gupta's contributions to this field ranged from the Punch-Marked Coins to Paper Money. He institutionalized the numismatic research in India, and in his own Gandhian way, never claimed credit for any of his contributions. I, therefore, congratulate the organizers, especially Dr Mahesh Kalra, who have worked tirelessly over the past many months to have us all here on the occasion of 102nd birth anniversary of Dr Gupta. Let us, therefore, begin this Conference by paying our collective homage to the memory of Dr Gupta.

Let me start by giving you a bit of background ş both about myself and also about my address to you this morning. Unlike most of you, my first introduction to numismatics was not through coins but through history books, where in one of the preliminary chapters, the sources of history are described, and, as it were, the numismatic sources are invariably summed up in a few lines. At that time like many students of my age, I did not realize what a tremendous amount of historical data these small metallic pieces hold.

I was fortunate enough to have my initial lessons in numismatics from the doyen of this field, Dr. Parmeshwari Lal Gupta, and whatever little I have been able to contribute to this discipline through my academic writings and presentations, is a tribute to his grooming.

Regarding Dr Gupta, many of you would be knowing much more than myself. Born on 24 Dec 1914, as an academician he distinguished himself as an acclaimed numismatist, historian, epigraphist, linguist, litterateur, and museologist. His published works, however, are not confined these disciplines but also include works on art and archaeology, sigillography, Political Science, Sociology, Law and popular Science. Dr Gupta also left his indelible mark on the sand of time as a freedom fighter, educationist, journalist and institution builder.

When I was approached to speak at this august assemblage I had initially thought of a topic based on coins of medieval India where use of coins in reconstructing history could be demonstrated, and which would have evinced interest of the numismatists, coin collectors as well as of the historians. However, since the Section President for the session on Medieval Indian numismatics, Prof. Ejaz Hussain could not attend this conference, I shall be chairing that session in his stead and I reserve my comments on medieval Indian numismatics for that occasion.

Accordingly, within the allotted time, and in my own limited way, I propose to encapsulate the vision of Dr. P. L. Gupta as far as the numismatic studies are concerned and try to draw the attention of the young scholars attending this Conference towards various dimensions of the numismatic research.

I

Numismatics, or 'the study of coins and medals' (OED) grew out as an academic discipline in Europe during the 16th-17th century out of an attempt to understand and organize the coin collected by various individuals and museums as curio pieces. Today, it covers a vast variety of currencies and coins of the past, ranging from the primitive money - from cattle, animal hides, salt, tools like arrow-heads, axes and knives; and the cowrie shells to metallic coins, paper banknotes, and today's electronic currency. In addition it also studies medals and tokens, in what is sometimes referred to as 'para numismatics'.

For reconstruction of history, the importance of the numismatic sources is too well known to be repeated here. 'Coins are primary evidence in all periods of history, but as we approach modern times this role becomes less and less important...'[1]. Nevertheless, the coins serve variously as corrective, supplementary, corroborative, or, at times, sole event of a historical event. I will fortify this fact by only one example from Indian context.

A very important chronological marker of the ancient Indian history is the invasion of Alexander in 326 BCE. Surprisingly, no ancient Indian text makes any mention of this event. All the historians of Alexander are from outside India and the earliest of whom, Strabo (64/63 BCE - c. 24 CE), was born about two-and-a-half centuries later! But then we have coins as the only contemporary visual account of the famous battle of Hydaspes fought between Alexander and King Porus of the Paurava kingdom. The names of a number of Indo-Greek rulers are known to us only through their coins. All this, and much more, you probably already know. I would, therefore, move on to sharing some thoughts about utilizing the numismatic sources as historical evidences.

For this purpose, it is important to realize the inter-dependence of numismatic studies and other disciplines. Here one of the crucial considerations is the provenance of a coin (or coins) and the circumstantial evidence of its discovery. Whether it was found in an archaeological excavation or as a result of clandestine digging? If it was found in an archaeological excavation, what were, if any, associated finds like potshards, artefacts or other materials objects. It is, therefore, important that the numismatist has a fair idea of archaeological processes and techniques so as to fully understand the importance of the numismatic find and utilize it as historical evidence.

Leaving aside the punch-marked coins (pmc) and early un-inscribed cast copper coins (euccc), most of the coins have inscriptions. In fact, the key to decipher two most popular Indian scripts - Brahmi and Kharoshthi – was provided by the coins itself. Here a numismatist not only doubles up as an epigraphist but also a paleographist. In fact 'numismatic paleography' needs to be taught as a separate paper to the students of Ancient Indian History and Archaeology.

Similarly, to properly understand and decipher the coin legends one must be fully conversant with the language and its grammer. Thus, for a majority of Brahmi coin legends a thorough understanding of Sanskrit grammar becomes a pre-requisite in the same way as a sound knowledge of Persian and Arabic is crucial for studying coins of the Islamic dynasties.

Next requirement is of having a fair knowledge about the metallurgy and coin manufacturing processes. The former is concerned with the properties of metals, their production and purification while the latter involves standardization of weight, fineness and coin impression through hammering ș whether with punches or with dies, casting, droplet technique, or milling. A keen coin-collector or a numismatist, for example, would readily identify a cast imitation of a coin which is ordinarily known to be die-struck. Such cast imitations usually lack the sharpness of the die-struck coins and their surface contains tiny marks caused by air bubbles.

Numismatic studies are directly linked with metrology, involving a scientific study of weights and weight standards. Till not so long ago, in fact till the introduction of the metric weight system in India in 1958, the weights throughout the country were expressed in terms of the principal coins, and, the *ser* and *man* were simply the multiples of the principal coin current in that area.[2] (Garg).

Equipped with these skills, a numismatist sets out to examine his or her evidence and employs a number of techniques such as hoard study, die-study and mint output analysis.

During the past few decades, one aspect of the contemporary coinage has increasingly attracted the attention of the historians dealing with the economic life of the period. And this is the monetary role of the coinage in the trade, commerce and state revenues, which has, in turn, produced some remarkable histories by many scholars.

While the economic historians analyze the role of coinage as a medium of exchange, standard of measure, store of value, and as a facilitator of trade and commerce, the numismatists, on the other hand, focus their studies on the physical or technical aspects of the coin. In other words, it is only when the coin has transcended its immediate role as the currency of the realm, that it enters the domain of numismatic studies. Seldom these two approaches intersect. While the study of coins has, over the last two centuries, developed into a full-fledged discipline, the vital evidence unearthed by the numismatists has, somehow, remained on the fringes of the mainstream historiography of India.

Apart from providing political and cultural evidence, the coins also have aesthetic and artistic value and as such they constitute a very important source for art historians, who have, so far largely concentrated on painting and sculptures and other visual arts, and have not integrated the numismatic art in their studies. The fact remains that the earliest royal portraiture, anthropomorphic representation of religious deities, finest examples of calligraphy, flora and fauna, costumes and jewellery, different symbols and motifs as well as other artistic designs and embellishments, all can be studied through coins. As P.L. Gupta records,

> "The dies from which coins were struck were the work of the artists of the day. So they reflect the workmanship of the artists and also the aesthetic tastes of the people of those times."[3]

II

The students of numismatics today face much less difficulties that were faced by their predecessors. Access to coin collections in museums has become quite liberalized. In the late 1970s, when Dr. P.L. Gupta conceived the idea of establishing a research centre devoted to research in Indian numismatics, the best alternative that he could think of to overcome this problem of accessibility, was to build up a photo-archive of coins deposited in various public collections. I remember my stint in the Nasik Institute from 1985-88, during which I visited several museums and spending days and months in meticulously photographing their coin collection and recording technical and other details. Even getting permission from many of these museums to photograph their coin collections was so difficult to obtain. Today, most of the large museums have digitized their collections which can be accessed easily. In addition, many private collectors are now sharing their collection on social media and in numerous coin exhibitions that are organized in various parts of the country throughout the year. Coin auction houses have multiplied and many of them regularly put up their sale catalogue online. In these days of demonetization, coins have also become a good investment option.

A direct result of all these developments is that more and more numismatic material is now coming in public domain for study and consultation by the numismatists. Organized sales and auction of coins and other numismatic materials have replaced clandestine sale and purchase of these artefacts, which was done in the past. And more and more people ș ranging from members of various coin societies to numerous FaceBook groups ș are now sharing their expertise, practically on an hourly basis.

I think, now is the time of consolidating all this acquired knowledge and integrate it in the historiography. It is the time of some Big Data analyses in the field of Indian numismatics, rather than confining our knowledge to purely numismatic pleasures of discovering an unrecorded coin type, a new mint, an unreported symbol or mint mark, or at times a new coin-legend.

I am sure that with an all new stream of young scholars and researchers, aided and guided by senior academics many of whom are present in this conference this morning, the Indian numismatic studies are all set to take a quantum leap.

I wish this Conference all success.

Thank You.

References

1. Grierson, Philip, *Numismatics*, Oxford University Press, Oxford.1975, P. 4
2. Garg, Sanjay, *The Sikka and the Raj: A History of Currency Legislations of the East India Company, 1772-1835*. Manohar Publishers and Distributors, New Delhi.2013, P. 188
3. Gupta, P.L., *Coins*, National Book Trust, New Delhi.1969, P. xi-xii.

Section - I

Ancient Indian Numismatic

1

Late Imperial Silver Punch-Marked Coin Hoards from Bengal:
An Analytical Study

Sandeep Pan

The term 'Bengal' here denotes undivided Bengal which is present day West Bengal and Bangladesh. Bengal never emerged as single political unit neither in the early-historic nor in the early-medieval period in the map of the sub-continent. This region was divided into several Geo political units and hydrography mainly defined the limits of these units. Bengal is divided into four major divisions[1]-

I. The area to the west of the Bhagirathi (which is a branch of Ganga)

II. The area lying to the north of Padma (a branch of Ganga)

III. The area between Bhagirathi and the Padma

IV. The area to the east of Meghna.

Issuing of metallic currency commenced in India sometime around c. 6th- 5^{th}century BCE. But Bengal started issuing coinage a little later from c. 3rd Century BCE onwards. Dr. Basu Majumdar has shown how monetization in Bengal commenced due to Mauryan contact. Thought this territory was located close to Magadha but the early Magadhan coinage did not influence the initiation of metallic currency here. Initially in small regions we find punch marked coins bearing less than five symbols. These are usually termed as janapada coins. On the basis of the variation of coinage pattern Dr. Basu Majumdar has traced three distinct zones or janapadas, one around present day Dacca i.e. the site of Wari-Bateshwar, second around Chandraketugarh and the third around present day Tamluk or ancient Tamralipta (Dharas hoard). These three regions had been issuing local or indigenous punch-marked coinage in less than five symbols pattern on the obverse. These punch-marked coins of both imperial and local variety being found together not only suggest that the impetus or influence for issuing the coinage came from Magadha but also reflects the interaction and network of these janapadas with the metropolitan and core region of the Mauryan Empire.

Imperial silver punch-marked coins in Bengal have been unearthed or reported from Lohapur (Birbhum District), Chandraketugarh, Murshidabad, Midnapur, Bankura, South Dinajpur, Bogra and Rajshahi areas[2]. But here in this paper i shall deal with only the Imperial punch marked coin hoards of Bengal. These include the Mahasthan Hoard I, Mahasthan Hoard II, Korabeg and Baigachha Hoard.

Mahasthan Hoard I[3] was discovered by a French-Bangladesh team during the excavation in the year 1995. The hoard consists of 93 silver punch-marked coins. Mahasthan Hoard II[4]consists of 275 silver punch-marked coins, discovered by a person during the time of digging for the cultivation of the land in 2006 in the Mahasthan area[5]. Korabeg[6] is located in 24 parganas, West Bengal and the hoard is consists of 57 Silver punchmarked coins. The hoard is found by a villager in 2004. Presently the hoard is preserved in the state archaeological museum, Kolkata. Baigachha[7] is located in Rajshahi District, Bangladesh. The hoard is found by chance by the villagers in 1987 while working in the bamboo garden. 33 Silver punch marked coins were stored in a copper or bronze pot.

I would like to revisit Mahasthan Hoard I, the only significant coin hoard recovered from excavated context. Some of the coins need fresh identification as these has been wrongly identified. I would like to follow the new updated version of Gupta-Hardaker[8]catalogue to identify the types.

These are as follows:

Fifty coins of Mahasthan hoard II published by Bulbul Ahmed, Md. Noorul Islam[9] and four coins of the Korabeg hoard published by Dr. Basu Majumdar[10] also need revisiting. These have been wrongly identified:

Hoard	**Acc. no**	**Previous Identification**	**New Identification**
Mahasthan	INIC 06.31, 32	Not identified	GH 416-37,450-63
	NIC 06.121-124	N. I.	GH 574(?),VIb, 570, VIb
	NIC 06.205-209,211	N. I.	
	06.212-229		GH 543,542-43, 542(?), 542-43, 542-543, 576-83, 576-82, 571-72, 571, 572, 547-67, 547-67, 547-67, 566 (?), 568-70, VI, VIbX9
	NIC 06.234,235	New type	GH 591,VII
	NIC 06.236-240	N.I.	GH VI(?), 552, 477/542, VI(?), 507-15

contd...

	NIC 06.242,244,246-49	N.I.	GH 507-15(?), 477-83/542-43, 507x4
	NIC O6.252,253, 263-265	N.I.	GH 485-86, 477-84/542-43, 480, 571-72, 467-71
Korabeg	13		GH 477-84 GH 480(?)
	24		GH 533-39 GH 537
	53		GH VI (?) GH 482/87/543
	56		GH VI(?) GH 570

A detailed analysis of the imperial punch-marked hoards reveal that the earliest GH type unearthed / reported from Bengal is 276 from Baigachha hoard, which belongs to the GH series II. Only four coins of GH series II and III (type 276, 277, 291, 320) are present in the late punch marked coin hoards in Bengal. It indicates that punch marked coins from the metropolitan reached Bengal at a later stage sometime around the circulation of GH series IV and these few earlier coins also reached along with the fresh GH series IV coins.

There are a few GH types which dominate at Mahasthan and among these is GH 481. Mahasthan hoard I consists of 18.08% GH type 481 while Baigachha hoard consists of 27.27% GH type 481. But interestingly Mahasthan hoard II consists of only 0.72% this particular type and Korabeg hoard doesn't have GH type 481. This shows a clear divide that north and east Bengal had a different bias whereas West Bengal has a separate pattern. GH type 481 did not even occur in Kathy White, Mir Zakah II, B. Birch, Kohler I and KOhler II hoard[11]. While Amaravati and Barwani hoards have 0.11%, 1965 UP hoard have 0.95% and Gorhoghat hoard have only 1.72% GH 481. It is worth mentioning here that this type occurs very rarely in other hoards and hence has a Bengal bias indicating towards its regional issuance.

Coming to another type i.e. GH 482 which has also been reported from some hoards in Bengal not exactly region specific but a certain pattern evolves as far their weight is concerned. At Mahasthan I (2.69 gms.) the average weights is low whereas at Korabeg (3.13 gms.) and Mahasthan II (3.05 gms.) weights are high. This reflects local minting of these types. Mahasthan adopted the pattern of retaining the purity and reducing the weight from *Karshapana* to a little less around a gram deducted. Basu Majumdar[12] suggests that this was due to the payment of a coining fee to the centre being deducted from the metal itself while coining. This was probably done in the local mints or indigenous mints. Kautilya suggests the location of such mints at highways.

Interestingly Mahasthan I, Mahasthan II and Korabeg hoards consists of 2.12%, 6.18% and 3.5% GH type 482, while Baigachha hoard does not have any. Amravati, Barwani and Rairah I hoard have 5.11%, 4.52%, and 4.90% GH type 482. But Kathy White, KOhler, Mir Zakah II, B.Birch and Rairh V hoard have 1.75%, 1.51%, 0.11%, 0.82% and 0.82% GH type 482.

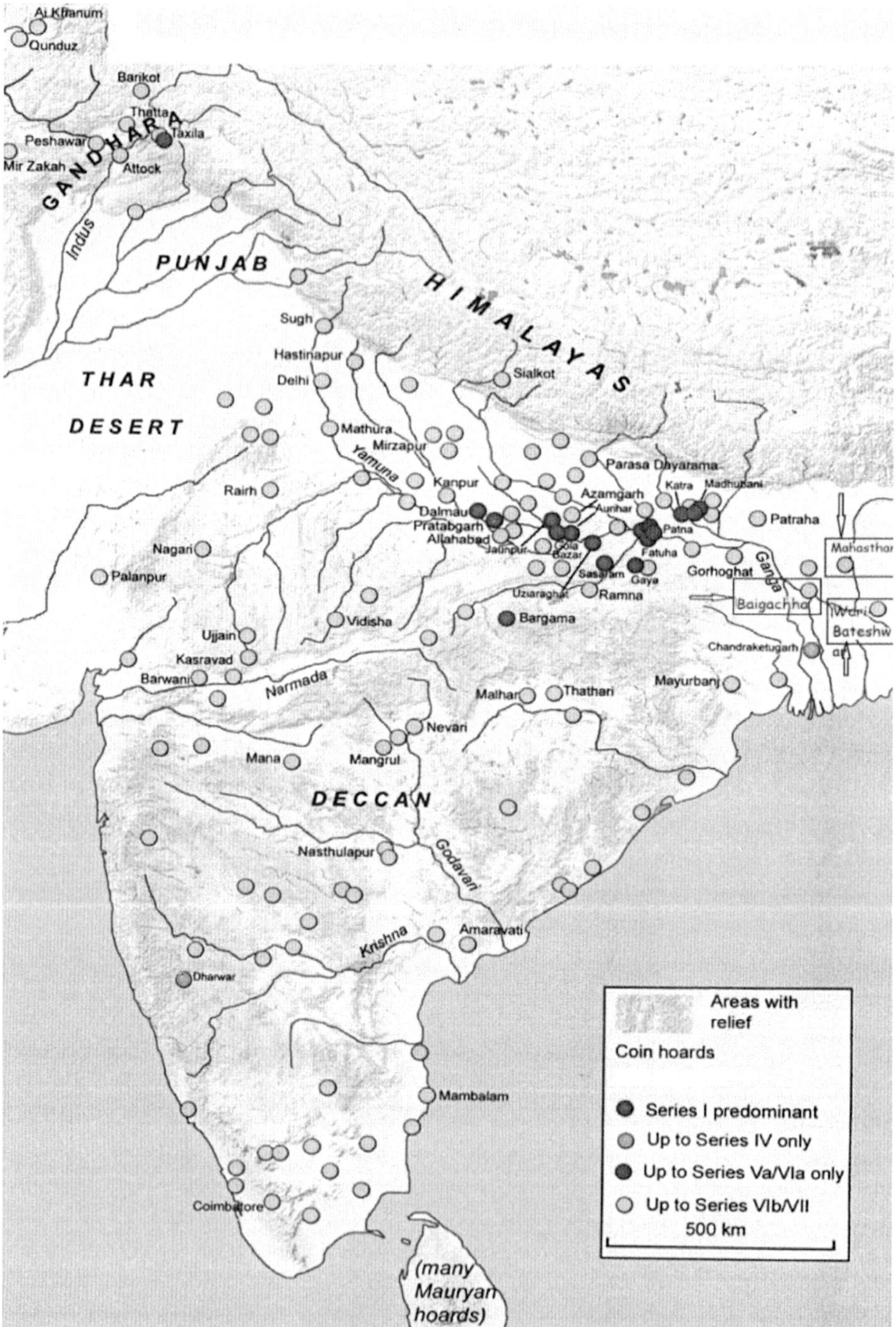

Major Imp PMC hoards find spot; arrow marks are

Indicating late Imp PMC Hoards from Bengal [edited map, img.I[13]]

The average weight of the GH type 481 in the Mahasthan hoard I and Mahasthan hoard II are 2.52 gms. and 3.06 gms. The average weight of the of GH type 482 in the Mahasthan I, Mahasthan II and Korabeg hoard is 2.53 gms, 3.06 gms, and 3.13 gms. So the weight of GH type 481 and GH type 482 in the Mahasthan hoard I is lower than the Mahasthan hoard II and Korabeg hoard. Interestingly GH type 481 and GH type 482 has almost similar weight.

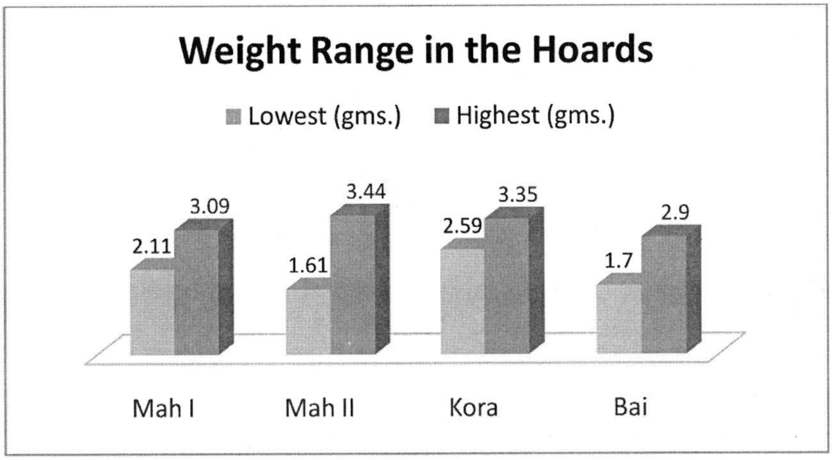

Salles and Alam[14] mentionedabout 7 nearly blank coins in the Mahasthan hoard from excavated context which also point towards local minting of these coins. Interestingly the weight of these "nearly blank punch makred coins" ranges from 2.1175- 2.6059 gms which again comply to the lesser weight pattern of north Bengal. These coins have been found along with other imperial punch marked coins. Condition of the rest of the coins is quite worn out and corroded which suggests their presence in the circulation process for a long period of time. Thus these may be considered as coin blanks prepared for minting but had skipped the process of receiving all the 5 punches but somehow were accepted in the process of circulation as money along with the rest of the coins. The details of the 7 nearly blank coins in Mahasthan Hoard I are given below[15]-

Acc. No.	Weight (gms.)	Condition
Mah95/727/21	2.60	Worn out
Mah95/727/76	2.28	Blank
Mah/95/727/69	2.51	Nearly Blank
Mah/95/727/66	2.31	Nearly Blank
Mah/95/727/56	2.25	Nearly Blank
Mah/95/727/33	2.58	Nearly Blank
Mah/95/727/23	2.11	Worn out

Another striking point is that the high occurrence of the GH type 543 in Bengal.Hoards from central and northern part of the sub-continent consist of low percentage of that particular type. Outside Bengal the hoards in which this type mainly occurs are Barwani(18.31%), Amravati (12.93%), H.W Kohler (37.87%), Bhalna[16] (10%) and Kathy White hoard(9.01%). If we compare Barwani, Amravati, Bhalna hoards with all Bengal punch marked hoards under consideration i.e. Mahastahn I, II, Korabeg and Baigachha hoards then we will find that all the late hoards from Bengal contain high percentage of GH 543.This is not due to regional bias as in case of GH 481 as it has the so called Taxila mark (✣✣✣) on the reverse. This mark indicates a trade linkage with Gandhara. B.N.Mukherjee[17] has shown how horses were imported from northwest and Ranabir Chakravarti[18] has published a sealing from Chandraketugarh in which a horse is being uploaded on a watercraft. These are clear indicators of an overland trade route from northwest to Bengal and then horses were exported to the southern part or peninsular south from ports in Bengal. To add to this another GH type which also has the so called Taxila mark (✣✣✣) as the control mark also has been reported from North Bengal. This is GH type 574 which is present only in Baigachha (3.03%) and Mahasthan hoard II (0.36%), type 575 only present in Korabeg hoard (1.75%) all this again point towards a connection with the northwestern part of the subcontinent.

Mahasthan I (17.02%), Mahasthan II (14.09%), Korabeg (8.77%) and Baigachha (36.36%) hoard. Barwani, Amravati, H.W. Kohler, Bhalna and Kathy White hoard contains 18.31%, 12.93%, 37.87%, 10% and 9.01% type 543. Bhalna hoard[19] is consists of 24.03% type 542 with 10% type 543.

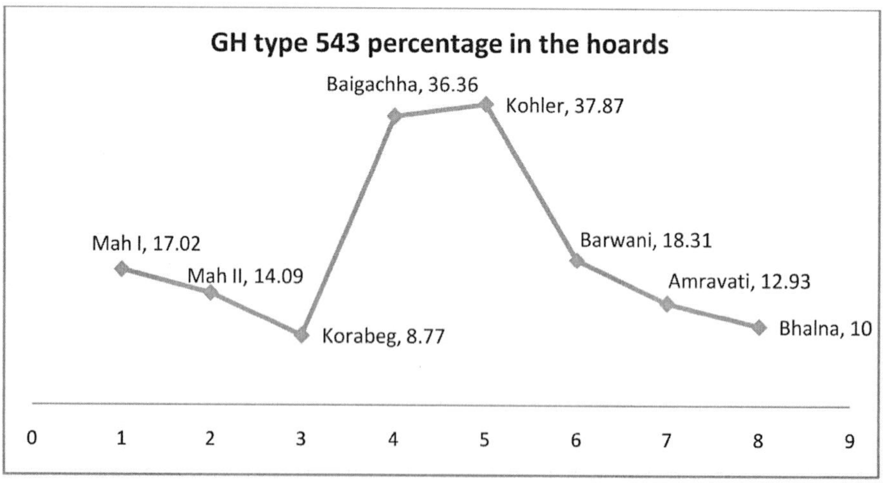

The average weight of the GH type 543 in Mahasthan I is 2.53 gms, Mahasthan II 3.08 gms and Korabeg hoard is 3.13 gms. The average weight of the coins of GH 543 of Mahasthan hoard I is much lighter than Mahasthan hoard II and Korabeg hoard, while the average weight of the coins of Mahasthan hoard I and Korabeg hoard is very close. The average of the type GH 543 in Bengal is still much lower than the other hoards such as Kathy white hoard (3.17 gms), Bhalna hoard (3.30 gms), Taregna[20] hoards (3.23 gms). The average weight of the coins GH 543 in Mir Zakah II hoard is 2.40 gms which is much lower than the other major hoards and close to the weight of Mahasthan hoard I.

Baigachha hoard is consists of 9.09% GH 552-553 while Mahasthan hoard I, II and Korabeg hoard doesn't have this particular type. Mahasthan hoard I is consists of 8.51% GH 553 with the average weight of 2.38 gms. Mahasthan Hoard II only has 0.36% of this particular type with the average weight of 3.44 gms. Korabeg and Baigachha hoard doesn't have GH type 553. Only Kathy White (0.35%), Mir Zakah II (0.01%) and Amravati (0.26%) hoard is containing GH type 552-53 or GH type 553. It is quite clear that Baigachha and Mahasthan Hoard I contain such a high percentage of GH type 552-53 and 553. Korabeg (5.26%) and Mahasthan hoard I (3.19%) contain decent percentage of GH 550. Mahasthan hoard I consists of only 0.36% GH 550 and Baigachha hoard doesn't have any of this particular type. Baigachha hoard consists of such a high 6.06% GH 509, while Mahastha hoard I, II and Korabeg hoard consists of only 1.06%, 2.54% and 1.75% GH 509. Mahsthan hoard I and Baigachha haord consists of 7.44% and 6.06% GH 344 respectively. But Mahasthan hoard II and Korabeg hoard doesn't have this particular type. GH 344 is occurs in Amravati (0.36%), Rairh hoard I (0.30%), Rairh hoard V (0.35%), Parasadayaram (1.19%), and Mirzapur (2.17%). So the ratio of GH 344 in Mahasthan I and Baigachha hoard is quite high in comparison with the other late Imperial Punchmarked coin hoards of the sub-continent. All these indicate a probable trade nexus in which Bengal was also linked and played a vibrant role while maintaining its own identity.

Major find spot of the GH 566 is Gangetic plain, from Haryana to Bihar and Rajasthan. GH 566 present largely in A/ Khanum and it is main type of Gohada hoard (611 coins)[21], covers 99.34% of the total total coins of the hoard. Interestingly GH 566 is absent from Mahasthan hoard I, Korabeg hoard and Baigachha hoard. Only Mahasthan hoard II is consists of 0.36% of GH 566. We are getting GH type 509 from Kathy White (5), Mir Zakah II (2), B.Birch (1), Amravati (103), Barwani, Rairh I, II, IV, V, Parasadayaram, Mirzapur and Taregna hoard. in compare with the other major late imperial Punchmarked coin hoards from the subcontinent. Hoards of Bengal contains decent percentage of GH 509.Only GH 509 and 543 is present in all four hoards in Bengal. So this two are the common type which circulated widely and largely in Bengal. Besides this we find that coins of series Va and VIb this two are the major coin series of all four hoards in Bengal. Series Va and VIb covers the large percentage of coins in the Mahasthan hoard I (69.14%), Mahasthan hoard II (63.26%), Korabeg hoard (40.34%) and Baigachha hoard (81.87%). Series IVd present in Mahasthan Hoard I (6.38%), Mahastn hoard II (10.90%) and in Korabeg hoard (8.77%), while Series IVd absent in Baigachha hoard. Series IVa is present only in Korabeg (7.44%) and Baigachha (6.06) hoard. Coins of

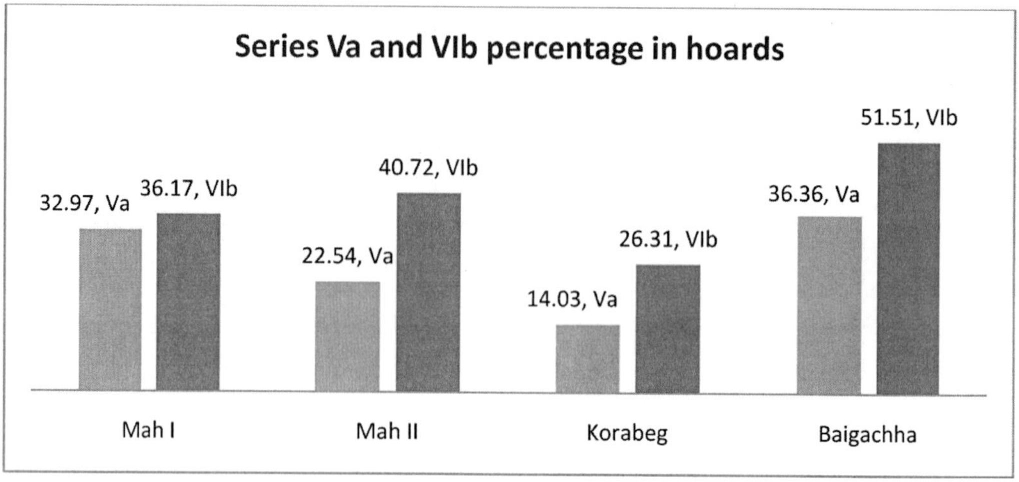

series II (type 276, 277) only present in Baigachha hoard (6.06%). Only one coin of series III (GH type 291) is present in Mahasthan hoard II. So hoards are showing some short of similarity in case of distribution pattern and from series IVa onwards we getting coins regularly from these hoards. Gupta and Hardaker[22] are of the opinion that series Va commenced with the accession of Chandragupta Maurya and series VIb circulated during the time of Ashoka. Though Elizabeth Errington[23] has put forward a different view, she argues that dating of Mauryan coinage will be from series III onwards. From the puchmarked coin hoards of Bengal we can trace that coins of series Va and VIb occupied the large part of the hoards. So during the time of the Mauryans imperial punchmarked coins circulated largely in Bengal. A clear picture emerges from the hoard analysis given below.

The average weight of the coins of Mahasthan I (2.49 gms), and Baigachha hoard (2.41gms) is much lighter than the normal *Karshapana* weight standard which is

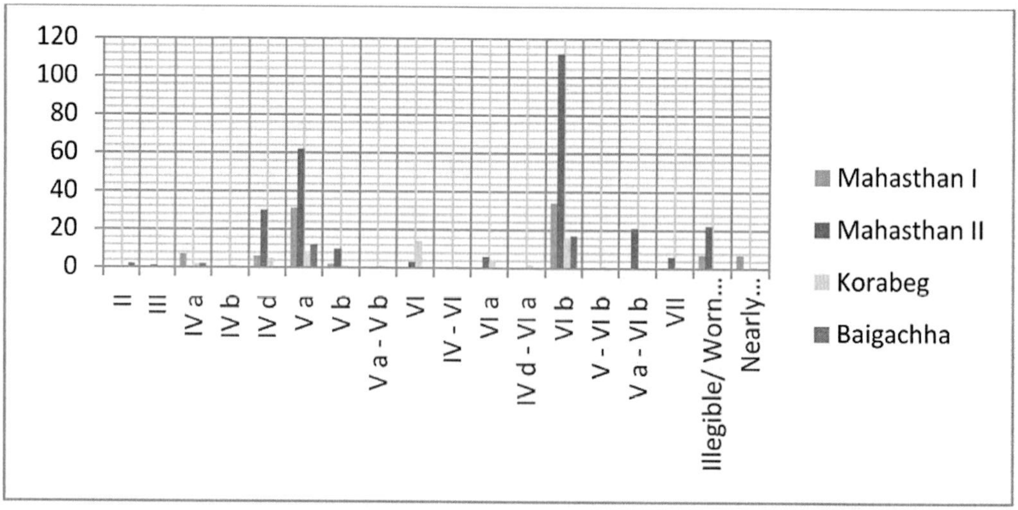

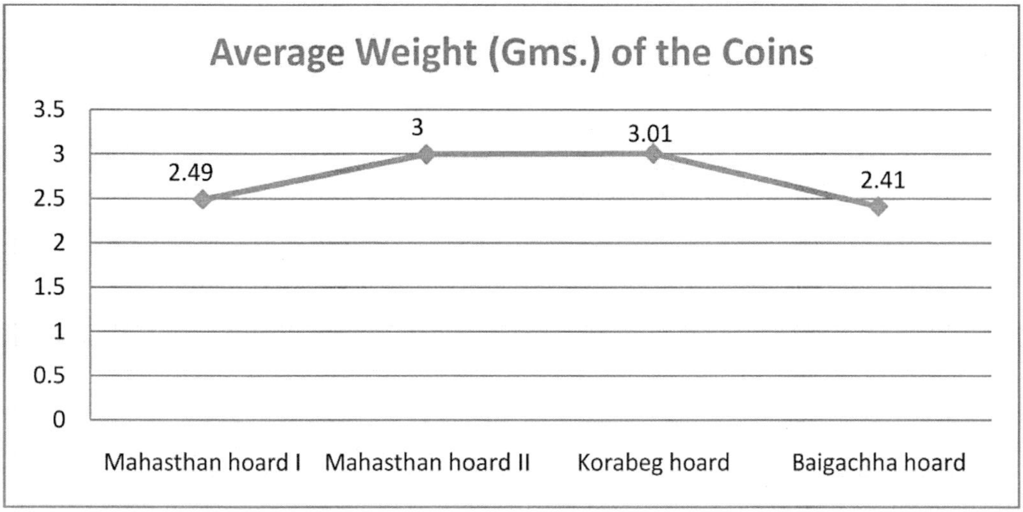

approximately 3.4 grams or 56.5 *Grains*. Mahasthan II (3.0gms), Korabeg (3.01gms) are closer to the *karshapana* standard. Basu Majumdar[24] has shown how these were two different patterns of minting. She argues that this is because of the penalty for the minting coins *anyatra* i.e. outside the Mauryan mints. *Arthasastra* refers to a penalty fees for minting coins outside the Maurya mints will be 25 *panas* or 0.5 gms silver.

The average weight of the coins of Mahashan I and Baigachha hoard is almost 1.0 gm. less than the normal *Karshapana* weight standard.

The average weight of the coins of Mahasthan I and Baigachha hoard are close and the average weight of the coins of Mahasthan II and Korabeg hoard is almost similar. The average weight of series IVa (7 coins) and IVd (6 coins) in Mahasthan I hoard is 2.44 gms. and 2.57 gms. respectively. All the 7 coins of series IVa this hoard are in good condition and all the 6 coins of series IVd is worn out but still the average weight of the

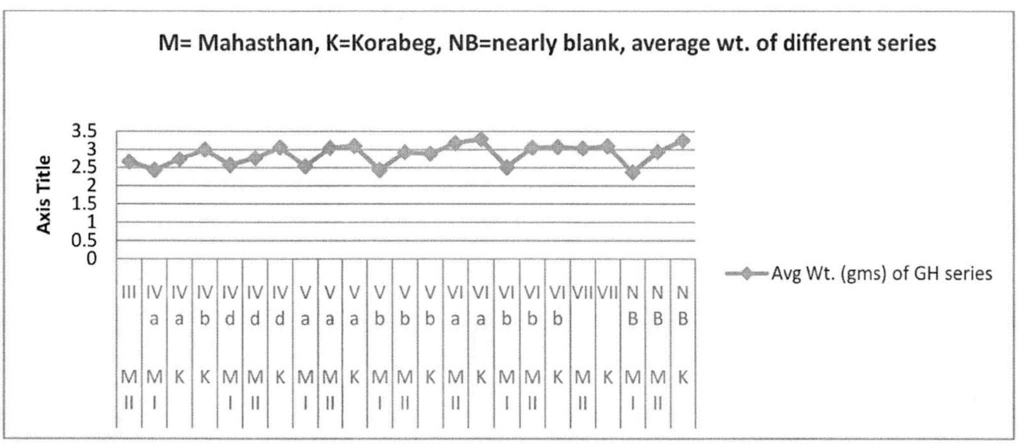

coins of series IVd is higher than the coins of series IVa. Probably the issuing authority intentionally issued the coins of series IVd in slight higher weight standard. Also the worn out condition of the coins of series IVd suggests that these coins were in circulation for a longer time. The average weight of the coins of Mahasthan I, II and Korabeg hoards are ṣ series IVd: 2.79 gms, series Va and Vb: 2.89 and 2.74 gms, series VIb: 2.87 gms. So the average weight of the coins of series Va and VIb is heavier than the other series. The average weight of the series VII in Mahasthan II (3.03 gms) and Korabeg (3.09 gms) hoard is heavier. the It is clear from the chart that coins of Mahasthan hoard II and Korabeg hoard is consistently maintaining a higher weight standard, especially Korabeg hoard. Mahasthan hoard I and Baigachha hoard is maintaining lower weight standard. Even the worn-out coins of Korabeg hoard is quite heavier 3.25 gms.

The worn-out coins of Mahasthan hoard II (2.93 gms.) maintaining higher weight standard as compared with the Mahasthan hoard I (2.37 gms). The coins of Korabeg and Mahasthan hoard II were issued in higher weight standard. The average weight of the

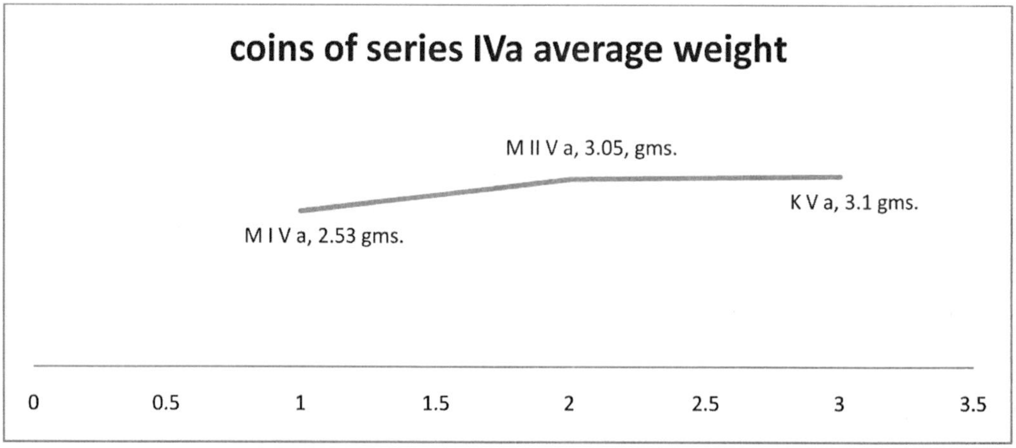

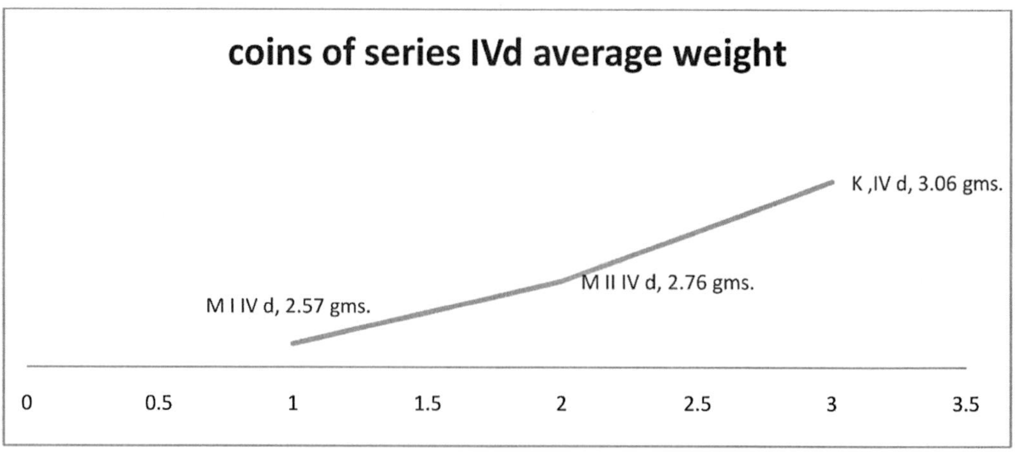

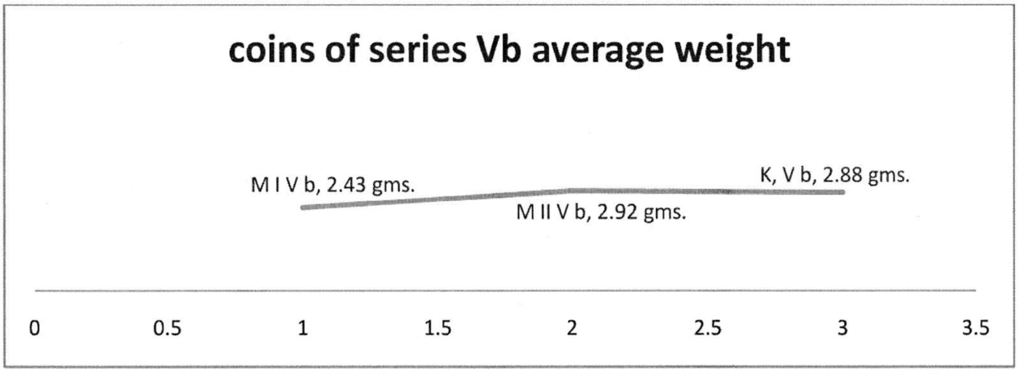

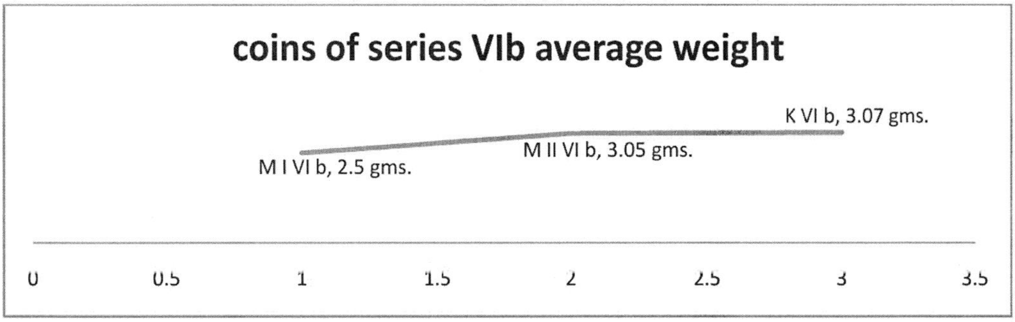

coins of Mahasthan hoard II and Korabeg hoard upto series IVd is issued in lighter weight standard but coins of series Va – VII is issued in heavier weight standard. But in the case of Mahasthan hoard I average weight of the coins of series III-IVd is issued in slightly heavier weight standard than the series Va – VII.

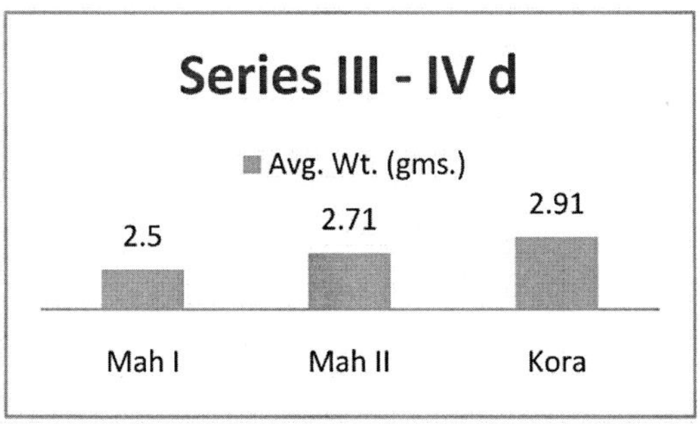

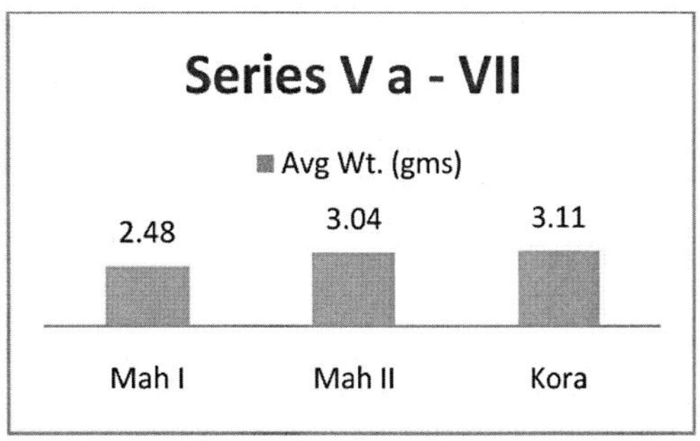

Thus from the above analysis we would like to place the hypothesis that Mahasthan II hoard does not belong to Mahasthan originally and is a displaced hoard. If displaced in the ancient period we will have to suggest that it belonged to a person hailing from a region in western part of Bengal. We have also shown how GH 481 emerged as a regional variety with Bengal bias. Our analysis also establishes and corroborates the fact of trade linkage of Bengal with north-western India as suggested by the presence of Kharoshti inscriptions, use mixed script (Kharoshthi- Brahmi) in Bengal also the horse sealing from

Chandraketugarh when see in conjunction with the presence of high percentage of GH 543 in Bengal hoards.

GH type occurrence in the hoards:

GH Type	Mahasthan I	Mahasthan II	Korabeg	Baigachha
276				1 (?) o/s 302
277				1
291		1		
320		1		
335-37			1	
340			1	
344	7			2
362			1	
367/380-83			1	
416	3	6		
416-37		1		
418-37/ 443/ 500			1	
422		2		
424		2		
425		2		
427	1	3	1 (?)	
428	1			
434			1	
442		3		
443		2		
446		1		
450		1	1	
450-61			1	
450-63		1		
456	1			
460		1		
464			1	

464-66				
467		**2**		
467-71		**1**		
468		**1**		
470		**1**		
475		**1**		
477		**4**		
477-84		**3**	**1**	
479	**1**	**3**		
480		**3**	**2**	
481	**17**	**2**		**9**
482	**2**	**17**	**2**	
482/87/543			**2**	
483		**1**		
484		**3**		
485		**1**		
485-86	**1**	**1**		
486	**1**	**2**		
488		**3**	**1**	**1**
489-91/579			**1**	
493	**2**	**1**		
496-99/504			**1**	
503		**5**		
504				
505		**1**		
506	**2**	**1**		
507		**4**		
507-15	**Y**	**7**	**1**	
509	**1**	**7**	**1**	**2**
510		**11**		

512		**1**		
514			**1**	
518		**3**		
518-19	**1**	**1**		
519	**3**	**2**		
521-22	**1 (?)**			
522		**1**		
523		**1**		
528			**1**	
530		**1**		
533			**1**	
488/527/533-39			**1**	
533-39			**2**	
534		**1**		
537	**1**	**1 (?)**	**1**	
538		**3**		
541/555-57			**1**	
542		**8**		
542-43		**3**		
542-82	**1**			
543	**16**	**41**	**5**	**12**
546		**1**		
547-67	**1**	**3**		
548		**1**		
548-49	**1**		**1**	**1**
550	**2+1(?)**	**1**	**3**	
551		**1**		
552		**6**		
552-553				**3**
553	**8**	**1**		

555		**1**	**1**		
558		**1**	**1**		
559			**3**		
563				**1**	
564		**1**			
566			**1**		
568			**7**		
568-70			**1**		
570			**3**		
571			**5**		
571-72		**1**	**1**		
572			**1**		
573			**1**	**1**	
574			**1**		**1**
575				**1**	
576			**1**		
576-82			**2**	**1**	
577			**3**		
582			**1**		
585			**1**		
586			**1**	**1**	
591	**1**				
595	**2**				

Coins with GH series and percentage:

GH Series	Mahasthan I	Mahasthan II	Korabeg	Baigachha	GH series % Acording to the hoards
II				2	6.06
III		1			0.36
IV a	7		2	2	7.44, 3.50, 6.06
IV b			1		1.75

IV d	6	30	5		6.38, 10.90, 8.77
V a	31	62	8	12	32.97, 22.54, 14.03, 36.36
V b	2	10	1		2.12, 3.63, 1.75
V a - V b			1		1.75
VI		3	14		1.09, 24.56
IV - VI			1		1.75
VI a		6	4		2.18, 7.01
IV d - VI a			2		3.5
VI b	34	112	15	17	36.17, 40.72, 26.31, 51.51
V - VI b			1		1.75
V a - VI b		21			7.63
VII		6	1		2.18, 1.75
Illegible/ Worn out	7	22			7.44, 8.0
Nearly Blank/Blank	7		1		7.44, 1.75
Total coins	94	275	57	33	

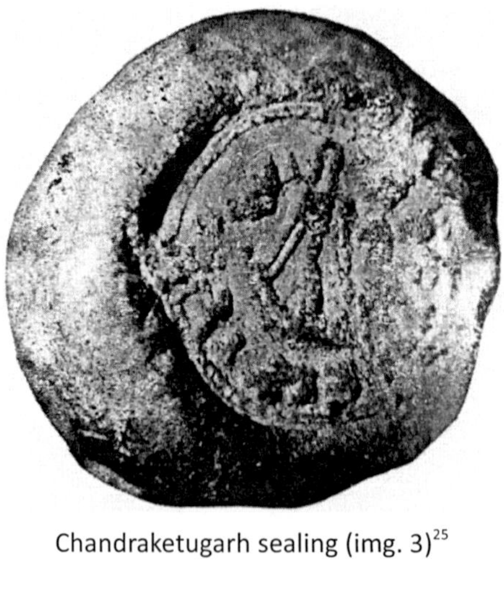

Chandraketugarh sealing (img. 3)[25]

References

1. Mukherjee, B.N., *Coins and Currency System of Early Bengal (up to c. A.D. 300),* Calcutta, Progressive Publishers, 2000, p.11.
2. Ibid.

3. Salles, J-F., and Md. S. Alam, (ed.,), *France-Bangladesh Joint Venture Excavations at Mahasthangarh: first interim Report 1993-1999*, Dhaka, Department of Archaeology, 2001, pp.238.
4. Ahmed, Bulbul and Md. N. Islam, *The Mahasthan hoard II of Silver Punchmarked coins*, Asiatic Society of Bangladesh, 2011.
5. This has been mentioned by the authors but this information does not match with the analysis and this hoard seems to be displaced or a collection pulled up from western part of Bengal travelled to this region in some point of time and was buried or was lost only recovered off late.
6. Basu Majumdar, Susmita and Roy, Amal, *Korabeg Hoard of Silver Punchmarked Coins*, Kolkata (CASTEI), Pratna Samiksha, New Series, Vol. I, pp.145-47.
7. Pan, Sandip, *Coins of Early-Historic Bengal*, Thesis submitted to the Calcutta University, for the M. Phil degree, 2014, pp.30-31.
8. Gupta P.L., and T.R., Hardaker, *Punchmarked Coinage of the Indian Subcontinent: Magadha-Maurya Series*, Nasik, IIRNS Publications Pvt. Ltd., 2014.
9. Ahmed, Bulbul, and Md. N. Islam, *The Mahasthan hoard II of Silver Punchmarked coins*, Asiatic Society of Bangladesh, 2011.
10. Basu Majumdar, Susmita and Roy, Amal, *Korabeg Hoard of Silver Punchmarked Coins*, Kolkata (CASTEI), Pratna Samiksha, New Series, Vol. I, pp.145-47.
11. Errington, Elizabeth, *A survey of late hoards of Indian Punchmarked coins*, London, Numismatic Chronical, pp.69-121
12. Basu Majumdar, Susmita, *Coins and currency pattern in early-historic Bengal ș An overview*, Numismatic Digest, Nasik, IIRNS Publication Private Limited, 2014, pp.27-28.
13. Gupta P.L., and T.R., Hardaker, *Punchmarked Coinage of the Indian Subcontinent: Magadha-Maurya Series*, Nasik, IIRNS Publications Pvt. Ltd., 2014, pp.16.
14. Salles, J-F., and Md. S. Alam, (ed.,), *France-Bangladesh Joint Venture Excavations at Mahasthangarh: first interim Report 1993-1999*, Dhaka, Department of Archaeology, 2001
15. Ibid.
16. IIRNS Library, Coin card access section, Nasik.
17. Mukherjee, B. N., *Coastal and Overseas trade in pre-Gupta Vanga and Kalinga, Trade in Early India* (R., Chakravarti ed.), New Delhi, Oxford University Press, 2010, pp.199-227.
18. Chakravarti, R., (ed.), *Trade in Early India*, New Delhi, Oxford University Press, 2010.
19. IIRNS Library, Coin card access section, Nasik.
20. Ibid.
21. Ibid.
22. Gupta P.L., and T.R., Hardaker, *Punchmarked Coinage of the Indian Subcontinent: Magadha-Maurya Series*, Nasik, IIRNS Publications Pvt. Ltd., 2014, pp.48.
23. Errington, Elizabeth, *A survey of late hoards of Indian Punchmarked coins*, London, Numismatic Chronical, pp.87-88.
24. Basu Majumdar, Susmita, *Coins and currency pattern in early-historic Bengal ș An overview*, Numismatic Digest, Nasik, IIRNS Publication Private Limited, 2014, pp.27-28.
25. Chakravati, Ranabir, Maritime trade in horses in early historical Bengal: A seal from Chandraketugarh, Kolkata, (CASTEI), Pratna Samiksha Vol. I, 1992.

2

The Elephant and Hill Uninscribed Cast Copper Coin and Their Presence in the Late 5th-4th c. BCE

Dr. Kurush F. Dalal and Raamesh Gowri Raghavan

Introduction

Amongst the earliest coins found in ancient India are coins made of silver and copper. They are made in two ways punch-marked or cast. Most of the coins from the earliest periods i.e. the 6th and 5th c BC are almost always uninscribed. The coins bear multiple devices on one or both sides.

Amongst the many variants is a type of coin called the UCCC or Uninscribed Cast Copper Coin. These coins are both square and round. The round coins are further subdivided into those with multiple devices on both faces and single bold devices on each face.

This paper deals with one of these sub-sub-types i.e. the Circular UCCC with single devices on both faces. The coin type is even more specific as it has two specific coins one on each face. On the obverse it bears an elephant facing left or right with or without rider and on its reverse a three-arched hill with crescent above it. This specific type of coin is called the 'Elephant and Hill type of UCCC'. It is found all over Northern, North-western and Central India. The coins were made in multiple clay moulds and are often found in joint pairs and rarely as trios. Almost all the coins bear a protrusion or two showing how they were a part of a much larger series of moulds all joined together by flow channels through which the molten copper flowed into the mould.

This type is also known as the 'Elephant and Chaitya type' and is classified as 'Series p/q' of Allan[1]. The elephant always faces left and the lower pair of 'hills' are clearly separated.

The Coins from Balathal

The Early Historic and Chalcolithic mound of Balathal was excavated by a joint team of the Deccan College Pune and the Institute for Rajasthan Studies (IRS), Rajasthan Vidyapeeth from 1993-94 to 2000 for 7 seasons.

The site of Balathal, Taluka Vallabhnagar, Dist Udaipur Rajasthan was first noticed by VN Misra during his survey of the Berach Basin in the early 60s[2]. The site was then revisited by Rima Hooja in 1980[3] during her doctoral research surveys.

Excavations were undertaken at the site for the following reasons (some scientific and some emotional) ş to understand better the Chalcolithic IRS in field methods and to establish their credentials in archaeology; Rajasthan was where VN Misra had started his career and this was where he decided he would like to carry out the last excavations as Excavation Director.

The seven seasons of excavations revealed a huge quantum of Chalcolithic data and also revealed a very clear EH stratum divisible into two phases and a small smattering a Medieval Occupation on the top of the mound[4].

The Early historical data could be divided into clear horizons where the earlier one represented by layers 3 and 4 was clearly demarcated from the upper by a cataclysmic fire which destroyed the site.

Layer 1 at Balathal yielded the remains of a small Early Medieval occupation in the centre of the mound. Layer 2 was an Early Historical occupation dateable to the Kushana period 1st c B C to 2nd c AD.

The entirety of layer 3 consisted of burnt wattle-and-daub debris with a huge amount of in situ Early Historical material. The ceramics from this horizon and the one above were studied by AR Dandekar (2002) for his PhD and the Artefacts were studied by the author[5].

Amongst the artefacts recovered from layer three were three copper cast coins. One was a small fraction of a round Elephant and Hill type of UCCC, a complete round Elephant and Hill type of UCCC and the third a much-weathered square copper cast coin with a very faint Ujjain symbol on one side. Two coins of the Elephant and Hill type were also found during intensive surface explorations of the mound. All the round UCCC were of a single type, the Elephant and Hill. This type bears on the obverse an elephant with rider facing left, the reverse bears a three-arched hill with crescent above it. The lower loops of the crescent are not joint in any of the examples and are slightly separated.[6]

Interestingly a terracotta sealing from the same layer also bears an identical motif, amongst others. It has been illustrated and published[7].

These coins were found in association with Black Slipped ware, Fine Grey ware and Red and Grey coarse wares. The fabrics and shapes especially the Pear-shaped pots,

Carinated pots with inward truncated rims, and the Fine Gray and Slipped Black Ware dishes with straight featureless rims all found parallels in sites dated between the 6th and 3rd c BC by various excavators. The artefactual data corroborated these facts[8].

Balathal is one of the most well dated excavations in the history of archaeology and there are over 50 C14 dates from the site.

All the Early Historical carbon samples from layer 3 have consistently yielded un-calibrated C14 dates between 400 and 280 BC (**Table 1**) thus giving us a secure window between the late 5th and mid 3rd c BC for both the layer and all the artefacts within including the coins. Thus, very securely dating these coins to the Pre-Mauryan phase at least and the Early Mauryan at the very least.

Table 1: C14 dates from Balathal

Sr. No.	Lab. No.	Tr.	Ly.	Depth in metres	Date in BP (Half-life 5730)	Date (A.D/B.C.)	Calibrated (Summary)
01	PRL-1848	C	2	0.50	1820±70	130 A.D.	
02	BS-1567	OA2	3	1.38	1900±90	50 A.D.	19 (100) 224 A.D.
03	PRL-1841	HX2	3	0.84	2110±60	160 B.C.	
04	PRL-2403	A3	3	1.05	2230±90	280 B.C.	
05	BS-1566	A	3	1.44	2280±80	330 B.C.	405 (379) 208B.C.
06	PRL-1849	C	3	0.90	2290±70	340 B.C.	
07	PRL-1983	A	4	1.77	2350±80	400 B.C.	
08	PRL-1850	C1	2	0.47	3530±70	1580 B.C.	

Discussion

Elephant and hill type coins identical to those from Balathal have been found from the excavations at Ahichchhatra[9], Kausambi[10], Kumrahar[11], Maheshwar-Navdatoli[12], Pataliputra[13], Adam[14], Pauni[15], Runija[16], Rupar[17], Sonpur[18], Taxila[19], Tilaura-kot[20], Tripuri[21], Ujjain[22] and Vaishali[23].

Apart from regular excavations, coins of the elephant and hill type have also been found at Kamrej[24], Kasarwad[25], Kausambi[26], Padmavati[27], Ujjain[28] and Vidisha[29].

These are some of the most common coins found all over Northern and Central India between the 4th and 3rd centuries B.C., fifty-eight similar are reported just from the 1912-13 excavations at Kumrahar and Bulandibaug (Pataliputra)[30].

Mitchener[31] identifies the 'elephant-and-hill' type of coins as Mauryan round cast copper coins. Lahiri[32] on the other hand ascribes to them a greater antiquity. He identifies these coins as the 'pre-Alexandrian coinage of India' on the basis of the writings of Alexander's historian Nearchus who says Indians used cast and not hammered copper coinage[33]. Lahiri thus is of the opinion that these coins belong to the 4th century B.C. and maybe even to the beginning of the 5th century B.C.[34]. This view is echoed by Gaur[35] who substantiates his views with excavated data from Atranjikhera where cast copper coins have been found in layers C14 dated to 540 B.C. (BM-194 540+-150 B.C.). K.A. Nilakanta Sastri[36] is also of the opinion that cast copper coins are contemporary to punch-marked coins.

Excavations at Ahichchhatra also seem to agree with this as the lowermost strata (Stratum VII and VIII), dated to 300 B.C. and lower, yielded only uninscribed cast copper coins. Of the 6 found in the lower most stratum (VIII) four belong to the elephant and hill type. Three coins from the next stratum (VII) also belong to this type.[37]

Conclusion

Taking into consideration the above-mentioned facts it seems quite suggestive on the basis of the elephant and hill type coins from Balathal, that the site of Balathal was probably established in the pre-Mauryan period. The early 4th century dates from Balathal further strengthens this hypothesis.

One of the main reasons for the confusion is that many of the sites are labelled Mauryan purely on the availability of NBPW. This is not necessarily valid as the NBPW levels from Hastinapura[38] and Atranjikhera[39] have been dated the 6th century B.C. and those from Rajghat[10]to 490±110 B.C. (TF-293) (Period 16) and 470⊥110 B.C. (TF-292) (Period IA). Period IC at Rajghat is ceramically very similar To Balathal (Abhijit Dandekar pers. comm). Further mention may be made here of the fact that a large number of excavation reports of sites bearing similar artefactual assemblages to those of Balathal were written prior to the large-scale use of C14 dating in India.

Thus, on the basis of the data and dates from the site of Balathal one can decisively say that the Elephant and Hill type of coins belong to the Pre-Mauryan and Early Mauryan Period and that we should start giving them their due place in Numismatic History.

Acknowledgements

The authors are very grateful to the organisers of the seminar - Dr Mahesh Kalra of CHAEN and Dr Suraj A Pandit of the Sathaye College for inviting them to present this paper.

The real thanks though are due to (late) Prof VN Misra and his team of archaeologists at the Balathal Excavations for choosing this site without which the data for this paper wouldn't have existed.

References

1. Allan, J. *Catalogue of the Coins of Ancient India*. London: British Museum. 1936, P 94-97.

2. Misra, V. N. *Pre- and Proto-History of the Berach Basin, South Rajasthan*. Poona: Deccan College.1967, P. 35-60.
3. Hooja, Rima. *Ahar Culture and Beyond*. Oxford: BAR International Series 412. 1988.
4. Mishra, V.N.; Shinde V. S.; Mohanty, R. K.; Dalal, Kurush; Mishra, Anup; Pande, Lalit and Khakrawal, Jeevan. *Excavations at Balathal: Their Contribution to the Chalcolithic and Iron Age Cultures of Mewar, Rajasthan*. Man and Environment XX (1): 48-80; Mishra, V.N.; Shinde V. S.; Mohanty, R. K.; Pande, Lalit and Khakrawal, Jeevan; 1997. *Excavations at Balathal, Udaipur District, Rajasthan (1995-97) with Special Reference to Chalcolithic Architecture*. Man and Environment XXII (2): 35-60.
5. Dalal, Kurush F.; 2001.*Early Historical Settlement of Southern Rajasthan (Mewar) With Special Reference to Balathal: An Artefactual Approach*. PhD Thesis, Pune: Department of Archaeology, Deccan College.
6. *Ibid*. P. 164-66.
7. Misra*et al.*, op cit. 1995.
8. Dalal.*op cite*. 2001.
9. Sharma, Y.D.,*Exploration of Historical Sites.* Ancient India (9). New Delhi: ASI. 1953, 138; Fig. 9.
10. Sharma, G. R..*Excavations at Kausambi 1949-50.* Memoirs of the Archaeological Survey of India No. 74.New Delhi.1969, 83, Pl. LIII. 12,13,14.
11. Altekar, A. S. and Mishra, V., *Report on Kumrahar Excavations 1951-1955*. Patna: K. P. Jayaswal Research Institute., 195993-4, Pl. LXXA.14.
12. Sankalia, H. D.; Subbarao, B. and Deo, S. B., *Excavations at Maheshwar and Navdatoli (1952-53)*. Pune: Deccan College., 1958; 71.15-20; PL XII-15-17,19,20.
13. Sinha, B. P. and Narain, L. A., *Pataliputra Excavation 1955-56*. Patna: Directorate of Archaeology and Museums.1970, 49; Pl. XXIV.7.
14. Nath, Amarendra; *Excavations at Adam (1988-1992)* (Vol 2). Memoirs of the Archaeological Survey of India No. 109: New Delhi., 2016, 717-19, Pl 17.30.
15. Deo, S. B. and Joshi, J. P., *Pauni Excavations (1969-70)*. Nagpur: Nagpur University., 1972, 32-3, PI. XLVI.4; Shastri 1974; 4-6.
16. Dube, J. N. and Muralidhar Reddy, B., *Some Coins from Runija Excavation-1981*.Journal of the Numismatic Society of India VLVII.1985, 22-3.
17. Sharma, Y.D., *Exploration of Historical Sites.* Ancient India (9). New Delhi: ASI. 1953, 124; Fig. 4.
18. Sinha, B. P. and Verma, B. S., *Sonpur Excavations (1956 & 1959-62)*. Patna: Directorate of Archaeology and Museums, Government of Bihar.1977, 68; Pl. XXIII.15-18.
19. Marshall, J.; 1951.*Taxila (3 vols)*. Cambridge: Cambridge University Press., 760-1, PI. 235.20-22.
20. Mitra, D., *Excavations at Tilaura-kot and Kodan and Explorations in the Nepalese Tarai*. Calcutta: The Department of Archaeology, His Majesty's Government of Nepal., 1972, 90,98: Pl. XXVI.18.
21. Dikshit, M. G., *Coins from the Tripuri Excavations (1952)*. Journal of the Numismatic Society of India XVI: 65-71, 1952, 65-70.

22. AARADG 1938-39; IAR 1956-57, 23, Fig.11.
23. Spooner, D. B., *Excavations at Basarh.*Annual Report of the Archaeological Survey of India 1913-14, 1917, 173; Smith, 1938, 202, PI.XXIII, Fig. 3.
24. Gadre, A. S., *Important Coins from Baroda State.* Journal of the Numismatic Society of India I, 1939, 24.
25. Disalkar, M. A. *Sixteen Copper Coins from Malwa.* Journal of the Numismatic Society of India 10, 1949:38, 41-2. Pl III.10.
26. Altekar, A. S., *Some new Coins from Kausambi.* Journal of the Numismatic Society of India XX, 1958, 149-50.
27. Trivedi, H. V., *Some More New Coins from Padmavati.* Journal of the Numismatic Society of India XVIII (2), 1956; 67, Pl.IX5.
28. Ramachandran, T. N., *A Recent Find of Coins from Ujjaiyini.* Journal of the Numismatic Society of India XIII (1), 1951, 75, Pl. v.9; Smith, 1938: 154 Reg. No. 29.
29. Jain, Balachandra, *Early Coins from Vidisa in the Raipur Museum.* Journal of the Numismatic Society of India XXIII, 1951, 305.
30. Altekar, A. S., *Coins in Kumrahar and Bulandibaug (Pataliputra) Excavations in 1912-13.* Journal of the Numismatic Society of India XIII (2), 1951, 144.
31. Mitchener, M, *Some Kausambhi,Rajgir and Mauryan Copper Coins.*Journal of the Numismatic Society of India.XXXIV (2), 1972, 157.
32. Lahiri, A. N., *Archaic Coins of Northern India.* Journal of the Numismatic Society of India XXXV (1), 1973, 30.
33. Lahiri, *ibid*, p.29.
34. Lahiri, *ibid*, 30.
35. Gaur, R. C., *Archaeological Significance of the Coins unearthed at Atranjikhera (Dist. Etah, U.P.).* Journal of the Numismatic Society of India XLVIII.1986, 69.
36. Sastri, K. A. Nilakanta, *Age of the Nandas and Mauryas.* Delhi: MotilalBanarasidass., 1967, 122.
37. Ray, S. C., *Cast Copper Coins from the Excavations at Ahichhatra 1940-44.*Journal of the Numismatic Society of India XLIX, 1987: 13-18.
38. Lal, B. B., *Excavations at Hastinapur and other Explorations in the Upper Ganga and Sutlej Basins 1950-52.* Ancient India 10 & 11. 1956.
39. Gaur, R. C., *Excavations at Atranjikhera (Early Civilisation of the Upper Ganga Basin).* Delhi: MotilalBanarasidass, 1983.
40. Narain, A. K. and Roy, T. N., *Excavations at Rajghat (1957-58; 1960-65) Part - I.* Varanasi: Banaras Hindu University. 1976, 25.

3

Wema Kadphises' Gold Coinage:

Reformation of Coinage in Ancient India from Silver to Gold

Venkitachalam Iyer

Introduction

The Yuezhi under the leadership of the Kushanas came from Central Asia and conquered all the earlier dynasties of the Northwest. The empire reigned from Central Asia to the North Western India. The first Kushana emperor Kujula Kadphises in 50 C.E., issued coins and adopted designs which were already in use. It was an extension of Indo Greek style coinage for more than three centuries who introduced bilingual inscription of Greek and Kharoshthi script on coins. This was later followed by Indo-Scythian and Indo-Parthian who ruled the region before Kushanas came to power. Coins minted were mainly in silver and copper. Wema Takto, son of Kujula Kadphises, minted coins with same design but discontinued silver coins and issued only copper coins.

Coins issued before Wema Kadphises, grandson of Kujula Kadphises, were majorly in silver or copper, but gold was rare and not minted in ancient India and found mainly with Roman and Hellenistic empire. But under the reign of Wema, we find majority of documented gold coins and few numbers of silver coins. The paucity of silver coins in Kushanas is an enigma.

Reformation of coins started with Wema Kadphises. Wema had introduced 7 types of gold coins, 1 type of copper and silver coins each. The paucity of Silver coins cannot be due to shortage of Silver, as silver coins were minted by multiple kingdoms who ruled along with Kushanas. In the North-west Indo-Scythian, Indo-Parthian issued only silver coins and they were also found in central, Western India and Deccan region which were issued by Nahapana and Satahavanas. These kingdoms were ruling beyond the boundaries of Kushana Empire. It is also strange while Wema minted gold coins and parallel kingdoms did not have even single known specimen of Gold coins.

Unlike gold and copper coins, we do know one specimen of Silver coin of Wema which is present at British Museum coin collection Museum number IOC.273.

(The coin can be viewed on British Museum's website at the following link: http://www.britishmuseum.org/research/collection_online/collection_object_details.aspx?objectId=672139&partId=1&searchText=Wema+kadphises&images=true&museumno=IOC.273&page=1)

Scholars also have discovered few specimens of silver coins of his successors. It suggests that silver coin might have minted for circulation in less numbers and may be issued in certain zones. Ancient India carried a flourishing trade with foreign countries and the Kushana Empire lay at the centre of the Silk route, beginning from China (Han dynasty) to Europe / Persia and further into the Roman Empire. Trading activities reached their zenith and had a great demand of luxury goods from India by the Roman aristocracy. Like the Roman rulers, the Kushanas used the art of coinage as a medium of manifestation of their royal power.

Before the advent of the Kushanas, the silver coinage of North-Western India had become heavily debased by the time of the Indo-Scythian ruler, Azes II, who was ousted by Gondophares I, the first Indo-Parthian ruler of the region. Silver coins minted by the last effective Indo-Greek ruler of the region, Hermaeus have high silver content. However, the coins of Azes II and Gondophores I are heavily debased.

A comparative study of certain groups of silver coins of Hermaeus, issued after his death indicate a gradual debasement of metal. History suggests of political unrest in parts of North-Western India towards the end or immediately after rule of Hermaeus. The lack of a strong political authority in a commercially important zone like North Western India probably tempted private moneyer's or/and irresponsible powers to mint coins, as they naturally wanted to make profit out of their business.

Conditions were thus ripe for the operation of an economic principle called Gresham's law after Sir Thomas Gresham, one of the masters of England's mint in the 16th century. This law enjoins that "all types of metallic money in circulation declared equal in value or purchasing power by the government must be kept equal in value or buying power. If they are not, the undervalued money will be hoarded, exported to places where it's true value will be recognized, or melted down for sale in the bullion market, while the overvalued, cheaper money, will be kept in circulation

"Is it just a happenstance that, the circulation of debased currency in that area (North-West) by the Scytho-Parthian?" More or so it could be considered as a fact, because of this menacing tendency of replacing good money by bad money became popular that ruler like Azes II could not check it.

Extant of Kushana Kingdoms (Annexure I: Map attached) from 200 BC to 100 AD, illustrates Kushanas has replaced Indo Scythian and Indo-Parthian.

MAP I: - https://www.cemml.colostate.edu/cultural/09476/afgh02-07enl.html

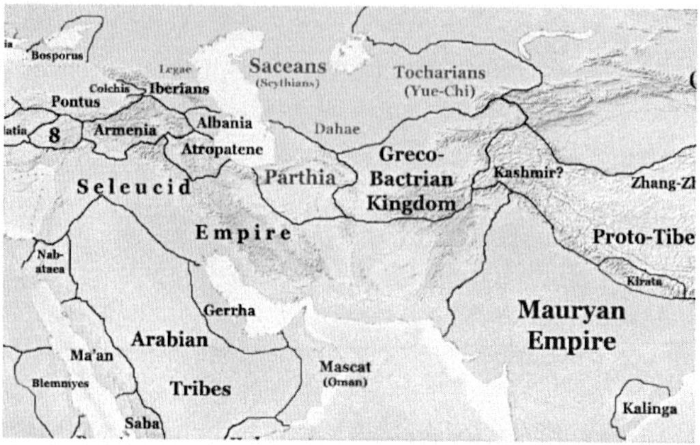

▲ 200 BC

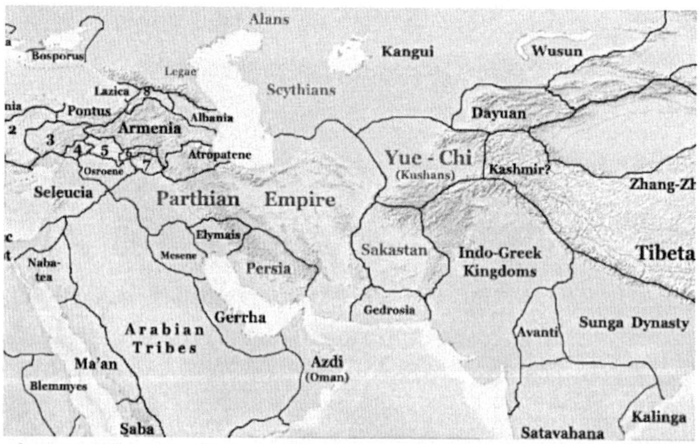

▲ 100 BC

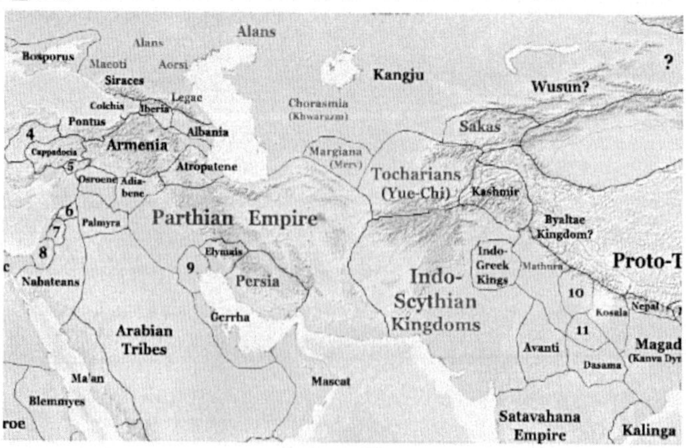

▲ 50 BC

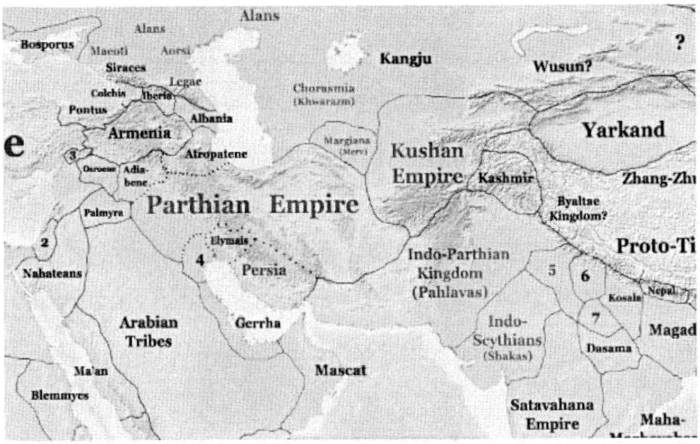

▲ 50 AD

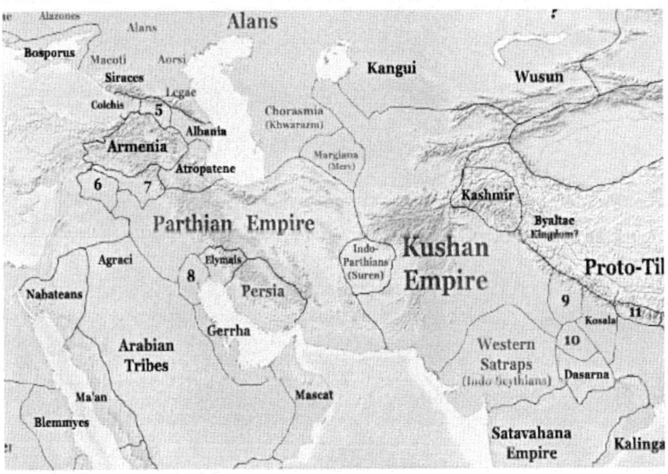

100 AD ▲

Kushanas under Wema conquered regions ruled earlier by Scythian and Parthian empire saw a good opportunity of Trade between Roman and Han Dynasty. Debased currency was in circulation and action was required to uproot it to bring certainty in the commerce and increase the economy of the empire. To overcome this they required cutting edge technology to beat the counterfeit / debasement of currency.

Wema had inherited a large empire with ample opportunity of Trade but no tradition of regular minting in gold, however clear precedents for the production of gold coinage is seen. The Hellenistic Kings of Bactria and Gandhara had issued occasional gold staters and in India the gold coins of Rome were imported and familiar to many users. Under the reign of Wema gold minting was introduced in small numbers and major denomination was dinar and few double and quarter dinar. Coins minted were primarily with portraying Shaivism on reverse. Technique / Technology of minting gold coins were definitely different from silver /copper issues.

Wema might have introduced gold coins for the following reasons:

1. New technology/metal to beat counterfeit coins, as gold was a costly metal compared to silver. Local moneyer couldn't have afforded to mint gold coins in large numbers unless authorized by empire.
2. Easy to carry gold coins in Trade as less coins would be required when compared to Silver coins.
3. Stable currency was required for comfort and trade, as silver was continuously debased.
4. To leave a royal mark and to portray power.

Conclusion

Gold coins minted were certainly for trade. However Sir Gresham's theory could be applied on Pre-Kushanas/Kushanas era of coinage.

References

Mukherjee B N, *Kushana Silver Coinage,* Indian Museum, Kolkata, 2004

Sharva Sathya, *The Kushana Numismatics*, Prananva Prakashan, New Delhi, 1985

Chattopadhyay Bhaskar, *The Age of Kushans – A Numismatic Study*, Punthi Pustak, Calcutta, 1967

Errington Elizabeth and Curtis Sarkosh Vesta, *From Persia to Punjab (Exploring Ancient Iran, Afghanistan & Pakistan)*, Csmvs, Mumbai, 2014

Bracey Robert, *The Coinage of Wema Kadphises,* https://www.academia.edu/2078734/The_Coinage_Of_Wema_Kadphises

Fernando López Sánchez, *The Mint Sites of The Kushān Empire, https://www.academia.edu/2078818/The_Mint_Cities_Of_The_Kushan_Empire*

Wema Kadphises Silver Coin image in the British Museum http://www.britishmuseum.org/research/collection_online/collection_object_details.aspx?objectId=672139&partId=1&searchText=Wema+kadphises&images=true&museumno=IOC.273&page=1

Map I https://www.cemml.colostate.edu/cultural/09476/afgh02-07enl.html

4

The Disappearance of Tusker Elephants on Coinage of Later Satavahana Kings:
Visible Signs of Polarity amongst Motifs in Coinage

Chaitanya Bhide

Vajra/elephant (Airāvata-Vāhana of Indra Dev[1]), has been found on the ancient Indus valley seals, punch marked coins and tribal coins and much later on Satavahana coins. Their First appearance of an Elephant on a Satavahana coins arose out of fierce expansionist policies of Satavahana King Satkarni I and that of Kalinga King Kharavela.

The original incidence of appearance of Elephant on Satavahana coinage occurs when Kalinga King Kharavela adopts the Srivatsa and Svastika (Svastisri[2] - Originally said to have been a Satavahana state symbol) on his coinage to openly proclaim his suzerainty over geographical area captured from SK-I and his allies Raikās (Khandesh-Ahmadnagar) and Bhōjakās (Berar) during his 4th regnal year. This rivalry arose along the length of Krishna river. Much later (Post SK-I, Queen Nagamanika as widow) most the lost territories were to be taken back under the backing of Satavahanas and allies, notably the Maharathis, who had family relations to Satavahana King SK-I by marriage.

King Satavahana started portraying '*Elephants*' (at times Tusker elephants) for the first time on Satavahana coinage in the region[3] (possible victorious war campaign). Kalinga was well known for the best type of elephants and ivory, hence there was a very flourishing ivory industry at Dantapura[4]. Elephants were later to become a common stay on coinage and seen at pillar capitals of Kārla, Bedsā, Nāsik, Amaravati, Sanchi etc.

Elephant type coins of Satavahanas are found in large quantities in hoards of Kalinga (Territories), which include regions of Core Kalinga, Nagarjunakonda, followed by

Kondapur, Warangal, Kotalingala, Peddabankur, and Kalinga border regions of Hyderabad (North of Dantapur) (Refer MAP I).

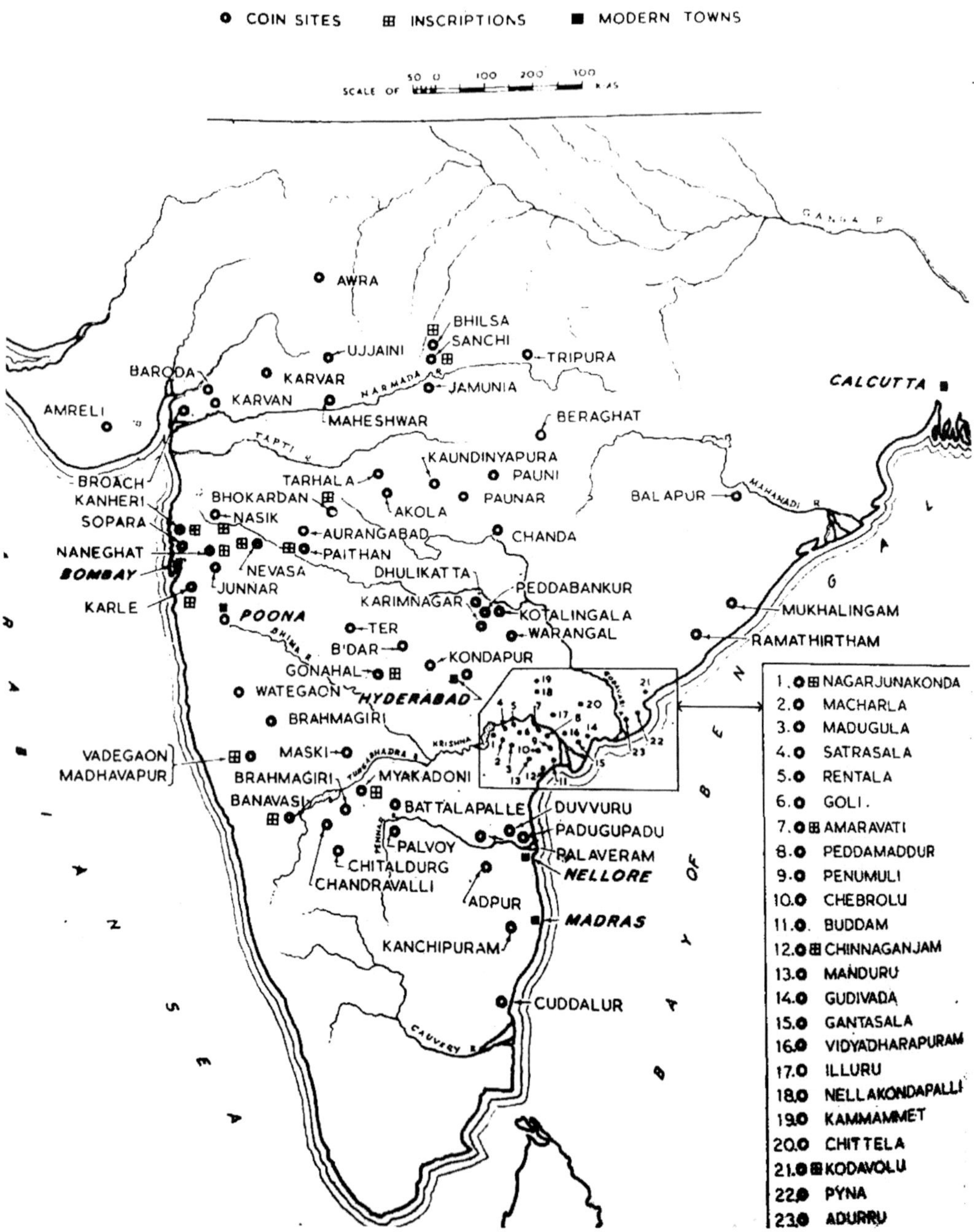

MAP I: **Directly from the book: Coinage of the Satavahana Empire by I.K. Sarma**

It must be specifically noted that the Tusker-Elephant type coins are found at the Warangal hoard, which could be directly attributed to the King Satavahana issuing Elephant type coins in the Kalinga region (Refer TABLE I). Elephant series for the early kings is found in the hoards of Warangal, Kotalingala and Kondapur. As time passed under the later kings, these elephant varieties are to be found in hoards all over the empire, *a specific geographic (concentric) spread is seen. Refer MAP II: - King-wise Concentric spread of Elephant series coinage.*

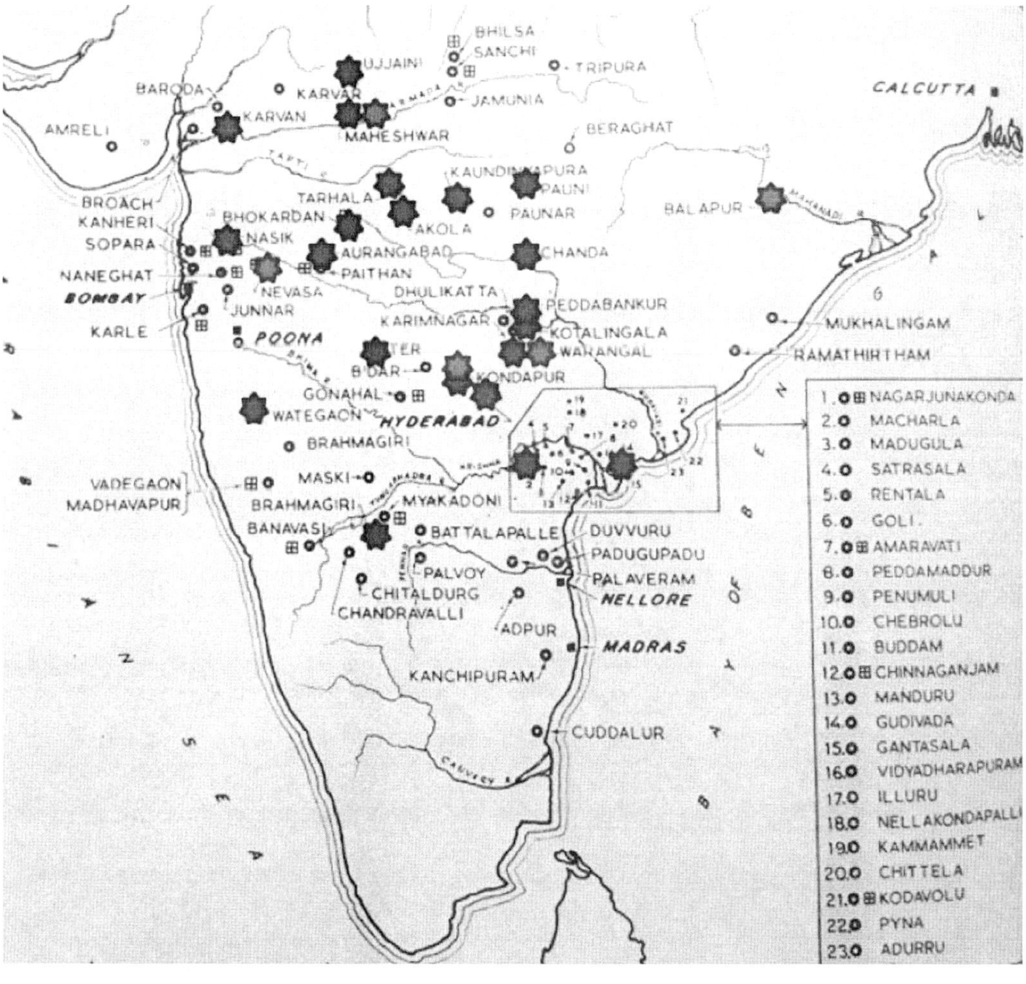

MAP II: - Geographically-Concentric Spread of Elephant Series of Satavahana Coinage. Chart prepared as per Hoard/Provenance Data from the book by IK Sarma (Data Finds till the 1980's Only).

Table I: Elephant Series Coins of Satavahana Kings[13] (Excluding the Coin details - Weight, Shape, Material) – (Timeline could be re-arranged with Simuka in 30BC, rather than the much earlier date noted by other scholars)

				Remark for Tuskers – ↑	
			Peculiar Variety –●	Jewelled neck Series – ↓	
King	**Era**	**Coin/No I K Sarma**	**Provenance**	**Obverse**	**Remark**
Siri Satkarni-I	189-179 BCE	– –			
Satavahana	179-161 BCE	B-1	Nevasa	Tusker Elephant - Walking right	↑ (11.59)
		B-1a	Nevasa	Tusker Elephant - Walking right	↑ (11.79)
		B-2	Nevasa	No Tusker	–
		B-2a	Nevasa	No Tusker	–
		B-3	Kondapur	Stout Elephant	●
		B-4	Warangal	Tusker Elephant - Walking right	↑ (7.12)
		B-4a	Nevasa	–	–
		B-4b	Aurangabad	–	–
		B-5	Akola	No Tusker	–
		B-6	Kotalingala	No Tusker	–
		B-6a	Kotalingala	No Tusker	–
		B-6b	Hyderabad	No Tusker	–
Sati Siri	–	B-7	Malwa	Crude Elephant Tusker - Right	↑ (6.54)
		B-8	Ujjaini	No Tusker	–
Kauisikiputra	–	B-9	Hyderabad	No Tusker	–
		B-10	Hyderabad	No Tusker	–
		B-11	Hyderabad	No Tusker	–
Satkarni - II	161-145 BCE	B-12	Pauni	No Tusker	–

		B-13	Kondapur	Stout Elephant to Right no Tusk	●
		B-14	Maheshwar Navdatoli	Elephant Tusker Walking Left	↑ (6.30)
		B-15	Nasik	No Tusker	–
		B-15a	Kotalingala	No Tusker	–
		B-15b	Kotalingala	No Tusker	–
		B-16	Western India	Tusker Elephant, Left	↑ (11.72)
		B-16a	Western India	Tusker Elephant, Left	↑ (11.72)
		B-17	Malwa	No Tusker	–
		B-17a	Malwa	No Tusker	–
		B-18	Western India	No Tusker	–
		B-18a,b,c	Karvan	No Tusker	–
		B-19	Kaundinyapura	No Tusker	–
		B-20	Western India	Stout Tusker Elephant to Right	↑ (7.90)
Sapilaka (Or King Apilaka)	87-75 BCE	B-22	Balapur	Elephant Tuskar Standing - Right	↑ (4.21)
Chhimuka Satavahana	40 BCE	B-23	Kotalingala	No Tusker	–
		B-23a...c	Kotalingala	No Tusker	–
Gautamiputra Satakarni	54-88 BCE	B-24	Nevasa	Stout – No Tusker	●
		B-25	Nevasa	Running Elephant	●
		B-25a	Ujjaini	Vajra - Peculiar – No Tusker	●
		B-25b	Peddabankur	No Tusker	–
		B-25c	Ter	No Tusker	–
		B-26	Nevasa	Stout – No Tusker	●
		B-27	Nevasa	No Tusker	–
		B-28	Ujjaini	No Tusker	–
		B-28a	Kathaiwada	No Tusker	–
		B-29	Bhokardan	Stumpy – No Tusker	●

		B-30	Aurangabad	No Tusker	–
		B-31	Kondapur	No Tusker	–
		B-32	Karavan, Kamrej	No Tusker	–
		B-33	Peddabankur	No Tusker	–
		B-34	Ujjaini	No Tusker	–
		B-35, 36	Kondapur	No Tusker	–
		B-37	Hyderabad	Stout – No Tusker	●
		B-38	Coastal Andhra	No Tusker	–
		B-39	Kamrej	No Tusker	–
		B-40	Nevasa	Playful Elephant - No Tusker	●
Vasishthiputra Pulumavi (II)	88-116 CE	B-41	Kondapur	No Tusker	–
		B-42	Nagarjunikonda	No Tusker	–
		B-43	Chanda	No Tusker	–
		B-43a	Chanda	Variant, Elephant - No Tusker	●
		B-44	Poona, Tarahala	No Tusker	–
		B-45	Chandravali	No Tusker	–
		B-46	Peddabankur	No Tusker	–
		B-47	Nagarjunikonda	No Tusker	–
		B-48	Hyderabad	No Tusker	–
Vasishthiputra Satakarni	116-145 CE	B-49, 54a	Nagarjunikonda	No Tusker	–
		B-49a, 50	Kondapur	No Tusker	–
		B-51	Peddabankur	No Tusker	–
		B-53	Nevasa	No Tusker	–
		B-54	Chanda	No Tusker	–
		B-55	Hyderabad	No Tusker	–
Vasishthiputra Siva Siri Pulumavi	145-152 CE	B-56, 57, 58, 58a	Wategaon	No Tusker	–

		B-59	Kondapur	No Tusker	–
		B-60, 60a	Hyderabad	No Tusker	–
		B-61	Peddabankur	No Tusker	–
Vasishthiputra Siva Skanda Satakarni	153-165 CE	B-62	Hyderabad	Jewelled Neck Legend - No Tusker	↓
		B-62a	Nagarjunakonda	Jewelled Neck Legend - No Tusker	↓
		B-63	Chanda, Tarhala	Jewelled Neck Legend - No Tusker	↓
		B-64, 64a	Wategaon	Jewelled Neck Legend - No Tusker	↓
		B-65	Bhokardan	No Tusker	–
Gautamiputra Yajna Sri Satakarni	165-194 CE	B-66	Nagarjunakonda, Banavasi	No Tusker	–
		B-67	Kondapur, Amaravati, Brahmapuri, Gudivada	Jewelled Neck Legend - No Tusker	↓
		B-68	Krishna District	No Tusker	–
		B-69	**Kondapur**	**Elephant Tusker facing right**	↑ **(14.12)**
		B-70a	Kondapur	Jewelled Neck Legend - No Tusker	↓
		B-71	Peddabankur	No Tusker	–
		B-71a	Hyderabad	Elephant to Right, Neck-Belt	●
Vijaya Satakarni	194-200 CE	B-72	Tarhala, Chanda	Jewelled Neck Legend - No Tusker	↓
Pulamavi-IV	203-210 CE	B-73	Tarhale	No Tusker	–
Rudra Satkarni	210 Onwards	B-74	Amaravati	Jewelled Neck Legend - No Tusker	↓
		B–74a	Godavari	Jewelled Neck Legend - No Tusker	↓
		B-75	Kanchipuram	No Tusker	–

		B-75a	Coastal Andhra	No Tusker	–
Saka Satkarni	– –	B-76	Tarhala	No Tusker	–
		B-76a	Coastal Andhra	No Tusker	–
Karna Satkarni	– –	B-77	Chanda	No Tusker	–
		B-77a	Tarhala	Jewelled Neck Legend - No Tusker	↓
		B-77b	Coastal Andhra	Jewelled Neck Legend - No Tusker	↓
Kumbha Satkarni	Till 220	B-78, 78a	Tarhala	No Tusker	–

Some of the distant hoards of having Tusker-Elephant type coins (Refer TABLE I) like Nevasa, Malwa, Maheswar-Navdatoli, and few western India hoards could be the result of trade, as it contains coins of later period. Balapur hoard could be attributed to trade as well as war campaign in the Kalinga border regions, since it had coins of later Kings (Apilaka) and is a Kalinga border territory.

The ***Tusker-Elephant series started by King Satavahana*** *is continued by many later kings, till King Sapilaka (Or King Apilaka[5]) who issued few of the* ***last in the series to be found at the hoard of Balapur*** *(Refer TABLE I - Marked by '! Symbol). Example, of King Satavahana Coins: - B1 (Fig.1) (Lead-Circular, 22 mm dia, 11.59 gms) & B-4 (Copper-square, 20 mm dia, 7.128 gms). All of the Tusker series of coins as marked in TABLE-I - '!, have a weight range of 6.5 gms to 12 gms, with only one exception of coin at Balapur having weight of 4.2 gms.*

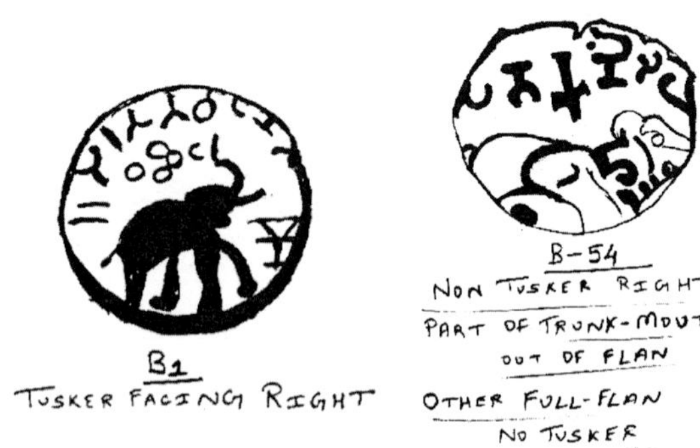

Fig.1: B1 -*Heavy-Tusker Elephant Variety,* King Satavahana &
B-54: - Non Tusker - King Vasishthiputra Satkarni[14]

Nearly 240 Years after king Apilaka, later King Gautamiputra Yajna Satkarni *issued a* ***Tusker-Elephant heavy type*** *B-69 (14 gms)(Fig.2), to be found at the hoard of*

Kondapur (Refer TABLE I - Marked by '! Symbol). Un-usually large size (heavier than earlier Kings/Varities).

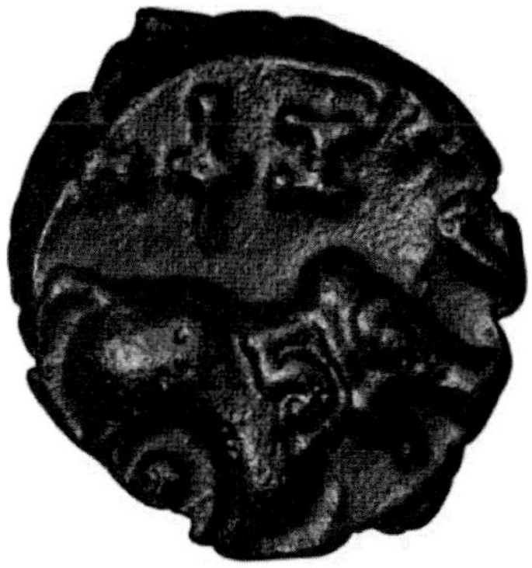

Fig.2: Heavy-Tusker Elephant Variety - of GPYS (IK Sarma)

Discussion: ***(1)*** *Gautamiputra Satkarni (GPS)* ***introduces matryonomic legends (Tuskers Disappear).*** ***(2)*** *GPYS re-introduces* ***Tusker-Elephant coins (after 240 Years).*** ***(3)*** *The period of 240 years is full of* ***Light-Tusker-Elephant variety***. (Fig.3)

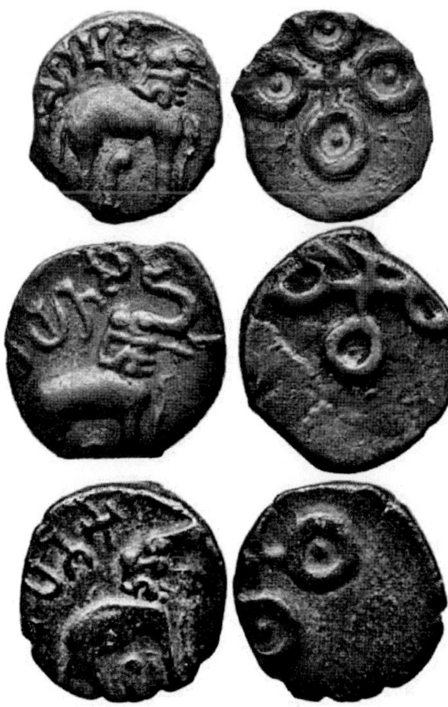

Fig.3: Light-Tusker Elephant Variety - i) Pulumavi, ii) Yajna, iii) Satakarni [15]
(Some are attributed to be minted by later feudatories/Contemporaries of Satavahana's).

(1) There are two short reigns of unconfirmed Kings after King Sapilaka (Or King Apilaka), then comes the reign of Gautamiputra Satkarni (SK-III - GPS). GPS introduces the matryonomic legends on coinages, first of its kinds on coinages. IK Sarma in his books quotes that "It appears that royal mothers were devotees of *rishipatnis* (seven great mothers), through whose grace their sons were believed to have risen to rule the earth"[6].

It has been noted by few scholars[7] that SK-I was garlanded by an female-elephant at the time of his coronation (a story noted from Muladeva in Devendra's commentary on the *Uttarādhyayana-Śūtra*). *The female-elephant are depicted on coins without tusks*[8] (Fig.4). Other animal motif such as that of the lion, which is in fact a attacking lioness as attributed by Dr. Gokhale, depicting aggressive position of the Satavahanas in the then political struggle between themselves and the Kshaharatas.[9] Notable reference of Ayodhya must be considered, rulers of Ayodhya were said to have inclined to a male-god, however the occurrence of elephant on coins seem to have something to do with representation of goddess Laxmi[10].

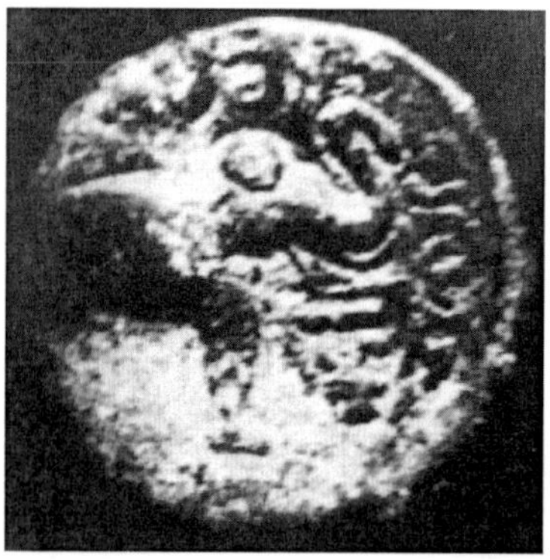

Fig.4: Non-Tusker Elephant Variety - of GPS/VPS (Marudharatrs Auctions) (Auction: 25, Lot 40)

Though there is paucity in the available evidence, it can said that there the kings showed unwavering reverence to the rishipatnis. This could also have been sublimated on the coinage in the form of the Non-Tusker-Elephant to attacking lioness. It is however difficult to ascertain this form inclination in case of other animals portrayed on coins.

(2) GPS was known to have completely defeated the King Nahapana, and conquered huge territories in all directions, however during the reignal years of his son VPP, strong evidence suggested scholars to conclude that a new Dynastic Line of Western Kshatraps under King Chastana took conquered vast territories reaching as far as north konkan, Ujjain, Pune, Nasik etc, pushing back the Satavahanas *(Post GPS & or Son VPP[11])* to a new capital. This downfall continued for some period when there we many wars to be fought between the two. The Satavahana's remained weak and ruled much south peninsular region un-till King Gautamiputra Yajna Satkarni (GPYS) took advantage of a weakened

power of Saka King Rudradaman, allowing him to recapture Ujjain and bringing back the Glory Era to the likes to his forefathers. The reappearance of Tusker Elephants on coins at the Kondapur Hoard (Much Earlier a Kalinga Territory) could simply be the Resurgent Satavahanas reflecting the glory era of their forefathers SK-II, King Satavahana and others. These coins from the hoard are unusually large of 28 mm dia & 14 grams (unusual size for circular Lead coins), closely similar to a variety of Non-Tuskers issued by GPS (B-36).

(3) For 240 Years form the end of reign of King Sapilaka (or King Apilaka) to reign of King GPYS there are several ***Light-Tusker-Elephant variety***. These could have been the result of ivory trade. This fact is evident from "Geography" by Ptolemy[12], who mentions this region as "Pytimdra", emporium (trade center) (Pithumda of the hathigumpha Insciption), though written at the time of 140 AD.

Moreover these Tusker verities belong to Vasishthiputra Pulumavi (II), Vasishthiputra Satkarni & Gautamiputra Yajna Satkarni. Most of these coins are Potin/Circular, 16-20 mm, 2.0-3.88 gms, no Square/rectangle of lead are to be found. Out of the 3 kings, 2 of them are known to have ruled a era of extreme conflict in the Empire, having been pushed back to south-eastern Maharashtra and Andhra Pradesh, and Kalinga region. The reason behind the ***Heavy-Tusker variety was lost.*** Some of the coins in Fig.5, belong to a much later period of decline of Satavahana, which can be attributed to the poor minting of these light weight potin varieties.

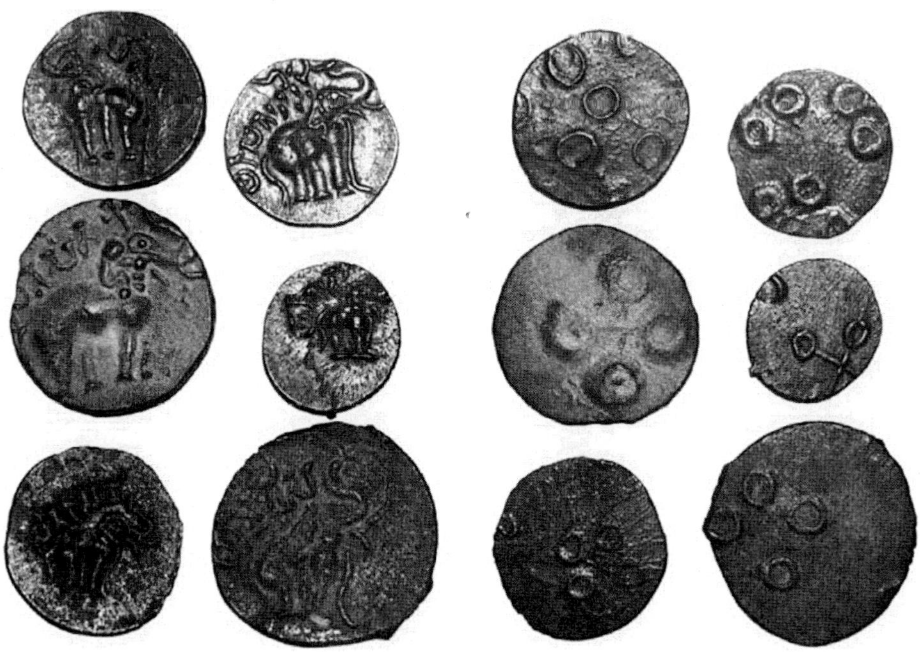

Fig.5: Light-Tusker Elephant Variety - of VPP & VPS.[16]

Conclusion

The Satavahana Coinage is very accurate when it comes to details, legends, motifs, other symbols. The mint masters carried out their task with full loyalty to their kings. Hence the above observed facts could not have been a result of negligence. But what was done was in the purest sense of reflection of culture and society on coinage. There is paucity of historical evidence for both Points 1.), 2.) and 3.), requiring some cultural/archaeological evidence as in the case of Point 1.) and evidence of campaign by GPYS in Point 2.).

However, it cannot be denied that the matryonomic legends on coinages was to pay obeisance to the mother, and ultimately to the rishipatnis. This idea was to be instilled onto the population of the empire through coinage having complete change of polarity in legends and also in certain motifs. The appearance of Tusker variety on VPP & VPS clearly seems to be a result of ivory trade, as both of these kings controlled areas in south-east Maharashtra and Andhra Pradesh along with occupied Kalinga-border territories and the coins are of lighter Potin issues. Which could be confirmed by the sudden appearance of a ***Heavy-Tusker variety*** under GPYS (With Triangle headed standard, feature - motif in early coinage).

GPYS could have carried out a small campaign in his time in the Kalinga region Or the resurgence resulting to the Kondapur finds of the tusker-elephant variety of unusually large coins. The size in itself provides for a specific event, prompting them to mint coins similar to the early King's. More evidence needs to be gather to fully ascertain certain aspects.

Many campaign/wars were fought in the area along the Krishna river.

- Tusker Elephant Hoards – All have weight range of 6.5 gms – 12 gms Nevasa & Warangal (Under King Satavahana) Kondapur (Post GPS), Malwa (Sati Siri), Maheshwar, Western IN (SK-II), Balapur (Sapilaka)
- Earliest Non-Tusker, Kotalingala Hyderabad, Kondapur, Akola, Nevasa under King Satavahan Malwa, Ujjain (Under Sati Siri), Hyderabad (Kausikiputra), Pauni, Maheshwar, Navdatoli, Nasik Karvan, Western India, Kaundinyapura (Under SK-II)

  Other Kings of Chhimuka, GPS, VPP, VPS, VPSS, GPYS, Later Kings issue Elephant Types – found – in hoards all over central India.

  Chart prepared as per Hoard/Provenance Data from the book by I.K. Sarma, Data of finds till – 1980 only

Abbreviations

GPS	Gautamiputra Satkarni;
GPYS	Gautamiputra Yajna Satkarni.;
VPP	Vasishthiputra Pulumavi;
VPS	Vasishthiputra Satkarni.

References

1. Bhaskar Chattopadhyay, *Coins and Icons, A study of Myths and Symbols in Indian Numismatic Art*, Punthi Pustak, Calcutta: 1977, p.40.
2. Sarma, I K, *The Coinage of Satvahan Empire*, Agam Kala Prakashan, Delhi 1980, p.70; C. Sivaramamurti, *Sanskrit Literature and Art Mirrors of Indian Culture*, p.98.
3. Sarma, I K, *Op. Cit.,* 1980,p.70.
4. Patnaik, Nihar Ranjan, *Economic History of Orissa, chapter: Economic Life in ancient Orissa*, p.24 & p.27.
5. Dutta, Mala, *A Study of the Satavahana Coinage*, Harman Publishing House, New Delhi 1990, p.270.
6. Sarma, I K, *The Coinage of Satvahan Empire*, Agam Kala Prakashan, Delhi 1980, p.62.
7. Shastri, Ajay Mitra, *The Age of the Satavahana: Chapter on Satavahana Coinage: Origins and Influences. Dr. Shobhana Gokhale*, Aryan Books International, 1999, p.281. (Chapter arranges data and timeline accepting Simuka in 30 BC, rather than the much earlier date noted by other scholars.)
8. Shastri, Ajay Mitra,*The Age of the Satavahana: Chapter on Satavahana Coinage: Origins and Influences. Dr. Shobhana Gokhale*, Aryan Books International, 1999, p.283.
9. Bhaskar Chattopadhyay, *Coins and Icons, A study of Myths and Symbols in Indian Numismatic Art*, Punthi Pustak, Calcutta: 1977, p.42 &p.249-251.
10. Shastri, Ajay Mitra,*The Age of the Satavahana,* Aryan Books International, 1999,p.52.
11. Shastri, Ajay Mitra,*The Age of the Satavahana,* Aryan Books International, 1999,p.132.
12. Sarma, I K, *The Coinage of Satvahan Empire*, Agam Kala Prakashan, Delhi 1980, p.42-286, (List compiled referring to Elephant Type of Coins of all Satavahana Kings).
13. Sarma, I K, *The Coinage of Satvahan Empire*, Agam Kala Prakashan, Delhi 1980, Coin B1-Eye Copy, Plate Section; Coin B-54 variety from my own collection.
14. Coin B1 - Eye Copy form The Coinage of Satavahana Empire, I K Sarma Plate Section; Coin B-54 variety from my own collection.
15. Bombay Auction Catalogue - Auction No: - 05, LOT No: - 23.
16. Arun Joy C, Paladka-Moodabidri - 9th August 2010 - *Blog-post*, Images (from collection).

5

Water Crafts on Coins, Seals and Sealings

Sreemanti Laha & Suvasree Chatterjee

The position of Indian subcontinent is such, that we have a huge maritime space because the southern part of the subcontinent is surrounded by three oceans namely the Indian Ocean, Bay of Bengal and Arabian Sea. In addition to this, countless perennial and non-perennial rivers, have given India a unique geographical character. This maritime space and riverine connections has been utilized to the fullest from the immense past. The principal objective of our paper is to explore water craft motifs on Indian numismatic specimens within the chosen time frame that is *circa* 3rd century B.C.E to 7th century C.E. This period has been chosen because there is complete absence of water craft motifs on Indian numismatic evidences prior or later to this period.

It is needless to say that coins are used as the medium of exchange. They also acted as the visual communicating media and at times also as advertising media. So symbols and scenes depicted on them were chosen very carefully. Each motif or scene bears a unique significance. The depictions of different types of water crafts on the coins, seals and sealings of an authority is a clear indication of communication and the trading relations with different areas inland or abroad and their building technologies. The find spots of these numismatic specimens indicate the area where those crafts were plying, and more over they provide us valuable information about the functions and contribution of these water crafts in ancient trade and communication of a certain area. Within the time frame of our study only some local punch marked coins of billon, some terracotta seals and sealings found from Chandraketugarh (North 24 Parganas), some silver punch marked coins of local type found from Wari-Bateshwar (Dhaka, Bangladesh) and also some Sātavāhana and Pallava lead coins from Andhra coast and Deccan have the depictions of water crafts on them.

Chandraketugarh is an archaeological site in West Bengal, with an expansion of 38 square kilometers, located in the district of North 24 Paragana about 35 kilometer north-east of Kolkata. River Vidyadhari is in its immidiate vicinity. According to some historians Chandraketugarh is identical with the port city of 'Gange' mentioned in various literary sources including Periplus Maris Erythrai. Though, this theory is not unanimously accepted. It was one of the most popular ports in early historic Bengal[1]. Some punch marked coins with 4 symbols on the obverse made of billon had been found from this site, which have depictions of water crafts on them. The reverses are either blank or with one or two unclear symbols. These coins are dated circa 400-300 B.C.E. Beside that we also get plenty of terracotta seals and sealings from this site having the depictions of water crafts dated approximately 300-400 C.E. Some of these punch marked coins and terracotta seals and sealings are preserved in State Archaeological Museum, Kolkata. The coins prove that this place had a money based economy and prosperous community.

Wari and Bateshwar are two adjacent villages under Belabo police station in Narasingdi district, some 4km south-west of Belabo town in Dhaka, Bangldesh. These two villages are on high land and surrounded by low marshlands. The confluence of Brahmaputra and Arial kha river is 5km North-East of Wari. From the bank of these marsh lands (which is now believed to be the dry bed of old Brahmaputra) innumerable of silver punch marked coins in earthen pots have been yielded. These coins also have 4 symbols on the obverse. The reverses are either blank or with some unclear symbols. As Dilip Chakravarti believes that Wari-Bateshwar gained prosperity around 3rd century B.C and it lasted for a few centuries.[2] The silver punch marked coins can't be dated before 3rd century B.C[3], thus the punch marked coins of Chandraketugarh and Wari-Bateshwar are contemporary. It is striking that the number of Wari-Bateshwar coins (few thousand) is greater than that obtained from other areas in Bangladesh which yielded similar coins. The National Museum of Dhaka has a large collection of Wari Bateshwar punch marked coins.[4] Except sun and six arms the main symbols of these coins are ṣ boat, bird, fish, hooked fish, lobster, etc. which clearly signifies maritime connections. It has been proven undoubtedly that Wari-Bateshwar was a maritime city or a riverine port[5] with a prosperous community and money based economy.

This is necessary to mention here that there was no unified geographical or geopolitical unit called Bengal from 600 B.C.E to 1300 C.E. The span of nearly two millennia witnessed the active presence of five sub-regions namely Pundravardhana, Radha, Vanga, Samatata, Harikela with their distinctive traits in political development, material milieu, and socio-cultural situations. Depending on the three different local coin types found from the Bengal region, there appears to be at least three different economical zones in Bengal issuing coinage of their own in this early phase. These areas are 1) Wari-Bateshwar village area, the coin of which area is attributed to Vanga sub-division by Basu Majumdar and Pan[6], 2) Tamralipta region (Midnapore), and 3) Chandraketugarh region.

The rest of Bengal used imperial silver Magadhan punch marked coins with 5 symbols. The local type coins of Chandraketugarh and Wari Bateshwar also has sun and six armed symbol which were prime symbols of imperial silver punch marked coins of Magadha-Maurya series. So Basu Majumdar and Pan have indicated a Magadhan influence and hence have dated them later. These local coins also followed the weight standard of karshāpna, but these are a little less than the weight of actual karshāpna (57.6 grains). The coins being less in weight have been explained by Basu Majumdar as the deduction of coining fee (for the permission of coining elsewhere or 'anyatra') from the original weight of the coin[7]. Basu Majumdar also believes that the symbols like boat, fish, bird, lobster etc which were closely associated with the daily life if the local people got a chance to be stamped on the coins because the coins were minted locally.[8] It is necessary to mention here that despite being the most popular and active port (during the time period of our study) and a separate economic zone, we don't get a single coin with boat motif on it from Tamralipta area. The actual fact is the whole hoard of punch marked coins of this time period found from Dharas (which is in Tamralipta economic zone) is lost except only one coin (which don't have a boat motif). So it will never be known until the discovery of another hoard of this period whether there was any boat motif used in the coins of this area or not. Due to the lack of proper evidences, the political scenario of Bengal in early historic phase is not very clear but the existence of three different types of local coins denotes that the total area of Bengal was divided into different political areas ruled by different authorities. But it's not clear if those areas can be called Janapadas or not[9].

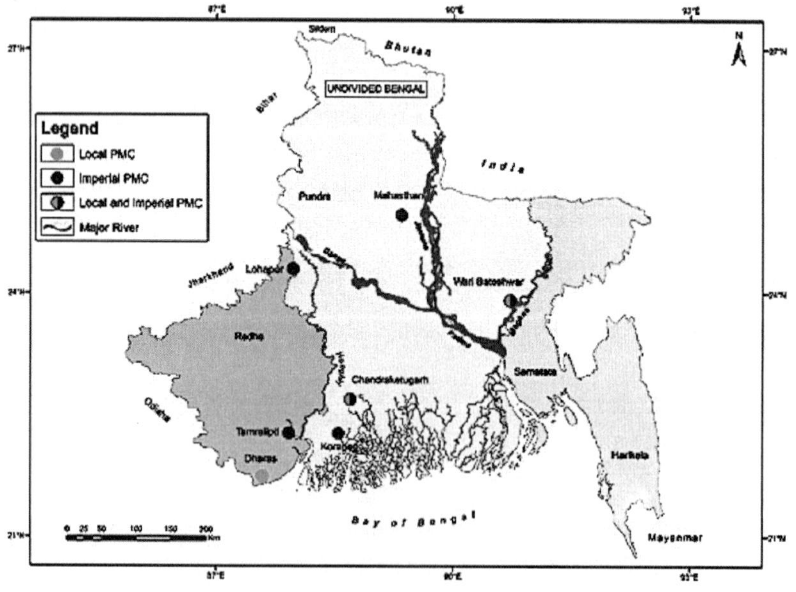

Map 1: Find spots of PMC from Undivided Bengal (600 BCE - 1300 CE)
Courtesy: Basu Majumdar & Pan, JBA 21, 2016, 68

Punch marked coins of billon found from Chandraketugarh shows a vessel with a cabin represented by two parallel horizontal lines, atop a long vertical line. The stern is raised high but it is bent at the end, giving the vessel a shape of a crescent. On the top right of the stern may be seen portion of a pole to steer the vessel. According to Ranabir Chakravarti, absence of an oar on these vessels may suggest that they were not used in sea voyages but on riverine routes[10]. A cabin is very unique in the representation of early Bengal boats which also proves that it is not a cargo ship and it is the oldest representation of a boat with a cabin.

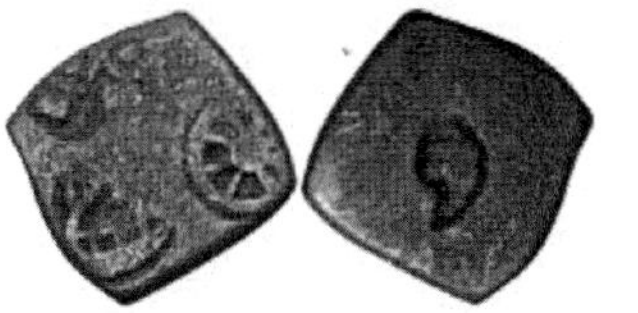

Figure 1: Punch Marked coin with boat motif from Chandraketugarh

Courtesy: Rajgor & Bhandare, *Punch Marked Coins in Early Historic India*, 2017

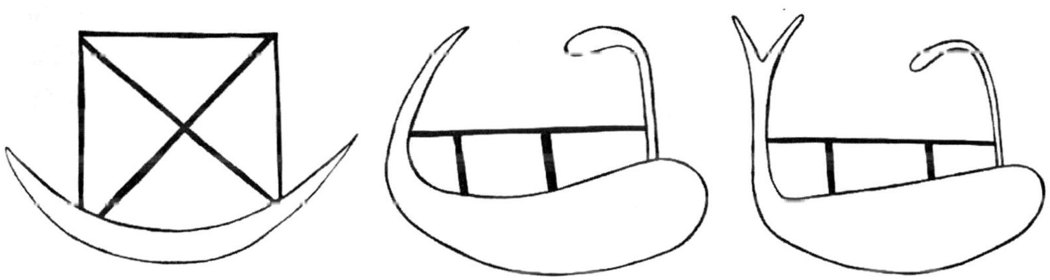

Figure 2: Line Drawing of water crafts found on Punch Marked Coins from Chandraketugarh

Interestingly enough in an article John Guy[11] described a boat model of early medieval period which looks like the boats depicted on the Chandraketugarh punch marked coins. Even to the present day such crescent shaped boats are used for fishing.

Contemporary silver punch marked coins of Wari-Bateshwar has depiction of another type of water craft on them. This also has a cabin like structure at the centre; its prow and stern are curved upwards. It has no mast, no sail is seen, and beams are also absent. This water craft also looks like a small boat; it is surely not a big ship or a large vessel which might be used for ferrying.

Then a seal impression from Chandraketugarh catches our attention. Here a water craft is clearly depicted, the left half of the hull of which is raised high and pointed at the end. There are three parallel and vertical bands between the port and the starboard side of the vessel. At the centre, the vessel stands a Central Asian man with a long cap. Near the

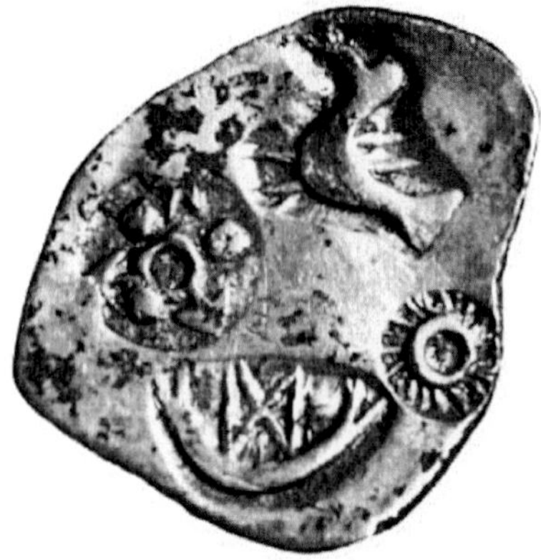

Figure 3: Silver Punch Marked Coins with boat motif

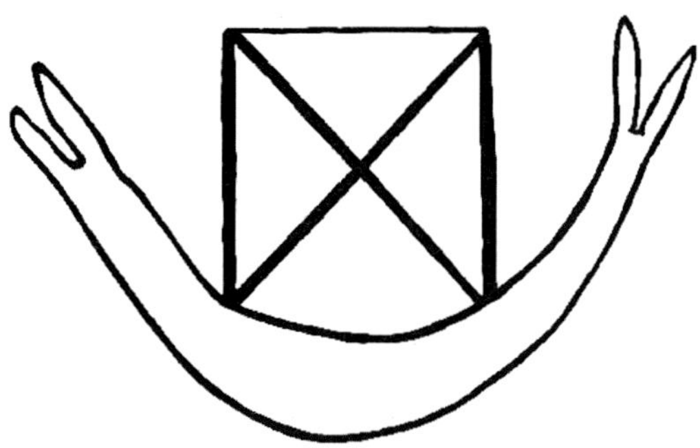

Figure 4: Line Drawing of the Water craft on silver Punch Marked Coins

Courtesy: Bose & Nasir, *Early Coinage of Bengal*, 2016

top of the mast, a pair of parallel rope comes down from a rectangular object on each side of the mast. The sail is not clearly seen. On the left hand side a rope hangs down from the ship, at the end of which an oval shaped thing is seen which appears to have been an anchor. B.N. Mukherjee noticed another similar anchor on the other side of the ship. Two anchors made historians believe in the stationary position of the ship at the port. B.N.Mukherjee also noticed a swastika on the same side of the sealing. On the right hand field of the seal impression there is a clear depiction of a horse with its head towards the mast. The horse is shown in profile, his elongated neck, eyes, ears, mouth, his torso, hind legs and tail is very prominent. Interestingly the motif of the horse is larger than the ship or the total scene. The artist seems to have deliberately enlarged the figure of the horse to drawn attention to the animal. This seal impression also has a legend in Bramhi-Kharosti script which says "Tasvodajana Hovaji(no) na Trapyagasa". Which means – "The ship of the class of Trappaga is belonging to or owned by the powerful Tasvodaja family. The seal impression from Chandraketugarh is one and only numismatic as well as archaeological evidence of Bengal taking part in horse trade.[12]

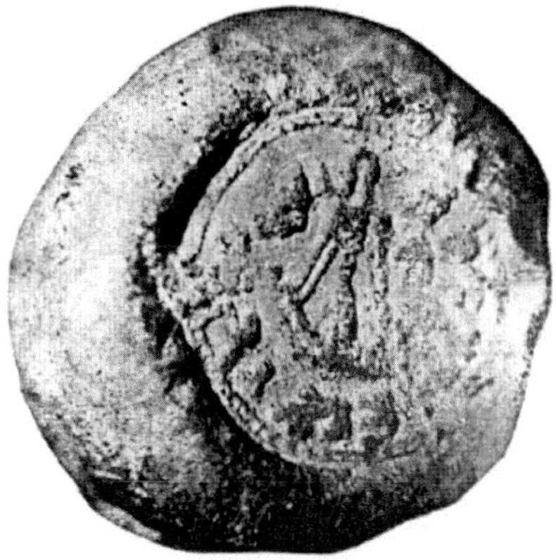

Figure 5: Sealing with boat motif on which central Asian man and horse are seen

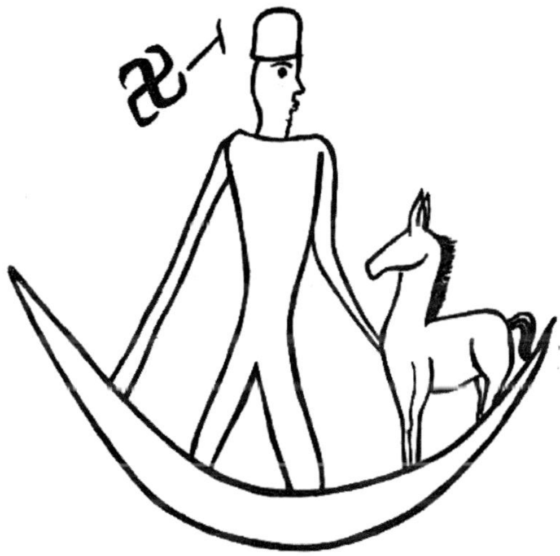

Figure 6: Line Drawing of the boat with Central Asian man and horse

Courtesy: Mukherjee, *Indian Museum Bulletin*,Vol.xxv, 1990

So, a kind of ship named Trappaga is clearly identifiable from the sealings, and it is doubtless that these ships were used in transporting horses. It is also seen that a family is the owner of this ship and were quite powerful. No doubt that this family was involved in horse trading. It is well known that horses were probably brought to Gandhara first from Central Asia by Kushana traders then were trained in India and then were brought to the ports of Bengal through inland routes. Then it was traded first to south India via sea routes and then was supplied to South East Asian countries[13]. In Periplus Maris Erythraei the anonymous writer mentions about a water craft named Trappaga (immediately identifiable with the ship named Trapyaga) and Kottymba which were employed by king Nambanus (Saka ksatrapa rular Nahapana that is) to guide foreign cargo ships to Barygaza

(Broach) and Trappagas used to go to Syrastrene (Saurastra, the Southern part of Kathiawad peninsula) to do their job. Periplus Maris Erythrai gives vivid description of how these ships used to understand the wind direction, tide of the water bodies and also gives information about how they guide those foreign ships through a difficult path to the port of Barygaza. These ships used to sail through the coast line of India and were able to go some extent into the sea. This water craft also looks bigger than the boats depicted on the punch marked coins mentioned above.Angavijja, a 4th century C.E jain text clearly classifies Trapyaka, Kottymba, Samghada as middle category ship which are higher than smaller crafts like Kattha and different from 'Pota' or large ships. It seems that these vessels named Trappaga or Trapyaga were medium sized vessels which were able to do coastal voyages but not appropriate for long sea voyages. Depending on the find spots of rouletted wares in the eastern coast. Ranabir Chakravarti and Asok Datta have shown that there was a strong coastal network during our chosen time frame[14], which was definitely possible because of these kinds of vessels like Trappaga.

Another terracotta seal impression from the same site shows a water craft with a single mast in the foredeck, a flag is attached to the mast, the bow and stern both are curved upwards. Beams are shown crudely. An oar is fitted to the stern. There could have been another oar which is not seen clearly. B.N. Mukherjee notices an auspicious sign on the right side of the mast but he has not identified the symbol. The legend says 'Jemdhas jujusya' which means '(ship) of Juja, the conquering king'. Identity of the king named Juja cannot be established historically but this ship is obviously a royal one. Here in lies the importance of this sealing because this gives the earliest definite picture of an Indian Royal Ship[15]. Here is a small contradiction to this statement i.e. the craft depicted in this sealing is not at all looking like a lavishly decorated royal ship. It is looking more like a small boat or 'Dinga' with one or two oar.

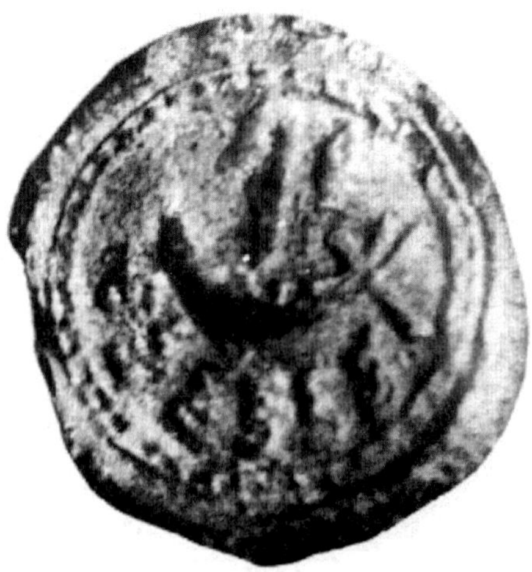

Figure 7: Sealing with a motif of a royal boat

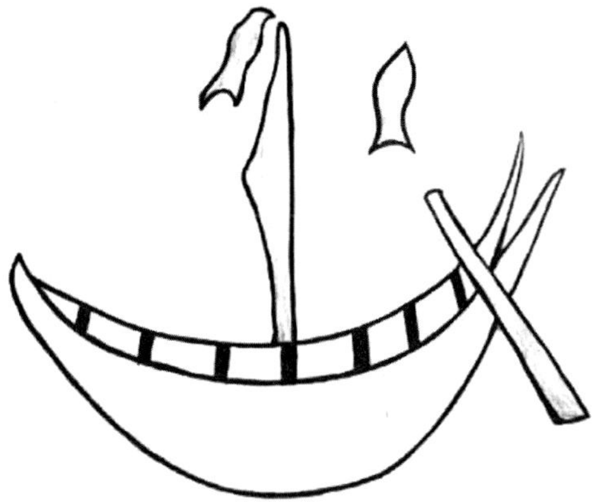

Figure 8 : Line Drawing of the Royal Ship

Courtesy: Mukherjee, *Indian Museum Bulletin,* Vol. XXV, 1990

There is another round shaped terracotta seal impression on which there is a depiction of water craft with its bow and stern curved upwards. The stern is fitted with an oar, beams are clearly shown. A tripod mast with a banner atop is erected at the foredeck. About a three quarter height of the mast there is a rectangular object with four holes, two on each side of the mast. It's difficult to identify this object but Dr. Schlingloff thinks that it is actually a folded sail. He also finds these kinds of things on the ship of Sātavāhana coins. Though the ship on Sātavāhana coins and Chandraketugarh coins, seals, & sealings are not identical. This seal impression has a stylized sheaf of paddy at the right hand field with a Brahmi-Kharosti legend 'Jidhatradhana jusatrasa Tridesojatra', which means the journey to three directions by Yaśoda, who was earned food wealth (i.e. whose wealth is earned by selling food)[16]. Here we find the mention of an individual named Yaśoda is having a ship who probably was a wealthy ship owner and engaged in trading grains. This water craft depicted here is that of a large vessel, at least bigger than the previously discussed royal boat.

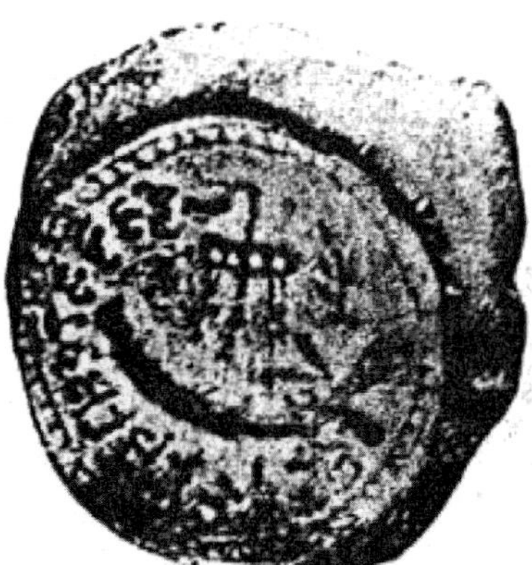

Figure 9: Sealing with a vessel and a sheaf of paddy

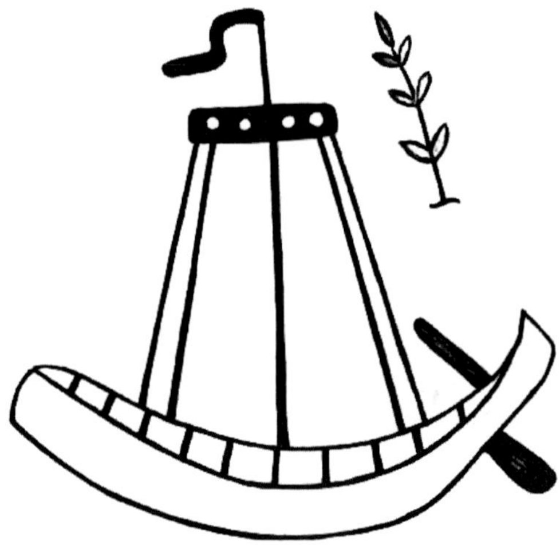

Figure 10: Line Drawing of the Vessel and sheaf of paddy

Courtesy: Mukherjee, *Indian Museum Bulletin*, Vol.XXV, 1990

Almost similar scene is found depicted on another seal showing a ship with a single mast on the foredeck and with clear representation of beams. B.N. Mukherjee mentions a flag fitted to the mast but it is very unclear. The stern is fitted with a steering mechanism which is represented by a vertical & horizontal line crossed at the centre though it is not clear whether it is a oar fitted with a horizontal handle or not. At the centre of this ship there is a disproportionately large basket from which a living plant is seen standing straight. The plant is still unidentified. Here again the enlargement of the basket of grain is intentionally done to draw people's attention to the goods. B.N. Mukherjee noticed the presence of a symbol that is a conch shell on the right field of the sealing. This according to him has a legend in mixed script (Brahmi-Kharosti) reading - 'Soridhajasa Dijammsa jaladhisakla', which means 'the ship Jaladhisakra (Indra of the ocean) belonging to the Dvijamma who is as famous wealthy'[17]. Here we see another wealthy as well as famous individual owning a ship, and obviously he is a merchant. Though B.N Mukherjee described this vessel as a sea going one but this water craft also looks like a small boat rather than a large vessel. The vessel which is called 'The Indra' of the ocean and which is going to three abroad countries is expected to be a large vessel. It is relevant here to say a few words about the plant depicted on the boat. If this plant is a trading good then most probably it is a medicinal herb. Ranabir Chakravarti[18] has shown that Bengal ports were famous for transporting herbs like Gangetic nard. Nard is not grown in Gangetic region, it is a plant of Himalayan region but because it was transported through Bengal ports it was named as Gangetic nard. Anonymous writer of the Periplus mentions about the Gangetic nard and its trade. The problem is this plant does not look like the plant of nard or any other herbs already known to historians as export goods from India or Bengal coast. A careful examination of the plant depicted here shows that it might have a symbolic significance like a Bodhi tree. As we all know that emperor Aśoka is said to have visited Tamralipta (which is a port of Bengal) on the occasion of sending a branch of Bodhi tree to Sri Lanka[19]. This kind of tree in railing is depicted in some other terracotta sealings found from Chandraketugarh.

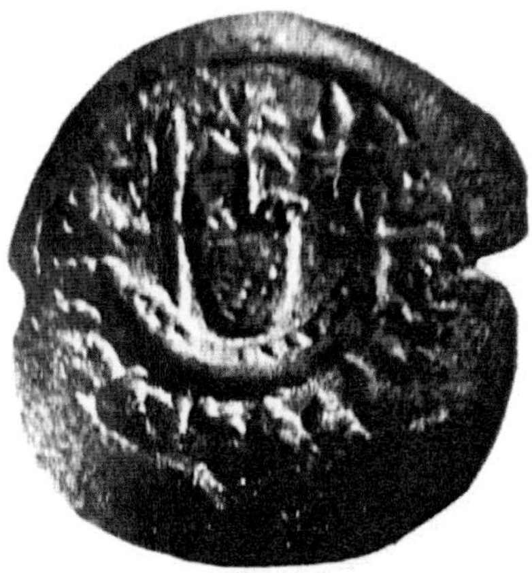

Figure 11: Sealing with the depiction of a boat with a plant in a basket

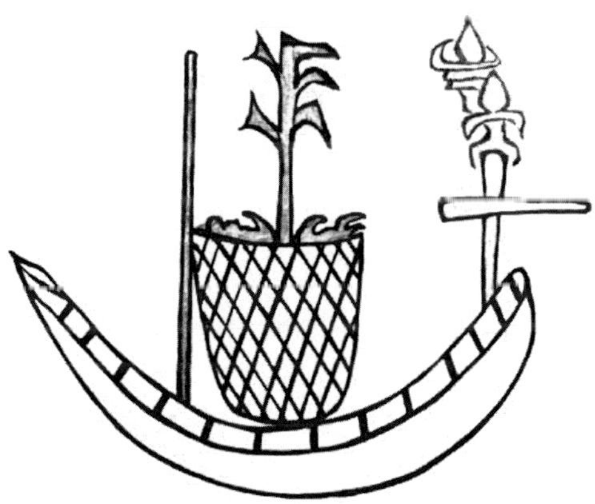

Figure 12: Line drawing of the boat with a plant in a basket

Courtesy: Mukherjee, *Indian Museum Bulletin* Vol.XXV, 1990

The Sātavāhanas were one of the most powerful rulers of ancient India within the time frame of 1st - 2nd century C.E. Among the later Sātavāhana rulers, only in the coins issued by Vasisti Putra Pulumavi and Yajñasri Satakarni have the depictions of ships on the obverse. This ship type coins were introduced for the first time in the history of Indian Numismatics by the Sātavāhanas. They used lead for minting this type of coins. A double masted ship is depicted on the obverse and the royal symbol of the Sātavāhana (Ujjain symbol) on the reverse. The ship type coins have been found at different points between Madras and Cuddalore and some of the coins of Yajñasri Satakarni have been discovered from Maharastra also. Rear and poops are different in shape, some has fan shaped projection. One or two oar towards the rear and a buoy between the bows can be noticed in some coins. Sometimes traces of the legend like 'yana Satakanisa' or 'Ra (no) Gotamipu(ta)...(na) Sata(ka)nisa' are seen. Ship with three masts, a tree near the ship and a wavy line beneath the ship are rare occurrence. On some coins of Yajñasri Satakarni a fish and a conch shell is seen beneath the ship with double masts. On one coin of Yajñasri Satakarni, a fleet of ships is depicted out of which one is large and others are smaller vessels. These might be a depiction of a coast where the large ship was anchored and the small boats are seeming plying towards the large ship for uploading or offloading goods. Another interesting thing about these coins are only two Sātavāhana ruler had ship motifs on their coins which is a clear indication of the increase of trade in their reign. Fish and the conch shell might be trading goods.

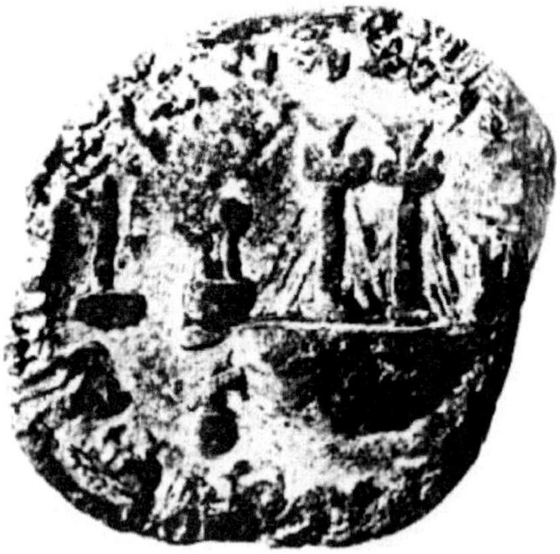

Figure 13 : Three ships on a Sātavāhana coin

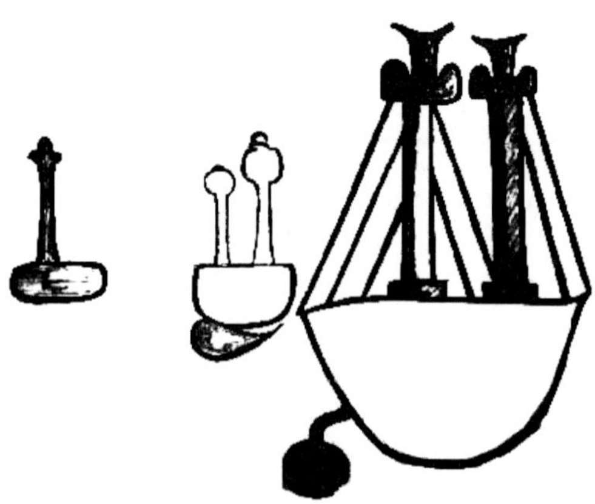

Figure 14: Line drawing of three ships found on a Sātavāhana coin

Courtesy: Mukherjee, *Numismatic Art of India*, Vol.II, 2007

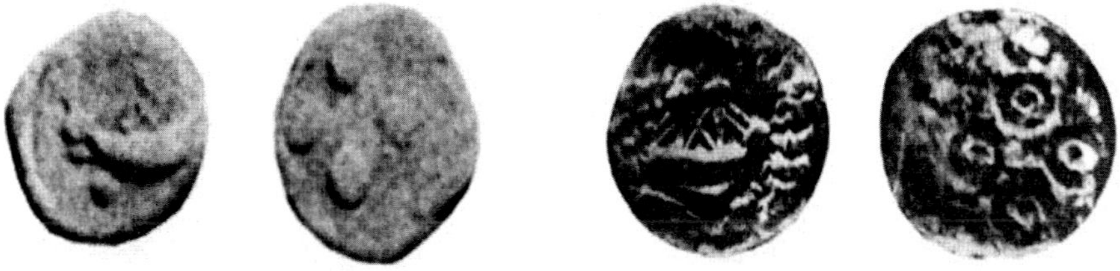

Figure 15: Sātavāhana coins with ship motif

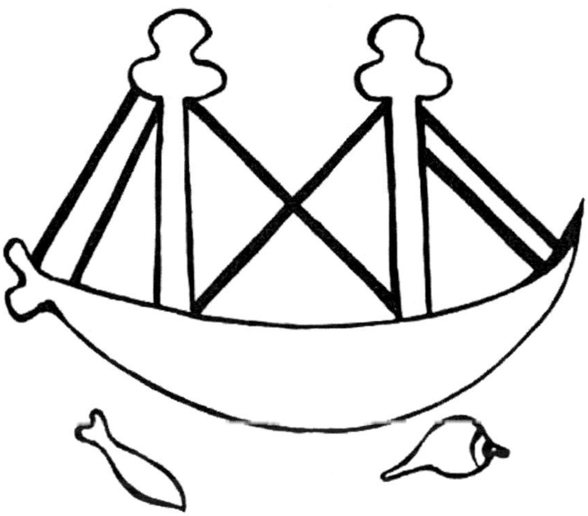

Figure 16: Ship motif depicted on Sātavāhana coins

Courtesy: R. Krishnamurthy, *The Pallava Coins,* 2004

Pallavas ruled in a portion of South India (Karnataka and Northern part of Tamil Region). They get prominence after the eclipse of Sātavāhana dynasty, of whom the Pallavas served as feudatories. They ruled from 275 C.E. to 897 C.E. but became a major power during the reign of Mahendravarman I (571-630 C.E.) and Narasimhavarman I (630-668 C.E.). Coins of Pallavas with ship motifs were also made of lead. On these coins a standing bull is seen on the obverse and a ship on the reverse. Most commonly ships with double mast are seen but some rare depictions of ship with single mast are also there. All the lead coins of Pallavas with ship motif can be dated to circa 3rd century C.E. just after the eclipse of the Sātavāhanas. Pallava coins with ship motif are found from different parts of Andhra coast. Interestingly, the ship type coins of Sātavāhanas circulated in that very area. So the ship motif of Pallava coins shows a continuity of motifs of the preceding authority as well as it proves that trade was one of the important sources of their wealth. Explicit temples made by Pallavas support this theory. These ships are crudely depicted but are surely different in appearance than the water crafts depicted on the numismatic specimens found from Bengal. These were obviously sea going large vessels, often decorated.

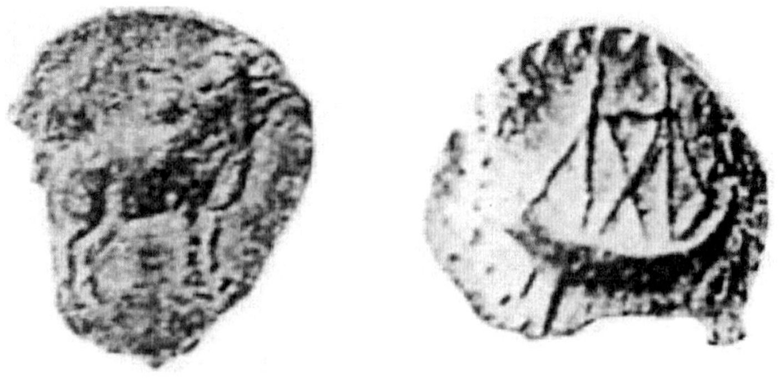

Figure 17: Ship motif on a Pallava coin

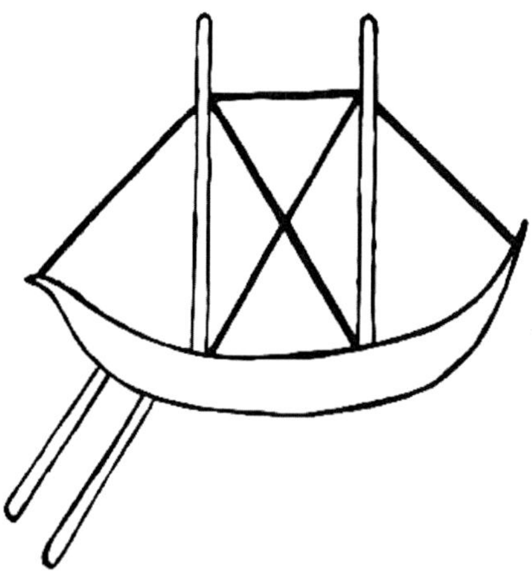

Figure 18: Line drawing of the ship in Pallava coin

Courtesy: R. Krishnamurthy, *The Pallava Coins,* 2004

So here we see three kinds water crafts – (1) small boats with or without cabin, (2) medium sized vessels, (3) large ships, and two kinds of owners – (1) royal family, (2) merchant family or individual. Interestingly Bengal area doesn't have any numismatic evidence with large ships depicted on them but literary evidences mention about large ships plying in coastal areas of Bengal.

In the **Rigveda** (dated circa 1500 B.C.E) there is a mention of a water craft named 'Satāritra Nau'. The name of the craft itself literary means 'a vessel/water craft with 100 oars'. Rigveda also mentions Eastern and Western oceans situating at two direction of this country. This information leads us to think that RigVedic people must have been accustomed with sea faring activities, but this cannot be proved. According to Ranabir Chakravarti there was not a single dock in ancient India where this huge ship with 100 oars can be anchored. He also says that it would have been impossible to anchor this ship even at Harrappan dockyard at Lothal. And sadly there is no other contemporary evidence which can prove the activity of sea faring at the time of Rigveda. In the **Arthaśastra,** the 3rd cent B.C.E text water crafts and the crew members are also mentioned. This text uses the term 'Nau/ Nauka' for all kinds of water crafts. But it clearly separates larger craft naming **'Mahānau'** from smaller crafts naming **'Kṣudrikā'.** It also says that Mahānau was used in large rivers having enough water even in summer and autumn and Kṣudrikās were used in small rivers affordable only in monsoon[20]. This text also mentions the duties of 'Nāvadhyakṣa' or superintendent of shipping assigns his responsibility for all navigation by sea, river and lake including fishing and ferry boats[21]. Megasthenes mentions about a neval division in Chandragupta's army[22]. Arian mentions about 800 vessels, Curtius and Diodorus mentions about 1000 vessels, and Ptolemy mentions about 2000 vessels all of which were made with Indian timber and by Indian craftsmen. Arian also mentions about construction of a dockyard. All these information lead us to believe that ship building industry thrived during the reign of the Mauryas.We have already mentioned above that Periplus Maris Erythrai also has mentions about large ships.

The contemporary text Milindapañha (1st century C.E) alludes to the regular sailing of a ship owned by a wealthy person to Vanga, China, Suvarnabhumi etc. this must be a large ship[23]. Strabo refers to the ascent of vessels from the sea by the Ganges to Palimbothra[24]. **Amarkośa** of Amarsinha, a 5th -6th century CE text, uses different words for different kinds of water crafts. Like "Udupa" - Rafts, "Nau/ Tarani/ Tari/ Droni" - Boats, "Pota" - large ships, "Potavanika" - Merchant vessel. This text also talks about one of such vessels which carry passengers. Some **Jātaka** stories (Janaka Jātaka, Mahājanaka Jātaka, Sānkha Jātaka, Valahassa Jātaka, Samudda Vanijja Jātaka)[25] tell us that some members of royal families used to play an important role in maritime voyages for trade in distant countries including Suvarnabhumi. In Kalidasa's 'Raghuvamsa', Vanga is referred to as 'Nau-Sadhanodyatan' which speaks of the skills of the people in the use of boats in all purposes including war[26]. Here it is very much appropriate to refer the Mahanavika Budhagupta of Raktmrittika whose name is mentioned in a 5thcentury fragmentary stone inscription found four Malay peninsula. Raktmrittika is identified with modern Murshidabad (Karnasuvarna) and the word Mahanavika means captain of a large ship, which means, at that time ships large enough to undertake long sea voyages used to sail from the coast of Bengal to South East Asian countries, of course for trading purpose. In this context we must remember the names of Chinese travellers like Fa-hien who started his journey from the port of Tamralipta to Sri Lanka, another traveller It-sing came from Malay to Tamralipta, and the very famous Xuan-Zang returned to china from Tamralipta, all in large ships[27]. Gate no. 2 of Sanchi (2nd century B.C), caves of Kanheri in Maharashtra (2nd century C.E), cave no. 2 of Ajanta (6th-7th century C.E) have sculptures and paintings depicting large ships. These are the oldest sculptural depictions of ships.

We have already discussed that different types of water craft motifs are depicted on the numismatic specimens of our chosen time frame, but none of them are sea going large ships. These are riverine small boats or coastal vessels. Interestingly enough these specimens also have depictions of export goods like horse and paddy on these small water crafts. If these goods were exported to south India and south-east Asia via sea routes it is surprising why we find depiction of such vessels which were unable to undertake long sea voyages. Here the question arises how could then those goods be transported to those countries. Probably, larger ships anchored in the high sea away from the delta region which was not navigable and hence small boats used to ply between the coast and the larger ship. This is the only reason why we find the depiction of smaller vessels or water crafts on the coins which local people might have seen regularly. Periplus Maris Erythrai gives us very interesting information about a very large ship named 'Kolandiophonta' which used to sail through Khruse and Ganges. There is description of another large ship named 'Sangara' which is built by tying up big logs of large trees. These ships used to undertake long sea voyages. There was frequent use of small boats also. Periplus Maris Erythrai mentioned, more than one time that big ships had to anchor at the sea port or coast because of the thick sediment on the riverbed. These small riverine water crafts used to play a major role in long distance trade and communication by bringing trading commodities from far away hinterlands to the sea ports via rivers. That was their most important role as a byproduct of which they contributed in maintaining communication between different inland areas of India[28]. Small boats were also used for ferrying passengers, fishing etc. Chandraketugarh and Wari-Bateshwar were feeder ports or important trading centers situated far inland from the coast but at the bank of the rivers (Vidyadhari and Brahmaputra respectively) where these small vessels used to anchor. It also seems that the Royal family and traders of these areas used to take part in loading the larger ships with export goods and distributing import goods to the inland areas rather than taking part in going to the abroad countries themselves. That is why small boats and vessels became so important to the issuing authorities that they decided to depict them on the coins and seals. Unfortunately there is not a single remain of ship wreck found from eastern coast which will of course obstruct our understanding of ancient Indian ship building technology. Bengal probably have its own ship building industry but in the absence of available archaeological data nothing much can be commented upon the boat building industry. However water crafts were a very important part of the coastal life and coastal network.

References

1. Ranabir Chakravarti, chapter 6 (Maritime Trade and Voyages in Ancient Bengal) in *Trade and Traders in Early Indian Society, Manohar,* New Delhi, 2002, reprinted 2007), pp.130. For details see B.N. Mukherjee, *Indian Museum Bulletin*, Vol.XXV, Indian Museum, Calcutta, 1990
2. Chakravarti 1992:59; 1995:217
3. Shahnaj Husne Jahan, Wari-Bateshwar: An Important Centre of Maritime Activities in Ancient Bengal, *Journal of Bengal Art,* Vol. 4, Dhaka,1999,207-216

4. Proper cataloging of these coins will help us in classification and further analysis of such coins
5. Ibid., pp.207-216
6. Susmita Basu Majumdar and Sandip Pan, Punch Marked Coins In Early Bengal: Issuance and Circulation Pattern, *JBA,* Vol.21, 2016, 55-78. K.G. Goswami, Excavations of Bangarh, Calcutta, 1948
7. Basu Majumdar, chapter 22 (Monetary History of Bengal : 'Issues And Non-Issues', *The Complex Heritage of Early India*, New Delhi, 2014, 585-605.
8. *JBA*, Vol.21, 2016, 55-78.
9. Basu Majumdar, Monetary History of Bengal : 'Issues and Non-Issues', 2014, 585-605. Basu Majumdar, *Banglar Mudra Babostha : Prachin o Adi Madhya Jug*, Kolkata, 2013.
10. Chakravarti, *Trade and Traders in Early Indian History*, 2007.
11. John Guy, A Boat Model and State Ritual in Eastern India, *JBA*, Vol.2, 1997, 99-110.
12. Chakravarti, *Trade and Traders in Early Indian Society*, 2007.
13. B.N. Mukherjee, *Indian Museum Bulletin,* Vol.XXV, Indian Museum, Calcutta, 1990.
14. Asok Dutta, Rouletted Ware in Bengal, Its Origin, chronology and Distribution: An overview, *JBA*, 2003.
15. Chakravarti, *Trade and Traders in Early Indian Society*, 2007.
16. Chakravarti, *Trade and Traders in Early Indian Society*, 2007. B.N. Mukherjee, *Indian Museum Bulletin,* Vol.XXV, 1990.
17. Ibid.
18. Ranabir Chakravarti, On board the Hermapollan: transporting Gangetic Nard from Muziris, Interrogating History : Essays for Hermann Kulke (Edited by Martin Brandtner and Shishir Kumar Panda), 2006, 147-163.
19. Mahavamsa, 19.
20. Chakravarti, *Trade and Traders in Early Indian Society*, 2007.
21. Enamul Haque, *Excavation at Wari-Bateshwar: A Priliminary Study*, 2001.
22. Ibid., 2001
23. Ibid., 2001.
24. Ibid., 2001.
25. R.K. Mookerji, *Indian Shipping*, 1912.
26. Haque, *Excavation at Wari-Bateshwar: A Priliminary Study*, 2001.
27. Chakravarti, *Trade and Traders in Early Indian Society*, 2007.
28. Wilfred. H. Schoff, *The Periplus of the Erythrean Sea,* 1912.

6

Dinaras in Early Bengal:
Circulation and Beyond

Soumya Ghosh

This paper attempts to revisit the issuance and the circulation of Dinaras in Early Bengal especially during the reign of the Guptas. But before delving deep into the issue let us now look at the political geography as well as the numismatic scenario of early Bengal before and after the rise of the Guptas. Here Bengal denotes undivided Bengal i.e. present day West Bengal and Bangladesh. Bengal was never a single entity before 11th century CE. In the ancient period it was a conglomeration of four sub-regions which was demarcated by the hydrographic units.[1] These are –

1) The area to the west of Bhāgīrathi
2) The area lying to the north of the Padma
3) The area between the Bhāgīrathi and Padma
4) The area to east of the Meghna

These different sub regions surfaced as a geo-political unit in different periods of time, some of which had a prolonged continuity whereas some were subsumed by other units. With the change in the political scenario often these geo-political units extended surpassing their core territory and often overlapped each other[2].

It is evident and well proven from different sources that major parts of Bengal i.e. sub-region 1,2, and 3 were under the Gupta domination from the first half of the 4th century CE to first half of the 6th century CE[3]. But the sub region which was situated to the east of Meghna comprising the Samatata area was not incorporated within their territory at least up to the end of the 5th century CE[4]. Even Samudragupta mentions it as *pratyantarājya* i.e. outside the frontier of Gupta empire[5].

Chart I :- Gupta coin hoards in Bengal

Hoard	Location	Sub-Region	Number of Issues Found[6]
Kalighat [7]	Kolkata W. Bengal	1	200
Madhavpur	Hooghly W. Bengal	1	13
Hasnan	Hooghly W. Bengal	1	11
Baincigram	Hooghly W. Bengal	1	7
Mainamati	Comilla, Bangladeh	4	4
Ahiran [8]	Murshidabad, W. Bengal	2	11

Chart II :- Inscriptions which resonate the Gupta political control over the parts of Bengal[9].

Name of Inscription	Time	Ruler	Location
Allahabad Praśasti [10]	2nd quarter of 4th c. CE.	Samudragupta	Varanasi, Uttar Pradesh
Meherauli Pillar Inscription[11]	...	Candra (Candragupata II ?)	Delhi
Dhanaidaha Copper Plate grant	113GE/433CE	In the time of Kumaragupta I	Rajshahi, Bangladesh
Damodarpur Copper Plate grant	124GE/444CE	Kumaragupta I	Dinajpur, Bangladesh
Kalai-Kuri Sultanpur Copper Plate grant	128GE/448CE	same	Rajshahi, Bangladesh
Baigram Copper Plate grant	128GE/448CE	same	Bogra, Bangladesh
Jagadishpur Copper Plate grant	128GE/448CE	Same	Rajsahi, Bangladesh
Paharpur Copper Plate grant	159GE /479CE	In the time of Budgagupta I	Rajsahi, Bangladesh
Damodarpur Copper Plate grant	163 CE/482CE	same	Dinajpur, Bangladesh
Damodarpur Copper Plate grant	broken	same	Dinajpur, Bangladesh
Gunaighar Copper Plate grant	507-8 CE	Vainyagupta (An Gupta Administrator)	Comilla, Bangladesh
Damodarpur Copper Plate grant	224 GE/543 CE	Viṣñugupta	Dinajpur, Bangladesh

It appears from the distribution pattern of epigraphic records and numismatic evidences that the sub-region 1 and 3 were under Gupta control.

Chart III :- different types of issues found in Bengal according to their issuers[12]

King	Type
Candragupta	King : Queen
Samudragupta	Archer, Standard, Aśvamedha
Candragupta II	Archer, Umbrella
Kumāragupta I	Archer, Elephant, Horseman, Lion Slayer, Kārtikeya
Skandagupta	King : Queen or King : Lakṣmī
Kumāragupta II	Archer
Vainyagupta	Archer
Narasimhagupta	Archer
Kumaragupta III	Archer
Viṣnugupta	Archer

Observations

I) All the rulers of the imperial Gupta dynasty issued coins and all of them have been reported from Bengal.

II) From the time of Candragupta II to Viṣnugupta parts of Bengal were under the political control of Guptas.

III) Archer type coins are the most predominant ones

In the period preceding the Guptas Bengal was issuing coins mainly in silver and copper. These were the punch marked coins and then early un-inscribed cast copper coins also circulated side by side with these silver issues. Besides this we also get billon coins from some regions of Bengal. Samatata was regularly issuing gold coins and it was a Kuṣāṇa imitation type. Along with the metallic currency Bengal was also using cowry-shells for the purpose of transaction.[13] Fashein mentions in his account in the 5th century CE the region of *madhyadesa* was using cowry currency[14].

It is interesting to note that the Gupta inscriptions mention the term '*rūpaka*' as coins which were used side by side with the dīnāras i.e. gold coins for the purpose of transaction[15]. These rūpakas are silver coins and may be assumed that the punch marked coins of the previous times were still in circulation in the region of Bengal. These may also be notional currency paid in cowries or *curṇis* (gold dust) equivalent to the valuation of the silver rūpakas. However we would also like to point out that few Gupta silver coins have also been reported from Bengal but their number is not significant enough[16]. The exchange rate of the rūpakas to the gold dīnārs as gleaned from the epigraphic records was 16:1[17].

The *kapardakas* or cowries might have formed the base of the economy in Bengal, at least partially and a part of the ordinary transactions in daily life was made through this medium. The cowries were not only a media of exchange in Bengal but also a vital element of long distance trade and transaction. Basu Majumdar and Chatterjee have shown that these cowrie shells of Cypreamoneta and Cyprea annulus variety were imported from Maldives though overseas trade in the Bay of Bengal network and part of these imported cowries were exported to China via Assam and Tibet[18].

The most interesting issue is that the Kuṣāṇa coins reached the extreme eastern segment of the subcontinent and influenced the coinage and currency system of this region i.e. Bengal. Samatata adopted the gold device of the Kuṣāṇa coins and minted its own currency in a local weight standard and the lower West Bengal also used the Kuṣāṇa copper currency as the model for its issues. These are the so called Puri-Kuṣāṇa coins[19]. This local derivative type of Kuṣāṇa copper currency continued throughout the Gupta and even in later period not only in the South West Bengal but in the neighboring Orissa, Bihar and Parts of Andhra as well. Basu Majumdar points towards a trend of imitation in Bengal in its different zones[20].

Cast copper coin based on the weight system of the silver punch marked coins was introduced in c. 2nd century BCE in western part of the Bengal (section 1 & 2). It continued up to the end of the Gupta rule (in at least section 1) though in 2nd century CE, in the South Western part of the Bengal it became, to some extent, metro-logically and typologically integrated with a copper series based on the imitations of Kuṣāṇa coins[21].

All of these have much significance. Firstly, regular imitation of Kuṣāṇa coins does imply the popularity and demand for the Kuṣāṇa coinage and at the same time the unavailability of sufficient coins at that area. Secondly demand of coins denotes the economic vibrancy of the area. Thirdly, issuance of copper currency indicates towards the easy availability of copper in the respective currency zone. It also indicates brisk day to day transactional activities at the mass level. Fourthly, though initially Kuṣāṇa copper coins were used then these were imitated and minted as per the Kuṣāṇa standard in this region but the region developed its own currency in the indigenous weight standard copying or imitating the original Kuṣāṇa device that had gained popularity.

In South-eastern Bengal which has been marked as sub-region 4) there was access to gold probably due to trade, gold coinage was adopted as the regular currency in this zone. It is needless to say that, initially these gold coins were minted by imitating the contemporary Kuṣāṇa coinage which reached this region through traders[22]. These were all crude imitations. These were minted for a long time till the Gupta coins in 4th -5th century CE started flowing into the region with its inclusion into the Gupta territory. These coins also influenced the currency pattern in this region and particularly the coinage under discussion. The Kuṣāṇa imitations with king sacrificing at the altar on the obverse and Nana or Ardokṣo on the reverse were influenced by the Gupta coinage and hence the obverse device of the freshly arrived coins with the Gupta archer type (depicting the king holding a bow on the obverse) was adopted as the principal obverse device of Kuṣāṇa imitations in Kuṣāṇa deity (which had undergone much degeneration in the process of its continuity. Scholars have already discussed the blending of the Kuṣāṇa and the Gupta device. The obverse was the imitation of the Gupta device and the reverse was the continuity of the Kuṣāṇa deity (which had undergone much degeneration in the process of its continuity as device for a long time). Basu Majumdar has shown these in their typological sequencing of continuity. Thus, a new pattern in imitation was adopted in south-eastern zone of Bengal. It has been mentioned as the Kuṣāṇo-Gupta gold coinage because of the blending of both the devices[23]. This special type of currency followed its own metrology adhering to a local weight standard i.e. 5.7 grams or 87.96 grains in average[24]. In the rest of the regions probably Gupta coins were the regular medium of exchange issued in *dīnāra* and later *suvarṇa* standard[25].

Thus in Gupta Bengal we get two distinct monetary zones one in north and south-western Bengal and the other in south eastern Bengal. On one hand South-western Bengal or lower West Bengal can be mapped within a broad copper using zone extended from Bhāgīrathi basin to Godavari basin. On another side south-eastern part formed a gold using zone with its distinct type and metrology. Samata region or the South Eastern Bengal had gradually evolved a separate currency system of their own which was moving parallel with the Gupta imperial dinar currency and therefore while the rest of the Bengal were using the Gupta imperial gold coins, in the South Eastern part of the region, that lies to the east of the Meghna (comprising Comilla, Noakhali in Bangladesh and also the western part of Tripura in india), their own coins of Kuṣāṇa-Gupta type were being circulated.

It is imperative to see how the monetization is reflected in the epigraphic records of this region. In this context we would like to mention that the inscriptions of Kumaragupta are replete with references to buying and selling of land in Pundravardhana region and *dīnāra* beign used for such transactions. These are known from the five Damodarpur copper plate inscriptions of the time of Kumaragupta and Budhagupta[26]. To this data we would like to add fresh information from a copper plate inscription of Vainyagupta originally issued by a hitherto unknown ruler named Nathacandra[27]. This has recently been published by Ryosuke Furui last year. It has been discovered from Comilla District in Bangladesh (i.e. Samataṭa subregion). In this inscription it is mentioned that, Vainyagupta revalidated a large donation of land measuring total 2455 droṇavāpa (120 at dakṣiṇamanḍala +717 at Vātaganga +518 at Vātaganga) in 184GE, which had been donated to a saAgha of Ajivikas by another ruler named Nāthchandra in 91 GE. It is interesting that 1225 droṇavāpa of land and 4 houses were record as purchased from more than 48 individuals and it was worth the price of 149 dīnāras in total. This is not only the earliest epigraphic record of Gupta period found in Bengal but also the largest land transaction in Bengal. Now, the question which rises here that what kind of coins are these dīnāras mentioned in this particular inscription. Definitely these were the ones which were circulating in the Samatata region. Originally, the term dīnāra came from the name of Roman denarius i.e. Roman silver coins. Though the Kuṣānas used this term which orinigally indicated Roman silver they named their gold coins *dīnāra*. Later Guptas followed them and used the term for indicating their gold coinage. In all other inscriptions of the Gupta period found in Bengal silver coins are called *rūpaka* but interestingly here it is mentioned as *māṣaka*. But the exchange rate is same in relation to *dīnāra* i.e. 16:1[28]. Thus, here we would like to conclude that any gold coin in Bengal was termed as *dīnāra* irrespective of its metrological differences and variations. For silver coins the term vareid from *karshapana* to *rupaka* and even *māṣaka*. With the discovery of the Nathacandra records a new dimension has been added to the monetary scenario of Gupta Bengal.

References

1. Mukherjee, B.N., *Coins and Currency System in Gupta Bengal,* New Delhi, 1992, Harman Publishing House, pp17-19; Basu Majumdar, Susmita, "Monetary History of Bengal : Issues and Non-issues'', Jha, D.N., eds., *The Complex Heritage of Early India Essays in Memory of R.S. Sharma,* Delhi, 2014, Manohar, pp.585.
2. Ghosh, Suchandra, *Exploring Connectivity Southeastern Bengal and Beyond*, Kolkata, 2015, Institute for Social and Cultural Studies, p.7.
3. Mukherjee, B.N., *Coins And Currency System in Gupta Bengal,* New Delhi, 1992, Harman Publishing House, pp.17-24
4. Sircar, D.C., Select Inscriptions Bearing on Indian History and Civilization, Vol I, Delhi, 1993, V.K. Publishing House, pp.340-4.
5. Ibid, pp.265; Chhabra, Bahadur Chand and Govind swamirao Gai, eds., *Corpus Inscriptionum Indicarum, Vol III*, Delhi, 1981, Directror General Archaeological Survey of India.
6. Mukherjee, B.N., *Coins and Currency System in Gupta Bengal,* New Delhi, 1992, Harman Publishing House, pp.50-1.
7. Basu Majumdar, Susmita, *Kalighat Hoard The First Gupta Coin Hoard From India,* Kolkata, 2014.
8. Banik, Subhasree, "An Analytical Study of recently Discovered Gupta Coins From Murshidabad, West Bengal", *Puravritta*, Vol.I, Kolkata, 2016, Directorate of Archaeology and Museums, Government of West Bengal, pp.57-75.
9. Chhabra, Bahadur Chand and Govind swamirao Gai, eds, *Corpus Inscriptionum Indicarum, Vol.III*, Delhi, 1981, Director General Archaeological Survey of India; Mukherji, Ramaranjan and Sachindra Kumar Maity, *Corpus of Bengal Inscriptions,* Calcutta, 1967, Firma K.L.Mukherhee, pp.41-6, 58-73.

10. Here king of Samataa was referred as *pratyantanrpati*. This indicates that the area to the west of Samataa i.e. South-eastern Bengal (sub-region 4) was already under Samudragupta. [Here it was proclaimed that king Candra had defeated an ally of the rulers of Vanga (i.e. sub-region 3)]
11. Here it was proclaimed that king Candra had defeated an ally of the rulers of Vanga (i.e. sub-region 3).
12. Mukherjee, B.N., *Coins and Currency System in Gupta Bengal,* New Delhi, 1992, Harman Publishing House, pp.49-50.
13. Mukherjee, B.N., "Monetary System in Bengal (upto C. A.D.1200)", *Coins and Currency System in Gupta Bengal,* New Delhi, 1992, Harman Publishing House; Basu Majumdar, Susmita, "Monetary History of Bengal: Issues and Non-issues'', Jha, D.N., eds., *The Complex Heritage of Early India Essays in Memory of R.S. Sharma,* Delhi, 2014, Manohar.
14. Mukherjee, B.N., *Coins And Currency System In Gupta Bengal,* New Delhi, 1992, Harman Publishing House, pp.58; Fa-hsien, *Fo-Kuo-chi*, Chuan XVI, J.Legee, A Record of Buddhist Kingdoms, etc., 2nd reprint, Delhi, pp.43.
15. Mukherjee, B.N., *Coins and Currency System in Gupta Bengal,* New Delhi, 1992, Harman Publishing House, pp.54-6.
16. Basu Majumdar, Susmita, "Monetary History of Bengal : Issues and Non-issues'', Jha, D.N., eds., *The Complex Heritage of Early India Essays in Memory of R.S. Sharma,* Delhi, 2014, Manohar, pp.591.
17. Mukherjee, B.N., *Coins And Currency System In Gupta Bengal*, New Delhi, 1992, Harman Publishing House, pp.54-6; Sircar, D.C., *Studied in Indian Coins*, Delhi, 1968, Motilal Banarsidas, p.75.
18. Basu Majumdar, Susmita, "Monetary History of Bengal : Issues and Non-issues'', Jha, D.N., eds., *The Complex Heritage of Early India Essays in Memory of R.S. Sharma,* Delhi, 2014, Manohar, pp.595-9.
19. Mitchiner, Michal, *Ancient Trade and Early Coinage Volume Two,* London, 2004, Hawkins Publication, p.1236; Mukherjee, B.N., "Coins of Early Bengal (SecondPhase)'', *Coins and Currency System of Early Bengal (up to c. A.D. 300),* Kolkata, 2000, Progressive Publishers, pp.26-30; Basu Majumdar, Susmita, "monetary history of Bengal : issues and non-issues'', Jha, D.N., eds, *The Complex Heritage of Early India Essays in memory of R.S.Sharma,* Delhi, Manohar, 2014, pp.589.
20. Basu Majumdar, Susmita, "Monetary History of Bengal : Issues and Non-issues'', Jha, D.N., eds., *The Complex Heritage of Early India Essays in Memory of R.S. Sharma,* Delhi, 2014, Manohar, pp.585-605.
21. Ibid, p.589; Mukherjee, B.N., *Coins and Currency System of Early Bengal (up to c. A.D. 300),* Kolkata, 2000, Progressive Publishers, pp.21, 30, 36.
22. Basu Majumdar, Susmita, "Monetary History of Bengal : Issues and Non-issues'', Jha, D.N., eds., *The Complex Heritage of Early India Essays in Memory of R.S. Sharma,* Delhi, 2014, Manohar, p.588.
23. Ibid, p.589.
24. Mukherjee, B.N., *Coins and Currency System of Post-Gupta Bengal (550-700 A.D.)*, Delhi, 1993, Munshiam Manoharlal and *Post Gupta Coinage of Bengal*, Kolkata, 1989, Coin Study

Circle, pp.1-46; Rodes, N.G. and S.K. Bose, *The Coinage of Assam*, Kolkata, Guwahati: Library of Numismatic Studies, 2003, pp.65-78; Mitchiner, Michal, *Ancient Trade and Early Coinage Volume Two,* London, 2004, Hawkins Publication, pp.1257-85 and *History and Coinage of South East Asia Until The Fifteen Century*, London, 1998, pp.91-95; Bose, S.K. and Noman Nasir, *Early Coinage of Bengal (c. 2nd Century BC – 10th Century AD),* Kolkata, 2016, Nabaloke Press, 142-90.

25. Mukherjee, B.N., *Coins And Currency System In Gupta Bengal*, New Delhi, 1992, Harman Publishing House, p.52; Altekar, A.S., *The Coinage of the Gupta Empire and its Imitation, Corpus of Indian Coins*, Vol.IV, Varanasi, 1957, pp.293-301.
26. Chhabra, Bahadur Chand and Govind swamirao Gai, eds, *Corpus Inscriptionum Indicarum,* Vol III, Delhi, 1981, Director General Archaeological Survey of India; Mukherji, Ramaranjan and Sachindra Kumar Maity, *Corpus of Bengal Inscriptions,* Calcutta, 1967, Firma K.L. Mukherhee, pp.41-6, 58-73.
27. Furui, Ryosuke, "Ājīvikas, Maṇibhadras and Early History of Eastern Bengal : A New Copperplate Inscription of Vainyagupta and Its Implications", *Journal of Royal Asiatic Society*, series 3, 26, 4 (2016), pp.657-81.
28. Ibid.

Section - II

Medieval Indian Numismatics

7

Revisiting the Repoussé Minting Technique

Abhick Sarkar

A coin is a metallic piece of prescribed weight, embellished with various types of design and legends. It was produced under the direction of a private or public authority for the use as a medium of exchange. Gold, silver, copper, lead, billon, bronze, brass were the metals used for minting coins in early and mediaeval India, among them silver, gold, and copper were the most important metals. As far as the minting of these coins is concerned we find the use of mainly four techniques throughout the span of history. Among these the die striking process the most popular technique. The least used technique is the repouśse. These four techniques are as follows:

1. Archaic multiple die striking technique popularly known as the punching technique.
2. Casting technique using moulds.
3. Die striking technique using a set of two dies upper die and the anvil die.
4. Repouśse techniqueusing a single die.

This paper concerns with this rare technique of repousse. The meaning of the word repouśse is hammered into relief from the reverse side. Thus the coins made with patterns in relief on one side only are known as repousse coins and the technique is also named similarly. Since the technique involves the process of embossing the device on one side by striking with a hammer on the reverse we have a debossed device of the obverse which is in intaglio. The process of embossing demands a thin flan to get a prominent obverse. All the repousse coins found till date are circular or round coins. As they are of a thin flan and are lighter in weight standard.

These coins are usually minted in noble metals i.e. gold and in silver. However a single repousse copper coins has also been reported from Malhar,[1] site located in the present day state of Chhattisgarh. As the repousse coins are thin and light the technique did not gain much popularity due to durability issues. It was adopted in mainly two regions: in ancient South Kosala or modern Chhattisgarh and its adjoining areas including portions of western Odisha. The second zone is south-eastern Bangladesh in the ancient territory of Harikela. Only a few late Harikela coins were minted using this technique and are quite crude.

Repouśse coins in South Kosala were the first of its type and were minted around 5th century CE by rulers named Mahendrāditya and Prasannamātra. The legends on the coins are in box-headed character of the Central Indian Brāmhī script. These coins were in circulation during the latter part of the fifth and early part of the sixth century A.D. We have two different series of these coins in circulation in two different areas, sometimes they overlap each other. The first series of these coins have *garuda* or *chakra* or both as device and this series belongs to the Śarabhapūriya kings of the Chhattisgarh region and the second series of these coins have Nandi or bull as device and belongs to the Nala dynasty of Bastar region. Among the Nala rulers mention may be made of the rulers named Varāharāja, Bhavadattarāja, Arthapatirāja, Nandanarāja and Stambha (rāja).

obverse reverse

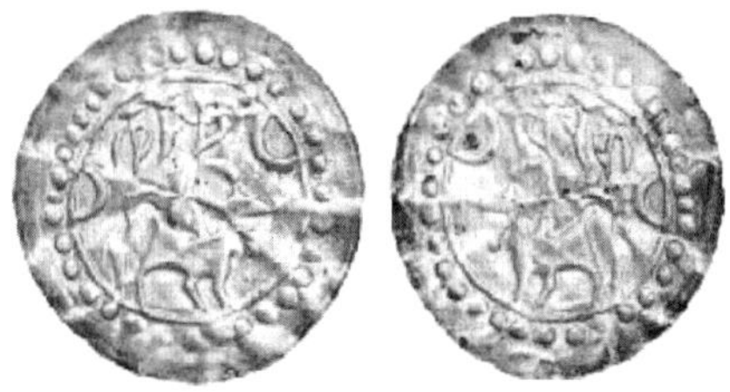

a silver repoussé coin of Harikela

obverse reverse

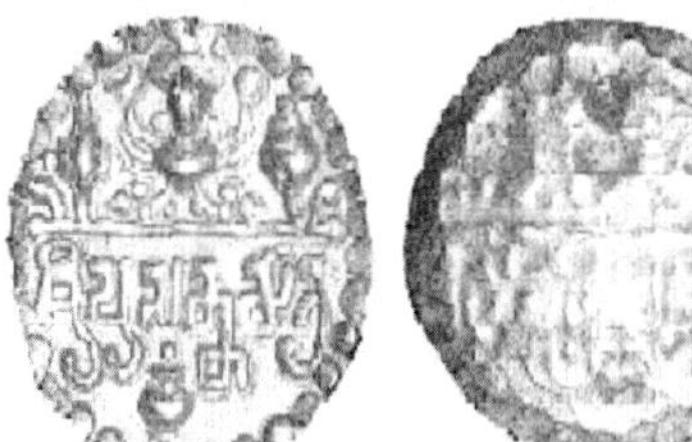

a gold repoussé coin of Prasannamatra

obverse reverse

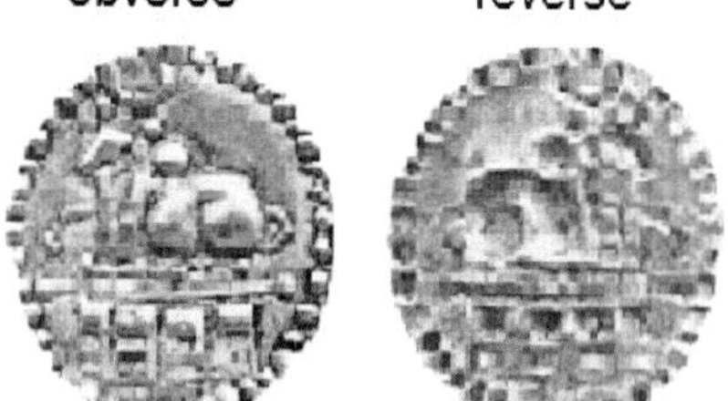

a gold repoussé coin of Varaharaja

Moreshwar Gangadhar Dikshit [2] used a term *utpīditankamudra* for this repouśse coins. Here the first half of this word *utpīdita,* stands for 'well pressed' and the second half stands for coining i.e. '*taṅka*'. According to B.N. Mukherjee "Apparently the thin flan of such a coin was placed on a piece of stone or metal displaying the positive impression of the device concerned either in high relief or in a sunken state. Then the thin blank was carefully hammered to receive one of its sides the positive impression of the device either in relief or as incised (depending on the manner in which it appeared on the matrix). Consequently, the other side of the thin flan got intagliated or raised traces of the device in negative."[3]

Moti Chandra and Parmeshwari Lal Gupta,[4] describing some ancient jewellery moulds, referred to similar specimens from Taxila excavations and quoted comments of John Marshall regarding their typology and mode of fabrication. John Marshal mentions the use of this process at Taxila for the manufacture of copper and bronze objects.[5]In this repouśse technique a thin plate of metal was heated and pressed down on a bed of pitch. On this plate the pattern was drawn and pressed out with a punch and hammer, and the process of heating and hammering repeated as often as necessary and then the plate was reversed and the face worked up with punches and chasing tools.

S. V. Sohoni[6] does not consider these as coins but as ornaments. He tries to relate these with the puttula in Bengali, and putati in Marathi evolving according to him from Sanskrit word puttalikā. According to T. P. Verma the process of making ornaments using similar technique is much more complicated and requires more attention and care. But he also states that 'The Indian goldsmiths still prepare ornaments in this way. But their technique cannot be called repouśse in the strict sense of the term. They make the ornaments of very thin fabric by fixing the gold flan on special kind of sealing wax and then carve the design by hammering gently. It is no wonder if these so called repouśse coins were manufactured by the goldsmiths in the same way.' At the same time also mentions that "it seems that the process of minting repouśse coins was not so complicated and was less time consuming because this much have been manufactured by dies with positive impressions on them, and, when these dies were hammered on the thin flan of the metal piece they got the positive impression on the back side."[7]

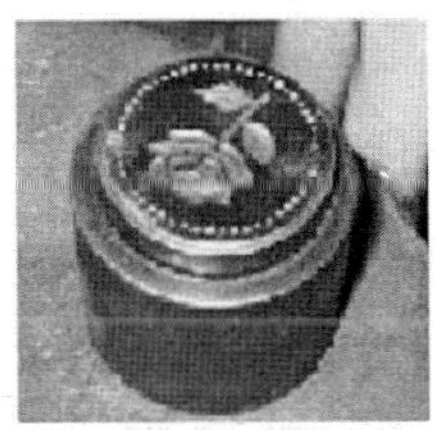

A modern die with shallow relief

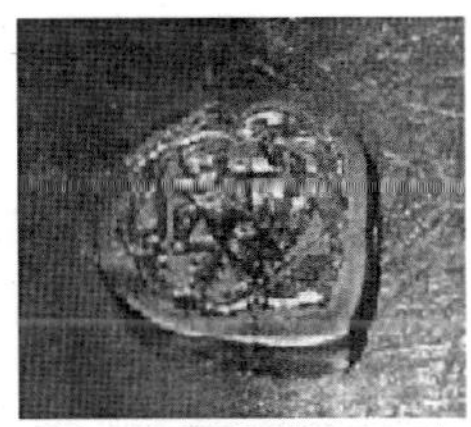

A modern die with deep relief

The engraving of the die of the repouśse coin has to be much deeper than the other dies used for die struk coins. The hammering has to be with more care and precision to receive proper pressure to receive the positive impression on the one side of the thin flan at the same time not to damage the flan which is much thinner than the normal case.

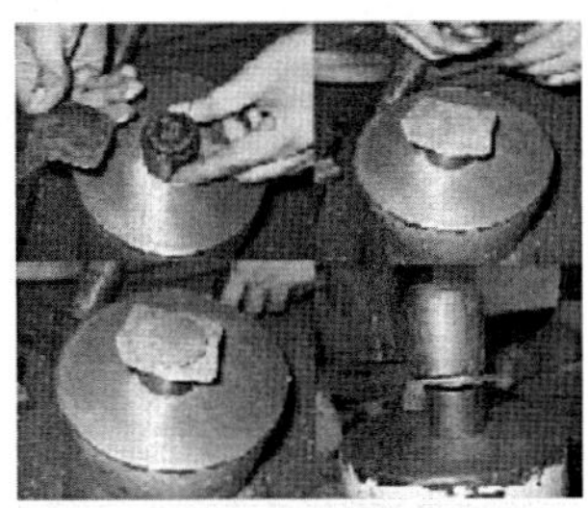

Placement of a Coin blank : Repousse technique

The die of the repouśse coin is placed on the anvil and on that die the coin blank is placed which would receive the device impression then a plain thin metal flan is placed on it, on top of the plain flan a piece of iron protector is placed which works as a shock absorber for the hammer blow. Then this whole unit receives a hammer blow from expert hands which know the pressure which this thin flan requires to receive the positive impression of the device. This minting technique of repouśse coin has been mentioned as time consuming by some but as it can be discerned from the description it is not time consuming. It only requires a little more care and attention. The prerequisite for this technique is pure metal with little alloy. In case of the coins of South Kosala the gold was procured from Mahanadi river bed and to this very little alloy was added. Thus here we have tried to demonstrate the technique on the basis of the practical minting and this has led us to clarify a few misconception which arose due to theoretical description and lack of practical minting experience.

The whole unit of the process

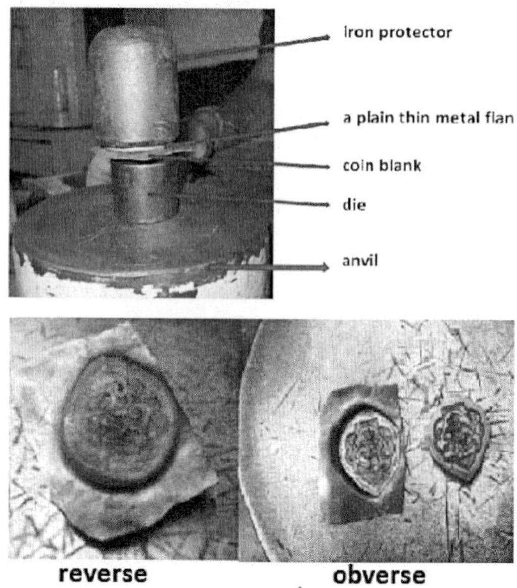

Acknowledgement

I would like to profusely thank Mr. Ravi Shankar Sharma for demonstrating the technique and also explaining the details and sharing his experience with me. Without his help this paper would not have taken shape.

References

1. "Attribution and Typology of the Sātavāhana coins", in Coinage of Sātavāhana and Coins from Excavation, (Ed. Ajay Mitra Shastri), Nagpur, 1972, p.4.
2. Dikshit, M.G., "*Madhya Pradesh ke Purātattva ki Rūparekhā*", Sagar, 1954.
3. Mukherjee, B.N. and Lee, P.K.D., "*Technology of Indian Coinage*", Indian Museum, Kolkata, 2000, p.18.
4. "Jewellery Moulds in Ancient India", *Bulletin of the Prince of Wales Museum*, No.8 (1962-64), p.11.
5. *Ibid*; Taxilla, II, Cambridge, 1951, p.617
6. *JNSI*, Vol.XLV, pp.156-157
7. "*The Repousse pieces of Mahendrāditya etc.*" JNSI, LIII, PP148-49.

8

Working Theory on Metrology of Ancient and Medieval Indian Coins: An Introduction

Mukesh Sharma

In the modern world of today, although credit and debit cards exists where money seems to live in some sort of cloud and appears without a physical presence, there is still cash money. That is to say physical objects still exist that carry a value. The value these days in circulating is merely what appears as a number or representation on the coin that tells us how much it is worth. We must know this to understand how much it can purchase. For the objects or things we have to purchase have a price because the barter system, in general no longer operates.

Today we have coins, paper money (notes) and cards. However if we go back just a couple of hundred years or less within the greater subcontinent other things existed. This money as we call it in general had no value (or denomination) stamped on it. It came in three metals although at times a composite metal (billon made up of silver and copper alloy). Gold was the most valuable, silver the second and generally copper was the lowest value.

In many areas there was also what is called humble money. That is to say they were not coins but were used by counting numbers of them to make a purchase. These could be caurie shells or bitter almonds for example.

Just like today people in small villages and large towns shopped for their produce and paid money. In fact just like today in historic times marketplaces were well organised with officials and guilds and organisations to not only protect the merchants but to also protect, as much as possible, the customers.

But here we now have a problem. There was no value written for much of the time on each piece of metal that was the coin. The value of the coin was in both the weight and (certainly for silver and gold) the fineness or purity of the metal. We know and understand two basic things about the purity of the metal.

1. In general throughout the ages purity was maintained at a high level.
2. Purity could be relatively easily tested by various touchstone methods.

So within the general marketplace we have moneychangers both great and small. Simple money changers regulated exchanges between, for, example, humble money and copper and between copper and silver. The higher end the shroffs or sarafs traded in all forms of money, gold silver, copper etc. and the letters of exchange for large sums of money called hundis.

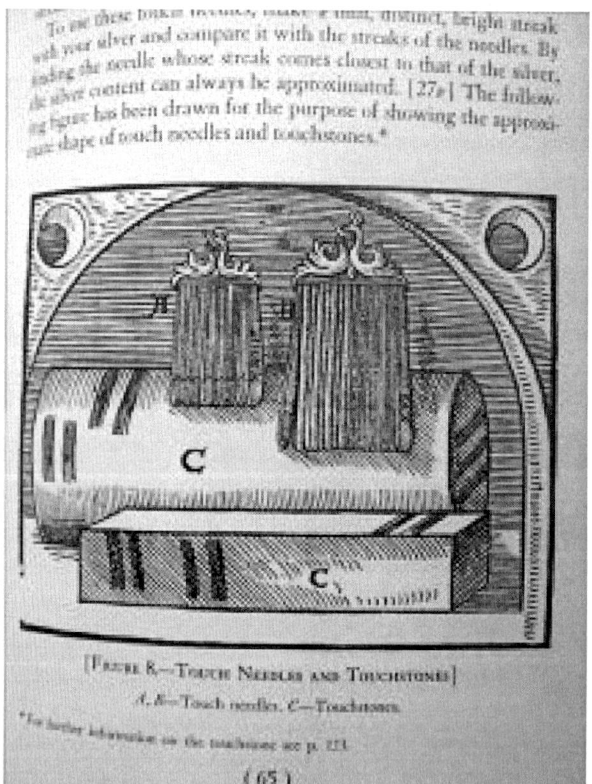

Fig. 1: Touchstone Techniques

The technique of touchstone testing has been known for many centuries. Accuracies of better than one percent metal content are achievable with practice and the simple equipment shown above.

It was simplicity itself. We had coins that could be tested for purity. But what about the weight of the coin? Again this would appear to be simple. But we know that weights in India if reduced to common terminology such as rati, tola, maund etc. varied from place to place. The great sub-continent was a number of local entities welded together by varying empires. Each district had its own practically unique system of weights and measures although the same names for the weights may have applied.

This is amply demonstrated when the British began their expansion within India and became somewhat confused by the weights and measures system as well the possible variance in the purity of precious metals in coins. The British system was based on uniformity. Uniformity was somewhat easy to maintain in a relatively small administration area of the British Isles where there had been for many years a centralised government however on the great sub-continent even in Mughal times there were differences almost everywhere.

Trade was not confined to regions of similar government. Trade took place across territories controlled by various rulers and also outside the general area of the sub-continent. Even though we know in Mughal times the coinage in the empire was controlled to some degree where all coinage used within the empire had to be Mughal issues. That is to say foreign coins had to be recoined for use the coinage of the sub-continent has much longer history than this.

We also understand that a silver coin, for example, of half the comparative weight of another silver coin of the same fineness was worth half as much as the full weight coin. This was true of all metals. But how was the weight gauged?

This then leaves two major outstanding questions.

1. How was weight gauged.
2. What was the conversion weight between coins of different metals (and humble money).

Weight was actually very simple. You had a simple balance scale. These can be made by anyone and can be accurate enough to determine comparative weights. A sample of the weight required can be made of anything. History tells us that these were made of metal, glass and many other objects. With this known weight on one side the coin could be compared. It was therefore easy to understand the comparative weight. A higher weight could purchase more, a lower weight less. It must be accepted of course that handmade coins did vary a little in weight so for standard transactions a little variance would be acceptable.

The bottom line is simple. It does not matter how many *ratis* (but which weight is a *rati*) or how many *tolas* a coin is said to be made of in weight. What matters is the purchasing power of a predetermined weight of the coin. Coin weights can vary and be changed within reigns as metals increase or decrease in comparative value. The purchasing power can be determined by comparative means.

Therefore, what is important is the relative exchange rates at any time between coin composition (types of metals) and the purity of those metals. From this we need to understand or determine the weight (in any scale) of a UNIT of any metal. When the unit is determined, we can have multipliers (heavier units) and dividers (lighter units). It does not matter whether these are weighed in *ratis, tolas*, grains or grams. It is the relative comparative weights that are important.

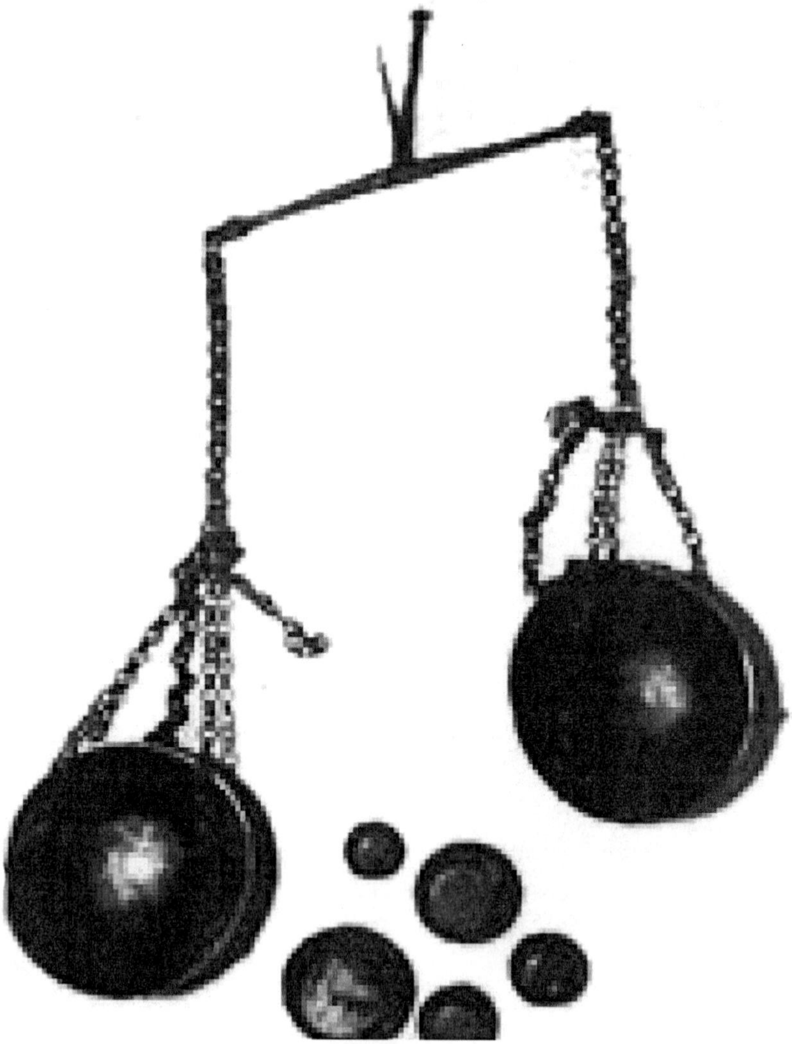

Fig. 2 : Simple hand held balance scale. A known weight is placed in one pan and the weight of an unknown object can be judged by balance.

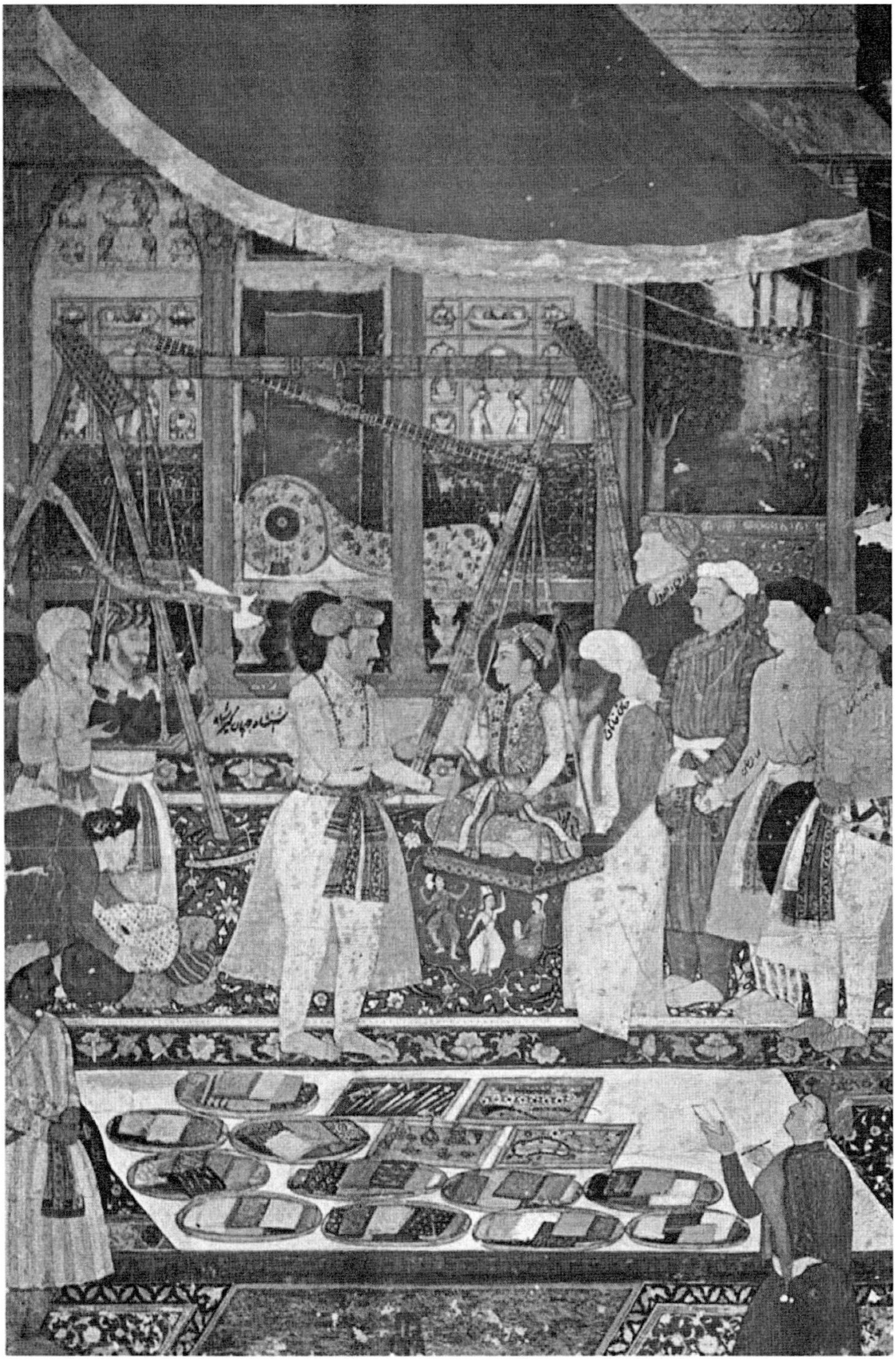

Fig. 3 : A larger and more complicated balance using the same mechanism.

A simple example of Jaunpur Sultanate coins is shown in the table below –

Sr. No.	Ruler	Weight of coin in grams	Remarks
01	Ibrahim Shah	9.07	-
02	Mahmud Shah	9.41	-
03	Husain Shah	9.76	No variance in weight except a gradual increase in weight over time

The above example shows the rise in eight of the standard billon UNIT of the Jaunpur Sultanate over the life of the Sultanate. Various theories have been advanced including a change from the standard weight of the northern *rati* to the standard rate of a southern or perhaps western *rati*. The actual weight is of no real consequence other than as a comparison to coins of a similar metal or the exchange rate to other metals. In true numismatic research, it is the comparative weights that need to be closely examined rather than theoretical thoughts.

There is a need across all sub-continent numismatics to define the standard unit of weight of various metals and describe similar metal coins as dividers and multipliers and to ascertain the real exchange rates between metals.

I am pleased to advised that this process has been in discussion with a major research group for two years and they have decided to use in their future publications (they have a formal publishing agreement worldwide) the term UNIT where applicable. It will also lead to a long series of research into comparative testing by modern and historic methods of testing for metal purity and a renewed effort in the research of comparative values between metals.

I am already thankful that the basic idea of this research project has been accepted by a numismatic group and will be used in future in their work.

Conclusion and Summary

1. The weight of the coins could vary at the will of the issuing authorities
2. For modern research, what is necessary is the comparative weights of the coins in the same metal
3. That for each series a measurement of the weight of a coin can be determined
4. This weight/standard will be called a Unit
5. There may be multiples or lower denominations of a unit.
6. The Unit may itself vary over a period of time
7. It is the relative exchange weight between metals of known weights (units) that is of utmost importance

8. For modern numismatic research, the old weight standards of ratti and tola for example are of no consequence.[1]

References

1. Editorial comment: The Editors disagree with this claim of the author of 'the ratti and tola standard being of no consequence' as the ratti (named Krishnala in the Vedic period and Surkh in the Mughal period due to its red colour) formed the basis of most Indian coin series right from the early Historic period till the early modern British period of Indian History.

9

A New Classification of Mughal Mints
with special reference to Mughal Deccan

Dr. Mahesh A. Kalra

Introduction

In case of studying the History of pre-modern Islamic Empires, their coins form an invaluable primary source for various reasons; chief among these is their association with the rituals of *Khutba* and *Sikka* used for legitimizing the rule of Islamic sovereigns in the Indian sub-continent since the Ghaznavid period; *Khutba*, being the recitation of the ruler's name in the Friday congregational prayers and *Sikka* being the inclusion of his name on the coins of the ruled region. In the past, both held comparable value in informing the local populace about the status of the current ruler. However, *Khutba* remained an oral recitation and hence short-lived in nature while *Sikka* (Coinage) acquired the position of a 'bulletin of the state' in metal preserved for posterity.[1]

Another reason for the importance of Islamic coins is the information inscribed on them apart from the sovereign's name which increases their value as primary sources; first is the date of issuing the coin inscribed either in words or numerals in the Hijri era (or other quasi-Islamic eras like the Illahi calendar of Akbar); second is the religious legends on the coins[2] and finally the most important feature is the inclusion of the name of the Mint town on the coin. In this respect, Mughal Coinage has attracted more than its fair share of attention since the early modern period as evidenced by the vast collections of Mughal coins in private hands and the coin cabinets of museums in India and Europe. The presence of coin enthusiasts both in the colonial administration and among private collectors with a good knowledge of Arabic and Persian ensured that these coins were recognized as tools of historical knowledge from the early modern period and hoarded in both private and museum collections.

The growth of the Mughal Empire under the Great Mughals was intricately linked to the rise of three types of urban entities; strategically-located cities like Kabul, Ahmadnagar, etc.; symbolic power centres like Lahore in the Punjab or Daulatabad in Deccan and lastly, market towns like Surat and Burhanpur which majorly contributed to the trade activities of the empire. The Mughal Empire was a conquest state which drew its strength from the conquest of kingdoms and states outside its jurisdiction through military campaigns followed by the establishment of imperial mints in the chief towns of the newly captured region. The names of these premier towns, christened as 'Mint towns', have been carefully studied and deciphered meticulously by modern numismatists since the nineteenth century as they are prominently inscribed on Mughal coins in all three metals. Mughal Mint town lists were thus compiled at the start of twentieth century by various numismatists in their catalogues.[3]

The Mughal Empire took three quarters of the sixteenth century to establish itself in north India to begin its expansion in the region of the Deccan south of Vindhyas towards the end of the sixteenth century under Akbar (c. 1556-1605). Beginning in 1590s, Akbar employed a host of political manoeuvres to establish Mughal presence in the Deccan. Deccan was ruled at this period by four major powers, the Faruqi rulers of Khandesh, the Nizamshahis of Ahmadnagar, the Barid Shahis of Bidar, Adilshahis of Bijapur and Qutbshahis of Golconda.

A careful study focusing on the surviving specimens of various mint towns with the various dates in Hijri era and Regnal Years occurring on them can be used for not only predicting the calendar of production of these mints but also the profusion or rarity of its activity. Based on this two-pronged data collected by the researcher during the reigns of a series of Mughal emperors, it has been used to classify the mint towns into two categories; Major Mints and Minor Mints.

An important aspect of all these scholarly works was to compile lists of Mughal Mint towns from which each Mughal emperor issued his coins. They not only utilized existing knowledge but also consulted primary works like the Ain'-i-Akbari to compare the list of mint towns. The earliest mint lists were compiled by both Lane-Poole and Rodgers; additionally, M. Longworth Dames[4] and Sir Richard Burn[5] both compiled updated mint lists. Rodgers' list of mint towns was augmented by both Wright and Whitehead; additionally, all three published a 'Mint Notes' section in their catalogues to showcase the existing knowledge about the location and history of important Mughal mint towns of the Empire including Mughal Deccan.

The attempts to study the pattern of Mughal mint towns again was a gradual study of mint towns in various reigns to identifying newly discovered mint towns with Persianate names which was heightened in the early twentieth century by the erudite studies of numismatic scholars like R. B. Whitehead[6], G. B. Taylor[7], William Irvine[8] and S. H. Hodivala.[9] These studies spurred a later generation of scholars to examine the new found evidence in light of surviving museum specimens of Mughal coins in major museums across the country and the British Museum to compile a relative output of these coinages. The first study was by Aziza Hasan which attempted a relative output of Mughal coins from various mints across the Empire (but majorly focussing on the North).[10] Though the methodology has been since criticized and debunked by many Western scholars viz. John F. Deyell[11] and Stan Goron, according to the author of this paper, the theory can be used to study relative outputs of the Mughal mints especially when compared with specimens available in the numismatic markets which increases the number of surviving specimens as well as stems the criticism of 'favoured and selected specimens in museums cannot reflect production' put by Dr. Deyell and Mr. Goron. (Fig. 1-2)

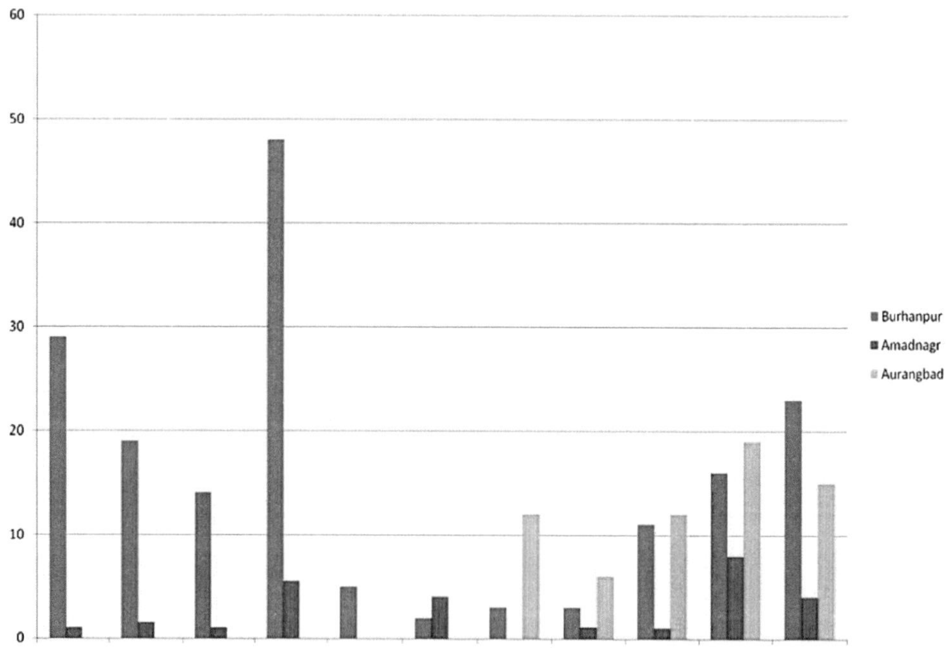

Fig. 1 : Bar Chart of Silver Rupee coins of 3 Major mints of Deccan based on Aziza Hasan's study

A New Classification of Mughal Mints

A careful study of the output of the mint towns (though indirectly) has been made by studying the relative survival of extant specimens in museums, private collections or hoards.

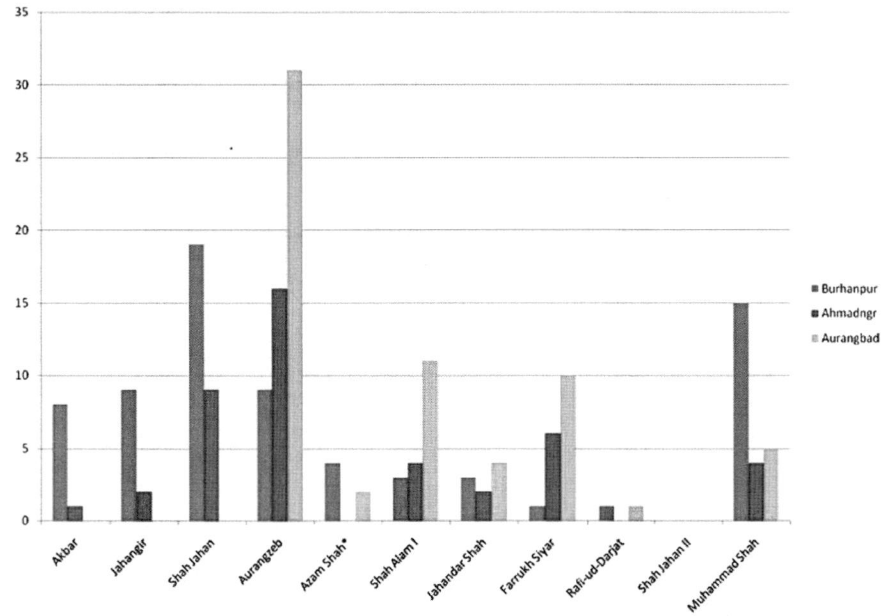

Fig. 2 : Bar Chart of Silver Rupee coins of 3 Major mints of Deccan found in collections of Central Museum, Nagpur

It reveals that the mint towns were of two types;

a) Major Mints which were economically important cities with huge volume of trade as well as velocity of the coins. These Major Mint towns had a huge output to supply the much-needed cash to the Mughal governor to monetize payments to the central treasury and facilitate trade payments to and from the region. This category of mint towns' importance is reflected by the survival of numerous extant specimens of coins covering the reign of several emperors.

b) Minor Mints are the second category of mint towns which were deemed mint towns where coins were minted for a very short period for various reasons elaborated below. Coins of Minor Mints are hence many times seen as 'rare' coins in modern numismatic circles due to the brief length of their issue as well as the lesser chances of the coin surviving to the modern period.

The author's study has been based on the Mughal coins issued from Mughal Deccan i.e. the expanding domain of the Mughals south of the Vindhyas from Akbar's reign till Muhammad Shah's reign to study the output of various mints lying in the Deccan region where the Mughal issued their coins from. Thus, the author has compiled detailed mint lists which table all possible mint towns which issued gold, silver and copper Mughal coins during the reign of each Emperor from Akbar (c. 1595 onwards) till the reign of Muhammad Shah (d. 1748) to study the relative output and survival of coins of various mints.

In his observation, Major Mint towns and Minor Mint towns can be further classified into sub-categories as described below.

Most Major Mints can be further classified based on –

- the number of surviving specimens for particular dates or Regnal years. An indirect way for collectors is the availability or rarity of a date/ regnal year
- the continuity of production throughout a reign/reigns
- the production of the Mint in three Metals

Thus, the following classification has been suggested by the author –

- **Major Mint 'Class A'** signifies which issued coins through most reigns in all three metals
- **Major Mint 'Class B'** signifies those mints which issued coins in all three metals but only during a certain reign
- **Major Mint 'Class C'** signifies mints which issued coins in a particular metal but throughout all reigns

The best example of 'Major Mint Class A' in Mughal Deccan was Burhanpur whose earliest coins were silver rupees and copper coins issued in Akbar's name with the date, Illahi 45 Khurdad (British Museum Collection) corresponding to May-June 1600. Though there are other Major Mints of Class A, Burhanpur stands out as its coins did not stop getting minted even during the most fragile periods of Mughal domination over the Deccan right from the reign of Akbar to Muhammad Shah. Burhanpur in particularly stood out due to its premier position as a trade town of exemplary resilience to any disaster or political catastrophe during this long period. This has been confirmed by the author's previous study contrasting the output of Burhanpur with other major towns of Mughal Deccan like Ahmadnagar and Aurangabad.[12] Other Major Mint Class A in Mughal Deccan is Aurangabad (Khujista Bunyad). In fact, both the mints, Burhanpur and Aurangabad were competitors both for Seat of Power position as well as Major Mint status. Both were equally prolific but the reasons were different; Burhanpur was first a major trade centre and then a seat of power till the period of Shah Jahan. Aurangabad's profile rose during Aurangzeb's era as it became the seat of power replacing Burhanpur due to its rising political importance. Aurangabad was renamed Khujista Bunyad from Aurangzeb's RY 32 and remained its name ever since. However, Aurangabad could not replace Burhanpur as the Major Mint Class A as its trade continued to dictate issuing of Mughal coins in all three metals.

The best example of Major Mint Class 'B' in Mughal Deccan is Daulatabad which became a Major Mint in the reign of Shah Jahan. Though Daulatabad Fort was captured from the Nizamshahis only in A.H. 1042 (1633), Shah Jahan issued silver rupees in the name of Daulatabad since his first regnal year A.H. 1037 with regular issues from A.H. 1045 majorly in silver but also in gold with few copper issues. However, Daulatabad stopped its issuing of coins after Shah Jahan's reign ended due to the decline of the city's political significance as a symbolic seat of power. Hence, Major Mints of Class B issued coins due to their politically importance during certain reigns; hence we see a major output from these mints in the reign of a certain emperor continuously throughout his reign with the stoppage of minting of coins from his successor's reign.

Major Mints Class 'C' are generally mints which issued throughout the reigns of Emperors usually in one metal. The best examples are Ellichpur and Macchlipattan which are both known for their prolific copper issues. Though beginning their issues in silver in the reign of Akbar and Aurangzeb respectively, Ellichpur and Macchlipattan became the Major Mints for copper coins in successive reigns of Aurangzeb's successors for providing the much-needed copper coinage for Mughal Deccan.

The Minor Mint category is applied to those mints whose coins are reflected by very few specimens in most reigns and issued for a limited period like a specific regnal year or Hijri year.These Minor mint towns issued coins specifically for three reasons;

a) Minor Mint Class A which issued coins to indicate their conquest by the Mughals with the date on the coin matching the specific year mentioned in other sources like Epigraphs and/or Contemporary Histories;

b) Minor Mint Class B which issued their coins for a specific purpose like paying the local army for the campaign and specific demand for money for monetizing the economy during the presence of the Mughal contingent.

A majority of Minor Mint towns belong to Class A viz. their coins were issued for showcasing their conquest by the Mughals. The best example is that of Asirgarh (Asir) which was captured by Akbar from its Khandesh rulers in 1600 and gold mohurs of the hawk type were issued with the specific date of Illahi Isfandarmuz 45 representing the conquest of Asir from Khandesh. (Fig.3) The date of this coin exactly matches the dates

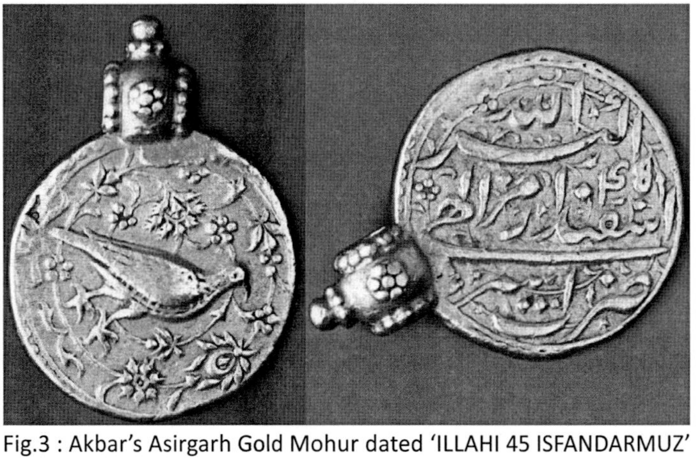

Fig.3 : Akbar's Asirgarh Gold Mohur dated 'ILLAHI 45 ISFANDARMUZ'
Image Courtesy: National Museum, New Delhi

on Akbar's epigraphs in the Asirgarh Fort announcing his conquest, entry into the fort and his leaving for the North.[13] Other examples of this category of Minor Mint towns is Shah Jahan's Aurangnagar Rupee and mohurs dated RY 15 symbolizing the conquest of Mulher by Aurangzeb from the local ruler of Mulher.

Minor Mint Class B towns were those which issued coins due to a probable demand from a local contingent for payment purposes especially with the Emperor camping in the area. The best example is Aurangzeb's coins from Islam Bandar (Rajapur) and Mahmud Bandar (Porto Nuovo), two port cities captured nominally by him during his long stint in the Deccan.[14] Another excellent example is a recently discovered 'rare' silver rupee of Gandikota mint issued by Aurangzeb in his thirty-ninth regnal year illustrated and sold by Oswal Auctions of Mumbai.[15] (Fig.4)

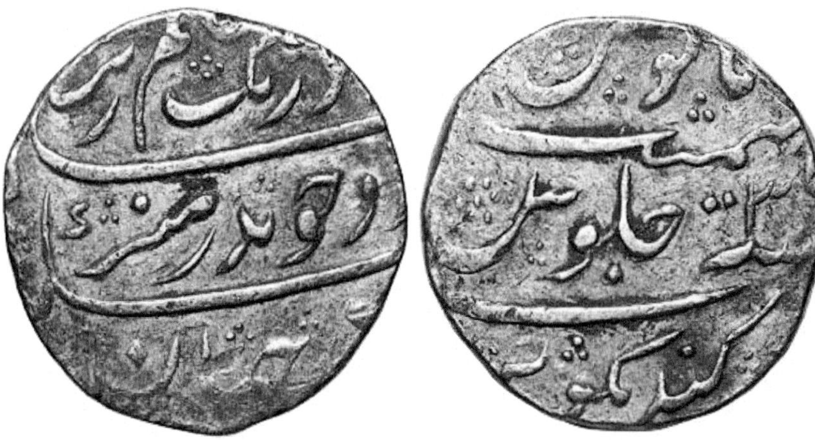

Fig.4 : Aurangzeb Silver Rupee Gandikota Mint Regnal Year 39
Image Courtesy: Oswal Auctions Auc# 61 Lot 371

Thus, the New Classification of Mughal Mint towns can be applied to other regions and areas under long domination of the Mughals by studying the relative survival rate of the coins in museum and private collections especially those in the public domain like auction catalogues of various auctioneers of Indian coins.

References

1. Stefan Heidemann, 'Numismatics' in the New Cambridge History of Islam – Vol. I – The formation of the Islamic World Sixth to Eleventh Centuries, ed. Chase Robinson, Cambridge University Press, New York, USA, 2010, pp.648-663.
2. In case of the Mughals, the first two Mughals Babur and Humayun stuck to the Islamic Kalima whereas Akbar and Jahangir veered towards variant religious legends or verses while Shah Jahan reverted to the Sunni Kalima. Aurangzeb and his successors strove to have Persian verses on their coins as a rule.

3. Stanley Lane-Poole, *The Coins of the Moghul Emperors of Hindustan in the British Museum* British Museum Press, London, 1892.
4. M. Longworth Dames, 'Some Coins of the Mughal Emperors' in NC 4th Series Vol II, 1902, pp.280-309. Published by: Royal Numismatic Society Stable URL: http://www.jstor.org/stable/42679818 Accessed: 28-07-2015 06:22 UTC. In addition to an updated list of Mughal mints, Dames gives a map showing the mints of the Mughal Empire.
5. R. Burn, 'Mints of the Mughal Emperors' in JASB, Vol. LXXII 1904, pp.75-107.
6. R.B. Whitehead, 'Mint Towns of the Mughal Emperors', JASB New Series Vol. VIII, 1912, pp.425-531.
7. G. P. Taylor, 'List complementary to Mr. Whitehead's Mint Towns' in NS to JASB Vol. XXII 1913 (127), p.178.
8. William Irvine, 'Mughal Mint Town, Firoznagar' *JASB NS* Vol. XIV (87) p. 580; 'Mughal Mint Town, Nusratabad (Dharwar) in *NS to JASB* Vol. XII (73), p. 381; 'Mughal Mint Town – Torgal' in NS to JASB Vol. VII (50) p.56.
9. S. H. Hodivala, *Historical Studies in Mughal Mint-towns and other Essays,* Sanjay Garg compiled and ed. Manohar Publications, New Delhi, 2014.
10. Aziza Hasan, 'Mints of the Mughal Empire (A Study in Comparative Currency) in *Essays in Medieval Indian Economic History – Indian History Congress Monograph Series* ed. Satish Chandra, Indian History Congress in association with Primus Books, 2nd Edition, New Delhi, 2014, (29th Session IHC) pp.169-192.
11. John S. Deyell, 'Numismatic Methodology in the Estimation of Mughal Currency Output' in *Indian Economic & Social History Review* 1976; 13; 393 DOI.
12. Mahesh A. Kalra, *'A Tale of three Mughal cities – the Mint towns of Burhānpur, Ahmadnagar and Aurangabad (c. 1601-1748)'* In: 'Studies in Medieval Deccan 14th to 18th Century: Festschrift to Dr. M. A. Nayeem', The Deccan History Society, Warangal, Telangana, 2015.
13. Syed Abdur Rahim, *Arabic, Persian and Urdu Inscriptions of Central India- A Topographical list,* Sundeep Prakashan, 2000 p.15.
14. Mahesh A. Kalra, *'Rajapur's transition to Islam Bandar and vice versa in the Mughal-Maratha War for Konkan c. 1687-1736 A.D.'* In: Konkan Itihaas Parishad's SHODH NIBANDH SANGRAH No.4, January 2015, ISBN 9789383871537.
15. Oswal Auctions # 61 Lot 371 www.oswal.auction.

10

Portugal Honours Garcia Da Orta:
The First Landlord of Bombay (Mumbai) with a Coin Issue

Adv. Ashok Shahani

The Government of Portugal has honored the first landlord of Mumbai GARCIA DA ORTA by issuing a 200 escudos coin in his name. There is also a stamp of Rs. 6/- issued by the Portuguese government in India. The Government had also issued a Bank note of 20 escudos way back in the year 1971 and it is since been demonetized.

The bi-metallic Copper-Nickel coin with a center in aluminum bronze ring having on the obverse side, a shield within a globe above the value with the legend "REPUBLICA PORTUGUESA". The reverse side has armored half-length bust of Garcia da Orta right holding a flower within a circle with the legend Garcia da Orta. The edge is segmented reeding.

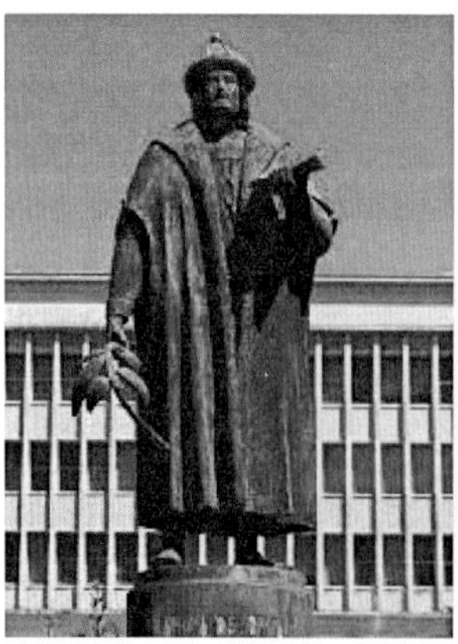

Fig.1: Garcia Da Orta

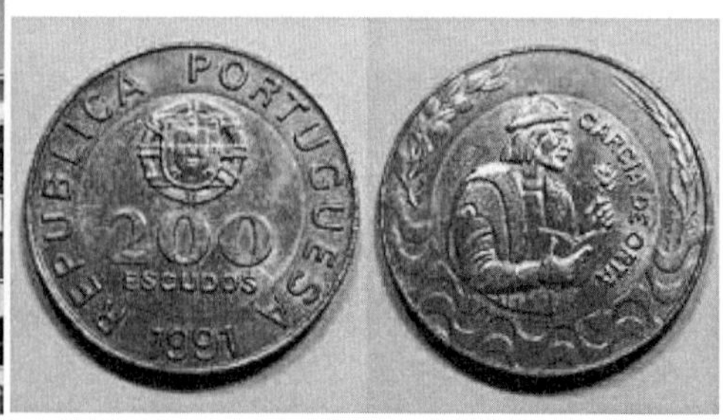

Fig.2 : Picture of 200 Escudos coin

Garcia da Orta (Garcia of the coconut groves) was a medical doctor by profession and training. He came to India in 1534 and leased the island of Bombay for 85 pounds from the Portuguese authorities as proprietor or Vazador in 1554. During the viceroyalty of Dom Pedro Mascerenhas, Bombay was granted to Garcia da Orta on a yearly basis for 85 pounds. It remained his property till 1570.He had a spacious garden where he grew medicinal plants and herbs.

In those times, the Portuguese had a base in Vasai or Bassein near Mumbao. He lived there and from there travelled frequently to Goa, which was in Portuguese hands then. By then he had also acquired riches and was a famous merchant there.

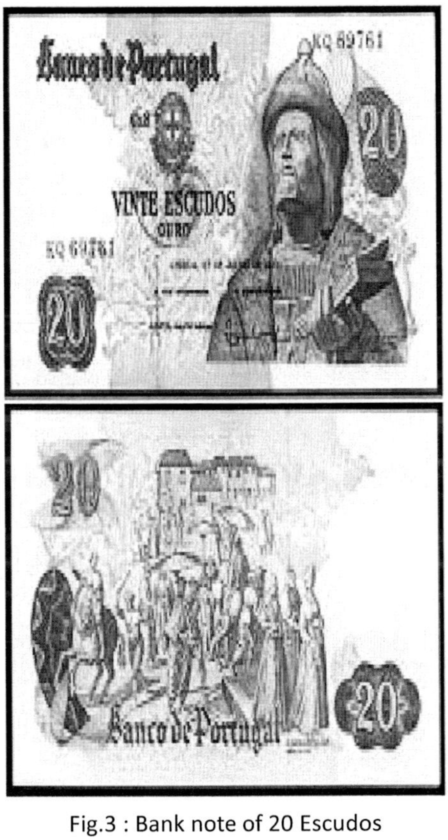

Fig.3 : Bank note of 20 Escudos

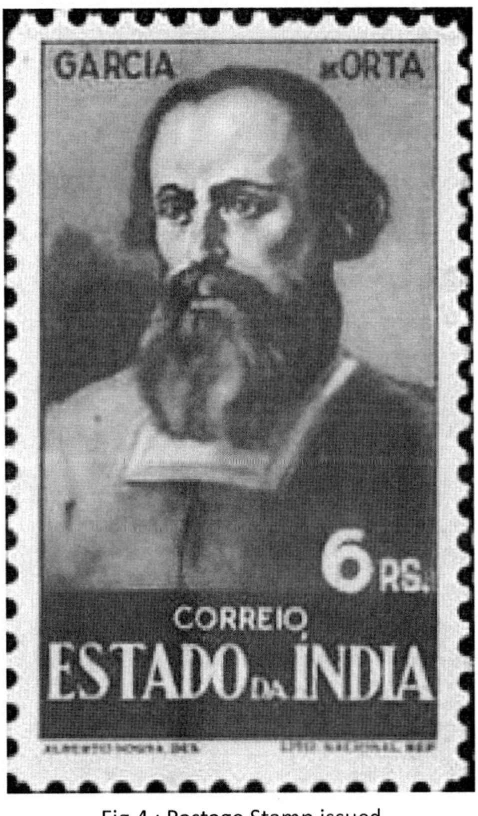

Fig.4 : Postage Stamp issued by the Portuguese Indian Government

His life and times

Garcia da Orta was born around 1499 in Castelo de Vide in the Alentejo region of Portugal. He was probably born in the Jewish quarter of that place. His family origins lay in Castille Spain from where his family had fled to Portugal. He was probably Sephardic Jew and whose family had adopted Christianity.

He studied Medicine from 1523 at Salamanca and Alcala de Heneres in Castile (Spain) and in 1530, he was appointed as the Professor of Logic at Coimbra University and was also honorary physician to King Joao III of Portugal.

His book on plants and drugs "Colloquies on the simples and drugs of India" published in Goa in 1563 with colorful drawing of plants was of great help to later physicians. He had also visited Ceylon to study medicinal plants especially for the use and treatment of snake bite.

Garcia da Orta stayed for seven years in Bombay (Mumbai). He flourished as a merchant and the owner of the island of Bombay (Mumbai). Garcia da Orta later on settled in Goa and died there in 1568.

Garcia da Orta stayed in a manor house located within the old precincts. This manor house with a spacious garden survived for a very long time but the record subsequently fades away. It was on one occasion also the residence of Sir George Oxenden, the first Governor of Bombay (Mumbai) in the year 1668. Till its subsequent alteration, it was a typical ground and one storied house with sloping roof and a veranda on both the sides. It later on became encompassed with other structures which formed part of Bombay Castle. The present location of the house can be roughly placed in the INS Angre complex, which is the headquarters of the Western naval command of the Indian navy. It also functioned as headquarters of the head of the East India Company and later on the Bombay provincial government.

His personal friend was Martin Affonsa D'souza, who was the governor of Portuguese India from 1542 to 1545. He was also friends with Burhan Nizam Shah of Ahmednagar and he acted as his personal physician.

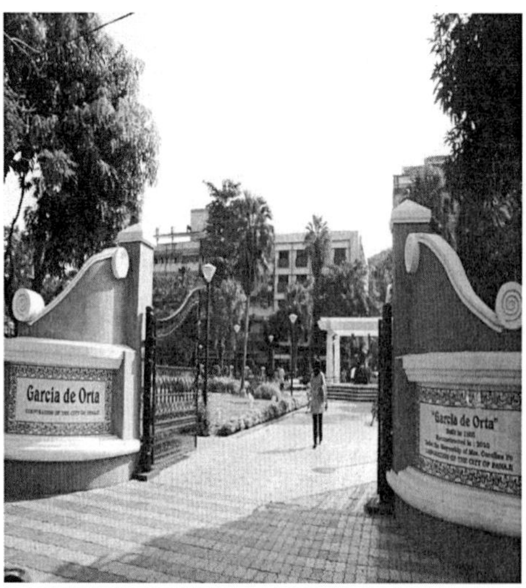

Fig.5 : Garden in Panjim, Goa, India

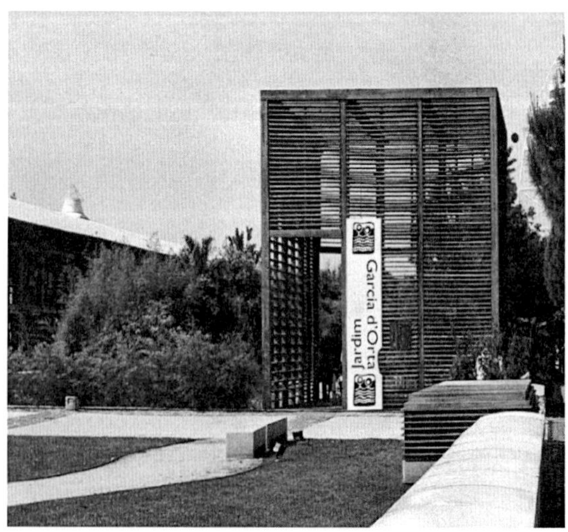

Fig.6 : Garden in Lisbon, Portugal

In 1554 he was granted a long lease of a part of Bombay (Mumbai). He had great knowledge of all the plants which came within reach from which drugs could be derived. He died at around in or about 1570 in Goa after practicing 37 years as a physician.

To honour his memory, there is a garden in Panjim, Goa named after him and probably his residence/villa was situated close by in the Jewish quarter. The garden is well preserved and is a popular venue for literary festivals. In Portugal, a garden in Lisbon, a high school in Porto and a hospital in Almada are named after him.

Section - III

Modern Numismatics

11

The Relevance of Mahatma Gandhi as a Numismatic and Philatelic Icon in the Twenty First Century

Dr. Mahesh A. Kalra

Mahatma Gandhi's assassination at the dawn of the Indian Independence crystallized his position as the Father of the nascent Indian nation with a number of honours and commemorations to this great son of India. Among several other paraphernalia issued in the Mahatma's honour were some private token medals issued probably at the time of Independence; among these a common type surviving is a cupro-bronze 'medal' with the image of Mahatma Gandhi with the Devanagari legend 'Mohandas Karamchand Gandhi - Rashtra Pita' and '15 August 1947' on the obverse; its reverse has an Utopian map of undivided India with the tricolour unfurling over it and the Devanagari legend 'Azad Hind' and '15 August 1947' inscribed over it. A variant of this medallion has 'MAHATMA

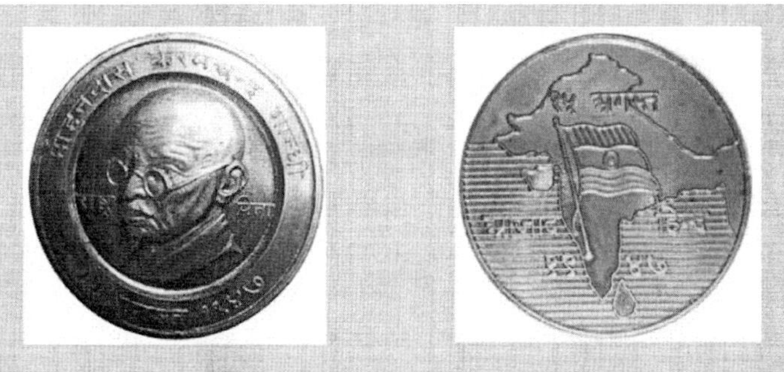

Portrait of the Mahatma with Devanagari Legend: Top : MOHANDAS KARAMCHAND GANDHI
Behind portrait RASHTRA PITA
Below: 15 AGAST 1947

Map of Undivided India with legends : 15 AGAST / AZAD HIND / 1947

Fig.1 : Mahatma Gandhi Bronze Medallion 1947 - Type I

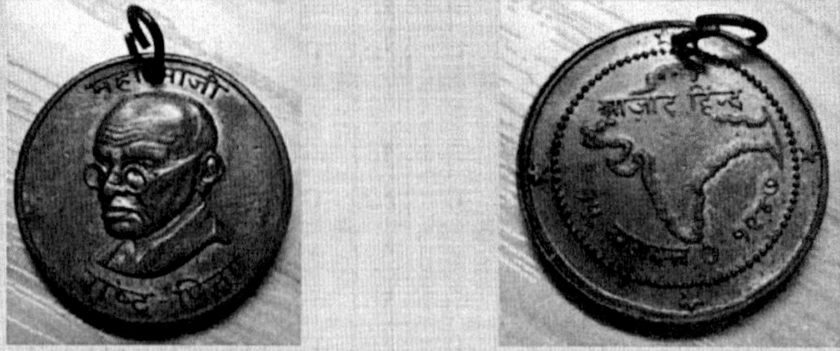

Portrait of the Mahatma with Devanagari Legend: Top : MAHATMA JI Below: RASHTRA PITA

Map of Undivided India with Devanagari legend : AZAD HIND / 15 AGAST 1947

Fig.2 : Mahatma Gandhi Bronze Medal 1947 - Type II

JI' inscribed instead of his full name with the same iconography repeated. A Pre-independence era medal commemorating the 75th Birth Anniversary of the Mahatma

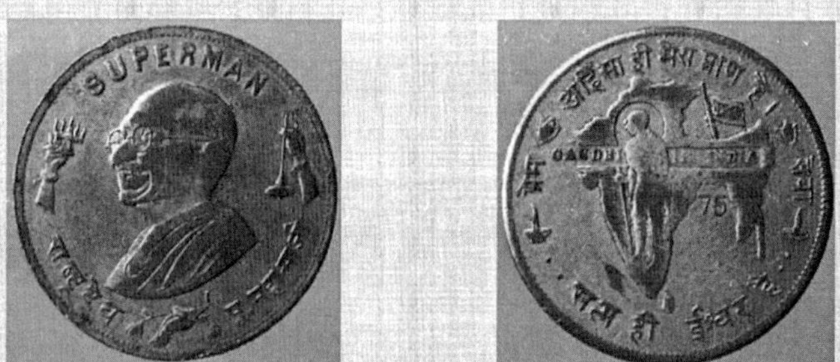

Image of the Mahatma surrounded by traditional Diya and Temple Bells and legend English 'SUPERMAN' and Hindi 'RASHTRA DEV PU. MAHATMA JI'

Image of the Mahatma looming large over the Map of Undivided India and Diyas and the Hindi legend 'PREM / SEWA / AHIMSA HI MERA PRAN HAI and below 'SATYA HI ISHWAR HAIN'

Fig.3 : A Pre-Independence token medal issued in honour of the Mahatma's 75th Birth Anniversary c. 1944

anticipated his imminent greatness with a term 'Super Man' in English and 'Rashtra Dev Pu(jya) Mahatma' in Devanagari with image of the Mahatma surrounded by diyas on the obverse; the reverse with the image of the Mahatma looming large over the map of undivided India, thus anticipating the Father of the Nation epithet that the Mahatma would earn.[1] Interestingly a '2 Anna' and '1 Anna' coin with the same map of undivided India has been also found among numismatic collectors predating the 1950 Republic of India Coinage issued as official currency by the Indian government.[2]

The official recognition of Mahatma Gandhi came on the first anniversary of India's Independence falling on 15 August 1948 which saw the release of the first-ever set of commemorative stamps issued in the honour of the Mahatma. These stamps were issued with his popular appellation 'BAAPU' in Devanagari and Urdu script legends to probably

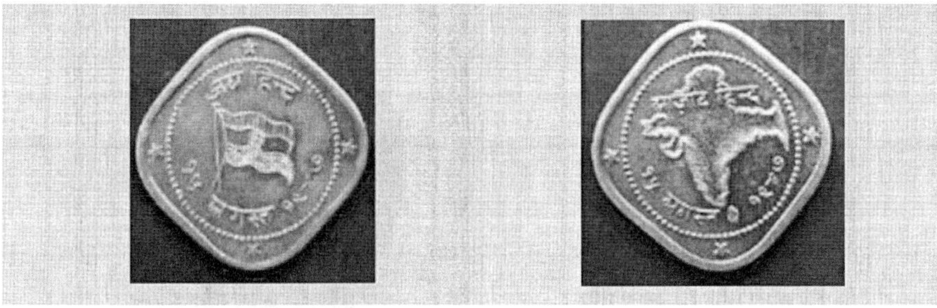

Fig.4: Mysterious 2 Anna Coin pre-dating 1950 Republic of India 2 Anna Series

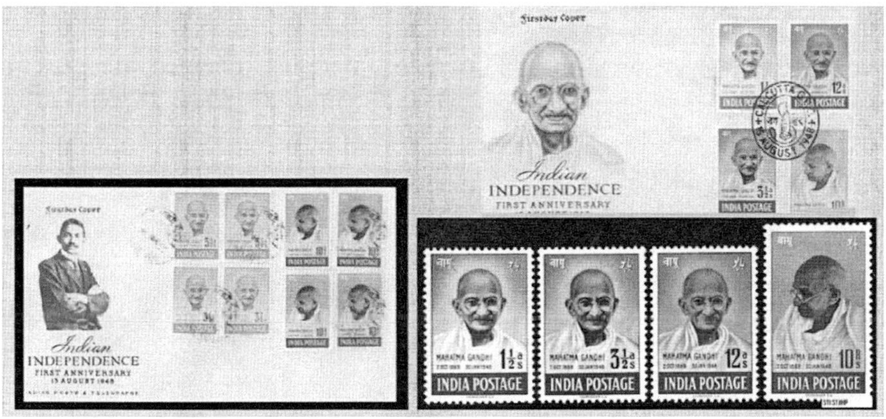

Fig.5 : First Commemorative Stamp Set 15th August 1948

position Mahatma Gandhi officially as an icon of India's Unity in Diversity to calm the embers of the smouldering communal tensions caused by India's Partition on religious grounds.[3] Thus, the early decades of India's independence saw Gandhi's installation as the official icon for various official purposes. However, a numismatic or Banknote commemoration still eluded the Father of the Nation as India adopted a new currency idiom on the declaration of the Indian Republic on 26 January 1950 with the adoption of the Ashokan Lion Pillar at Sarnath as the main emblem of the Indian Nation among other numismatic devices like the Bull on the base of the same pillar.[4] Similarly, the Banknotes issued by the Republic of India first considered replacing the British monarch's image with that of Mahatma Gandhi but finally adopted the Ashokan Lion Pillar emblem as its main notaphilic device.[5]

During the first few decades of India's existence as a Republic, the world around it was changing in rapid strides as the Cold War divided the world into two antagonistic blocs of power between the USA backed NATO and USSR. The scenario's grim nature made the world recognize the effectiveness of Gandhi's methods of non-violence as some countries including India formed the Non-Aligned Movement (NAM). More importantly, many political movements in India's neighbourhood and abroad took cue from Gandhi and used Satyagraha as a mean to highlight colonial, racial, class and gender biases in Asia, Africa, Europe as well as the Americas. These movements turned Mahatma Gandhi into an international icon of non-violent resistance to injustices committed round the world. Apart from South Africa where Gandhi left an indelible mark and footprints for Nelson Mandela to emulate, other African nations used Gandhian symbolism in their fight against colonial powers to achieve Independence from them in the fifties. Thus, many of these countries viewed Gandhi as a benevolent figure advocating international peace and brotherhood. In the West, the fifties and sixties was a period of the rise of Gandhism in both British and American political circles where the radical protest movements adopted Gandhi's Satyagraha as the main tool of protest. His role was however scarcely acknowledged as a primary mover due to religious and cultural differences perceived by the protestors especially his advocacy of vegetarianism and celibacy. Notably, Black Rights' Champion, Rev. Martin Luther King Jr. acknowledged Christ as his main inspiration while barely admitting that Gandhi's methods showed him the possibility of using peaceful methods of protest.[6]

In India, many changes in the official and public perception of Gandhi as a symbol of Indian values enshrined in the Indian Constitution especially the focus on Ahimsa or Non Violence. Unfortunately, tectonic changes in the political scenario after Nehru's death in May 1964 led to the Congress Party split with the Young Turk section favouring Nehru's daughter and heir to his political legacy, Indira Priyadarshini Gandhi in 1967. However, the tradition of Mahatma Gandhi was kept alive by few Gandhians like Vinoba Bhave and Jaya Prakash Narayan (JP) who organized non-violent resistance to both capitalist and communal forces alike through movements under the banner of Shanti Sena and later the Bhoodan and Gramdaan Movements in the late fifties and sixties.[7]

Thus, in this markedly changed scenario, the centenary of Mahatma Gandhi was celebrated in 1969-70 in the whole country and abroad. In India, there was the release of a commemorative set of coins and banknotes celebrating the life of the Mahatma with great gusto. The set of commemorative coins were issued from the Bombay Mint which was chosen for commemorative coins for the country in 1964 when it issued a similar set on 14 November 1964 in the memory of the late Pandit Jawaharlal Nehru. Thus, the four denomination set of 10 Rupees, 1 Rupee, 50 Paise and 20 Paise were issued on 2 October 1969 to commemorate the centenary of the Mahatma. The coins had the image of the Mahatma with Hindi/English legend 'MAHATMA GANDHI' and his life span '1869-1948' inscribed on the obverse in the exergue. The Ten Rupee coins had 80 per cent silver and 20 per cent copper alloy.[8] Similarly, banknotes were issued in the honour of Mahatma Gandhi in the denominations of One Rupee (legal tender) signed by the Secretary of Finance I. G. Patel and other denominations like 2 Rupees, 5 Rupees, 10 Rupees and 100 Rupees with an image of Mahatma Gandhi seated in deep contemplation at the Sabarmati Ashram on the reverse.[9]

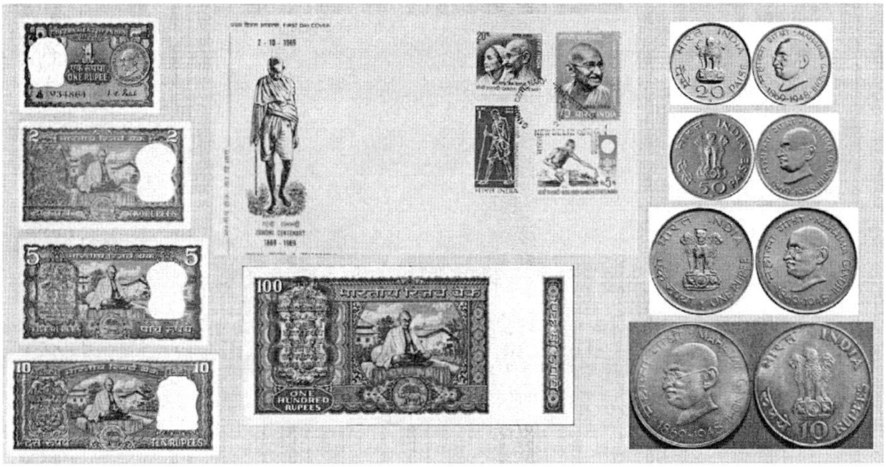

Fig.6 : Commemoration of Gandhi Centenary in India 1969-1970

The impact of International Gandhi movements was seen in his centenary year when 34 countries issued commemorative stamps in Mahatma Gandhi's honour. Leading the way was India with four stamps in the denomination of 20 paise with the image of Mahatma Gandhi and Kasturba Gandhi, 75 Paise with front profile of Mahatma Gandhi, 1 Rupee with a Dandi March silhouette of Mahatma Gandhi and 5 Rupees with image of Mahatma Gandhi at the Charkha and with Sun and Lotus symbolising Truth and Non-Violence.[10] Of the 34 countries listed by Mani Bhavan's catalogue, the countries can be divided into South Asian (Bhutan), West Asian (Iran, Sharjah & Dependencies, Southern Yemen, Syria, U.A.R.), African (Burkina Faaso, Cameroon, Congo, Gabon, Mali, Mauritania, Mauritius, Morocco, Niger, Senegal, Somalia, Tchad, Togo, Upper Volta), Western (Cyprus, Great Britain, Germany, Greece, Ireland, Malta) Soviet bloc (Hungary, USSR), Atlantic (Brazil, Chile, Dominica, Grenada, Guyana, Mexico, Suriname, Trinidad

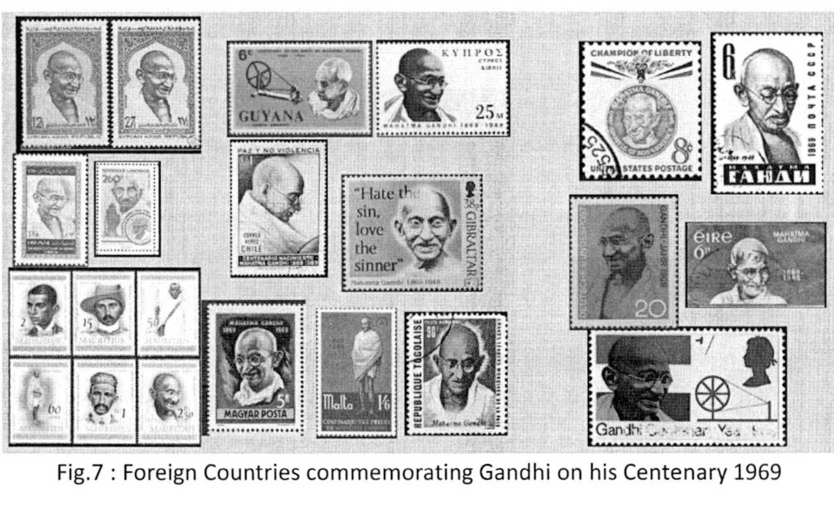

Fig.7 : Foreign Countries commemorating Gandhi on his Centenary 1969

& Tobago, Uruguay, USA).[11] The array of diverse countries which issued these commemorative stamps points to the spread of Gandhism in some form or the other in different parts of the civilised world through various media.

In India, post the Centenary, the rise of the JP Movement in the early nineteen seventies plunged the Indian Republic into its gravest crisis, the Emergency. The application of Gandhian methods by JP and his call for 'Total Revolution' was one more example of Gandhi's relevance to the Indian people as they opposed the forces behind the Emergency with all might till it was released in 1977. The JP Movement resulted in the formation of a national government by the Janata Party which was a coalition of various socialist and centre-of-right parties like the Jana Sangh. The Janata Government however fell too fast to leave an imprint of its Gandhian legacy on coins and stamps though its leader was a veteran Gandhian. The Janata Government's fall brought Mrs. Gandhi back to power in 1980 and following her tragic assassination the country faced more tumult in the 1980s and 1990s with rise of regional parties forming coalition governments at the centre. The corruption scandals in the nineteen eighties and nineties made Gandhian values look pale and of a different age.

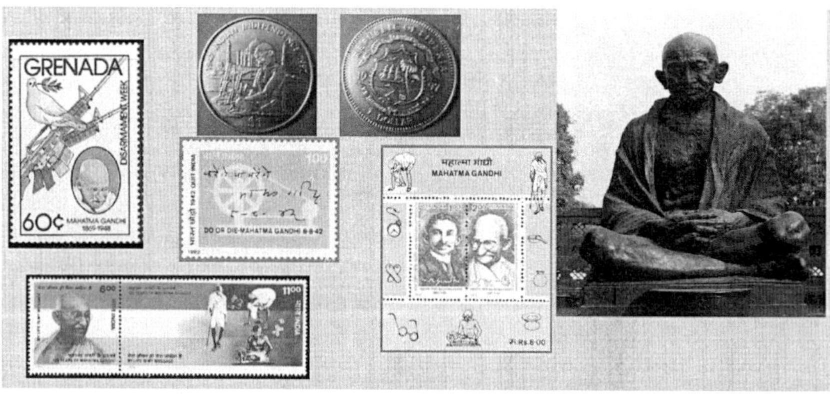

Fig.8 : Relics of Gandhian Symbols on Coins, Postage in the 1990s

Significantly, the Reserve Bank of India introduced a 500 Rupee Banknote in 1987 with the image of Mahatma Gandhi on the obverse with a reverse scene of him leading a group on the Dandi March. Around 1996, the Reserve Bank of India ironically introduced Mahatma Gandhi as the main icon on all Indian Banknotes in a series known as the Mahatma Gandhi series. Importantly in this series, even the watermark was changed from the Lion Pillar emblem to a portrait of Mahatma Gandhi.[12] Thus, the Mahatma has remained central to the Indian political ethos despite the decadence of the Indian political system. However, he also remained the main fount of its revival as many opposition groups when grappling issues turned to the Mahatma for inspiration as seen in the case of the newly formed Bharatiya Janata Party formed in 1984 and reduced to mere 2 seats in the Eighth Lok Sabha. The Party's Constitution speaks of its commitment "to Nationalism, National

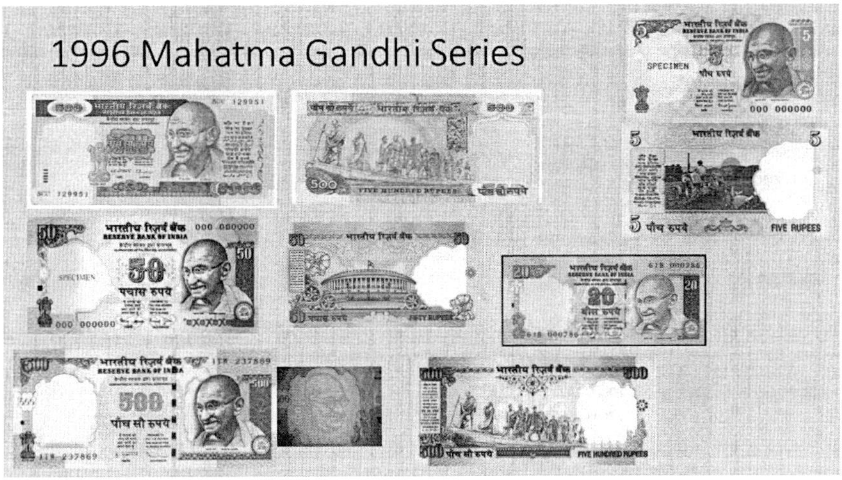

Fig.9 : 1996 Mahatma Gandhi Series of Indian Bank notes

Integration, democracy and 'Gandhian approach to socio-economic issues leading to the establishment of an egalitarian society free of exploitation, Positive Secularism and value based politics. The party stands committed to decentralisation of economic and political power."[13]

The rise of two diametrically opposite national political parties again in the twenty-first century and more significantly their recent embittered battles for political space may leave us despairing of Gandhian values and its relevance. Also, the rise of regional satraps in various states has led to the rise for replacement of Mahatma Gandhi with other national leaders by regional parties. However, the commitment of both leading national parties to Gandhian values and recognition of his importance to the Indian ethos has scuttled all moves to replace the Apostle of Non-Violence with other worthy leaders of the National movement.[14] Thus, the future of Mahatma Gandhi as a numismatic and philatelic icon looks only set to more heights in view of his impending 150th Birth Anniversary in 2019. The event which would be important for leaders across the political spectrum would

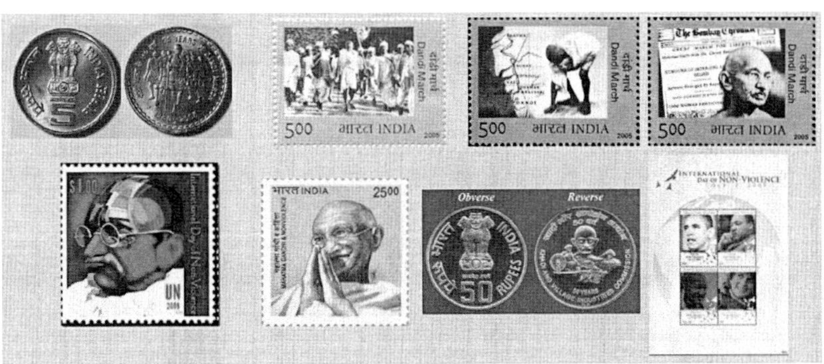

Fig.10 : Gandhi's Numismatic/Philattelic representation in the 2000s

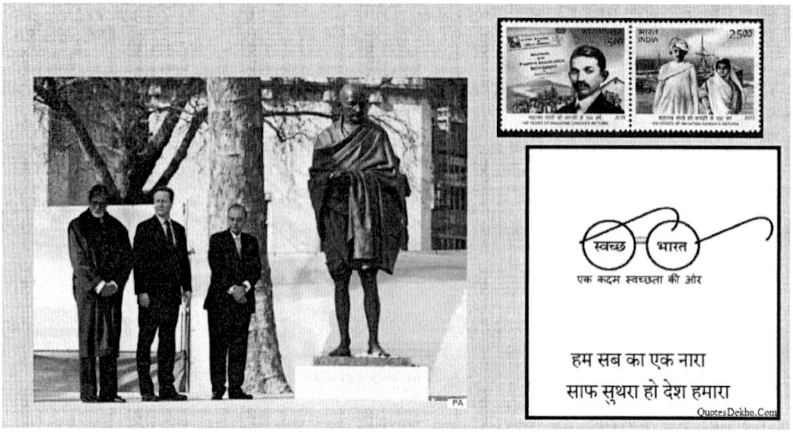

Fig.11 : Gandhi Statue at Parliament Square, London 2015

hopefully lead to a further increased focus on the Mahatma's legacy as an icon of global peace, environmental cleanliness and ethical and moderate behaviour in politics across the globe.

References

1. http://www.worldofcoins.eu/forum/index.php?topic=1658.0 Discussion on tokens of Gandhi with images of prominent types.
2. George S. Cuhaj & Rajender Maru eds *South Asian Coins & Paper Money ș Indian Edition including Undivided India Prior to 1947 AD,* Krause Publications, Iowa, USA, 2013, p. 475. KM# 4.1 (2 Annas 1950): "A similar shaped independence commemorative issued in 1947, bearing a map of India, circulated to some degree as a 2 anna coin." There is also a similar note under KM 3.1 (1 anna 1950), so there must also be slightly smaller independence medallions with a scalloped edge.
3. 'Gandhi Birth Centenary Postage Stamps – 1969' published by Usha Mehta for Mani Bhavan, Gandhi Sangrahalaya, Bombay, 1972, pp.10-11. The stamps were issued in the denominations of 1¾ annas, 3¾ annas, 12 annas and 10 Rupees with similar images and legends except the 10 Rupee stamp.
4. P. L. Gupta, *Coins,* The National Book Trust, New Delhi, first published 1969, Reprint 2013, pp.224-25
5. Bazil Shaikh & Sandhya Srinivasan, *The Paper and The Promise – A Brief History of Currency & Banknotes in India,* 3rd Edition, Department of Currency Management, Reserve Bank of India, Mumbai, 2009, p.43.
6. Sean Scalmer, *Gandhi in the West – The Mahatma and the Rise of Radical Protest,* Cambridge University Press, first South Asia Edition, New Delhi, 2011, pp.137-205. Scalmer traces the rise of small movements in both USA and U.K. In U.K. the Peace Pledge Union formed in 1951 for opposing nuclear armament of Great Britain dubbed as 'Operation Gandhi'; in USA the Afro-American Civil Rights movement which began the anti-segregation bus boycott under the leadership of Dr. Martin Luther King Jr. in December 1955.

7. David Hardiman, *Gandhi in his time and ours,* Permanent Black, New Delhi, 2003, pp.191-207.
8. Gupta, *Coins,* p.229.
9. Rezwan Razack, *A collection of facts about Indian Paper Money*http://indianbanknote.blogspot.in/2012/01/collection-of-facts-about-indian-paper.html.
10. *Gandhi Birth Centenary,* p.14.
11. Ibid. pp.18-58 with colour plates.
12. *The Paper &...,* pp.47-48.
13. *http://www.bjp.org/images/pdf_2012_h/constitution_eng_jan_10_2013.pdf* vide Article IV Commitments p.1.
14. http://www.dnaindia.com/money/report-don-t-replace-mahatma-gandhi-with-other-leaders-on-banknotes-rbi-panel-2041223.

12

India Post: Themes and Biases in Commemorative Stamps Issued From 1995 To 2015

Raamesh Gowri Raghavan

Introduction

The use of postage stamps as propaganda material goes back a long way̧tone might even say to 1840 in fact, when Sir Rowland Hill introduced the first ever postage stamps, the one-penny black and the two-penny blue[1]. Not only did he draw upon prevailing practices in currency design by putting the face of Queen Victoria on the stamps, but the very purpose of these pre-printed 'stamps' as bearers of witness to the sanction of the state on what is effectively a proof of postage paid was to give the state a square inch share of voice (and revenue) on private communications.[2]

The most significant unintended consequence of issuing postage stamps, as more countries started issuing them following standardisation and/or nationalisation of mail/ carrier systems, was the emergence of the stamp collector. The rise of this phenomenon, and the consequent rise of dealers, auction houses and cataloguers, led to the rise of the commemorative stamp̧tthe ultimate subversion of a state tool for propaganda. As countries used the opportunity provided by these few square inches to promote their cultural achievements and tourist potential to foreigners (before the rise of the audio-visual medium) as well as to promote state objectives (nationalism, civic pride) or the objectives of the parties controlling the state (communism, national socialism), it fuelled further mania among collectors[2]. Indeed, some of the most collectible stamps to date are those issued by the Soviet Union and Nazi Germany[3].

India has never shied from the game, issuing its first commemorative stamp on 15 August 1948, in memory of Mahatma Gandhi[4]. But being a democratic dispensation such

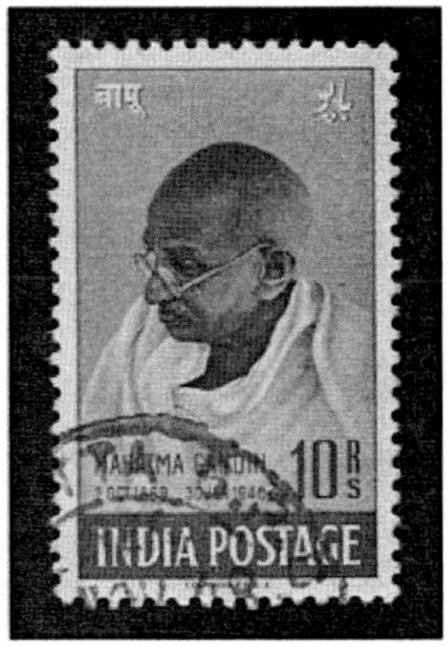

Fig.1: Independent India's first commemorative stamp issued in honour of Mahatma Gandhi on 15 August 1948. India's first definitive series would follow a year later, depicting various monuments.

as India, do they also serve as vehicles of subtle or overt propaganda for the people in power? For not only does democracy offer the opportunity for propaganda of state objectives (e.g. family planning, 5-year plans, secularism) but also offers the ruling political party to shape national opinion in favour of itself. Postal stamps, by commemorating issues and personalities, offer a strong mass vehicle for such propaganda.

As an avid collector of Indian postage stamps since 1995, I decided to draw upon my personal collection to answer this question, with particular reference to the period 1996-2016. This period has seen a wide fluctuation in the natures and ideologies of parties that governed India, in stark counter-position to nearly one-party rule by the Indian National Congress in the period 1947-95, interrupted only by small episodes of multi-party 'Janata' coalitions.

Table 1: Governing Coalitions and their Periods of Rule

Governing Coalition	Period	Prime Minister	#Stamps issued
United Front	1996—1998	H. D. Deve Gowda, I. K. Gujral	106
National Democratic Alliance (NDA-1)	1998—2004	A. B. Vajpayee	268
United Progressive Alliance (UPA)	2004—2014	Manmohan Singh	339
National Democratic Alliance (NDA-2)	2014—present	Narendra Modi	71

In this paper, I examine the distribution of themes reflected in 820 commemorative stamps issued by the Department of Posts, Government of India over a twenty-two-year period from 1994 to 2016. The analysis has been carried out by looking at both the complete distribution over 22 years and also by segregating them into periods corresponding to governing coalitions. *The period from 14/12/1994 to 4/5/1996 has been omitted for periodic analysis due to insufficient data (38 stamps were issued in this period), but has been included in the overall analysis.*

Materials and Methods

Out of my personal collection, 820 commemorative stamps issued by the Philatelic Bureau, Department of posts along with accompanying brochures and lists of stamps were examined, tabulated and categorised. These stamps were acquired through a subscription programme with the Philatelic Bureau, General Post Office, Mumbai that I have pursued for over 20 years. By regularly depositing money in a Postal Deposit Account (PDA), I am able to automatically purchase stamps and brochures every quarter and have them mailed to me by registered post. The record is not complete for the period, with a few gaps here and there due to reasons such as non-receipt of mail, non-renewal of subscription etc. While it was possible for me to supplement the record by looking up lists of stamps published across various philatelic websites, I took the decision to apply my analysis to stamps whose existence I could confirm by physical possession, and also because there is no way to verify the contents of websites except by looking at the stamps themselves. Nevertheless, a number of websites were used for references of spelling, attribution, correct date of issue etc, including that of the postal department itself[5] and other collector/amateur websites[6,7,8].

The dates of issue and names of the icon depicted on the stamps were then tabulated in a worksheet using Microsoft Excel software (file available with the author on demand). 'Icons' here are defined as any person, institution, event, monument or living being that is considered noteworthy or important enough to be commemorated by issuing a stamp.

Subsequently, the stamps were categorised on the following bases:

- *First*, I determined whether the stamp represented any one of the following five categories:
  - *Human beings:* notable people from various walks of life
  - *The Indian State:* civil and military establishments, services, agencies
  - *Institutions:* libraries, schools, colleges & universities; hospitals and vaidyasalas; trusts and foundations; associations and charities
  - *Abstract themes:* commemorative days and events
  - *Other:* wildlife, national parks, cultural practices and anything that did not fit the above 4 categories
- *Second*, the icons were classified as being Regional, National or International icons. If the icon was regional, the state of the icon was recorded.
- *Third*, the nature of icons from various walks of life were determined, by making references to the brochures as well as looking up state[5] and amateur websites[6,7,8]:

- *Military:* forces, regiments, ships, missiles, war commemorations
- *Civil State:* courts, legislatures, agencies & their Jubilees, both state & central
- *Political:* persons & events
- *Social, Cultural and Traditional:* festivals, objects, traditional crafts, dances etc.
- *Religious:* theologians, priests & gurus, institutions & their anniversaries
- *Literary:* writers, poets & playwrights
- *Financial:* banks & NBFCs, MFs & Insurance companies, regulators, and financiers
- *Nature/Environment:* national parks, activists, wildlife, fossils
- *Music/Films:* musicians, personalities associated with film-making
- *Press:* newspapers & media houses, journalists
- Art: painters, sculptors; paintings & sculptures
- *Sport:* sportspersons; sporting events
- *Industrial:* industrialists, companies, infrastructure
- *Historical/Mythical:* persons and events
- *Science/Technology/Medicine:* persons, organisations, research institutes, conferences
- *Education:* libraries, schools, colleges and universities; teachers, professors and founders of educational institutions
- *Law:* lawyers

Furthermore, the whole data was also reanalysed by taking only sections of it that corresponded to the tenures of ruling coalitions (Table 1). The tripartite analysis mentioned above was carried out.

Finally, the data was also examined for the following themes:

- Forces-wise distribution of military icons
- Faith-wise distribution of religious icons
- Statewide distribution and skew of regional icons

Results

Analysis 1: Icons by Category and Walks of Life (Figs 2 & 3)

Although humans are the most popular category, accounting for over 50% of the stamps in the period across regimes, a marked decline is seen in their proportions over the years, as a greater proportion of stamps have been issued favouring government establishments and other institutions. This decline is starkly observed in the current regime (Fig. 2e). That said, all comment on trends seen during the current regime must be subject to future re-examination, as

(a) the number of stamps issued is small (71) and

(b) trends may reverse or otherwise change as the regime prolongs.

Among the many walks of human life, the press, the arts, sports and the legal & financial professions are highly under-represented; while literary figures (both Gyanpith award winners from several Indian languages and also popular and classic writers) and film folk (inclusive of various regional industries and not just the Hindi film industry) are however, well-represented. A spike is particularly seen in the tenure of the UPA, when a flurry of stamps was issued to commemorate 100 years of Indian cinema.

Religious and historical/mythical icons occur in high frequency; they occupy the highest percentages in the NDA-1 and NDA-2 periods. Further analysis of religion is presented later on in this paper.

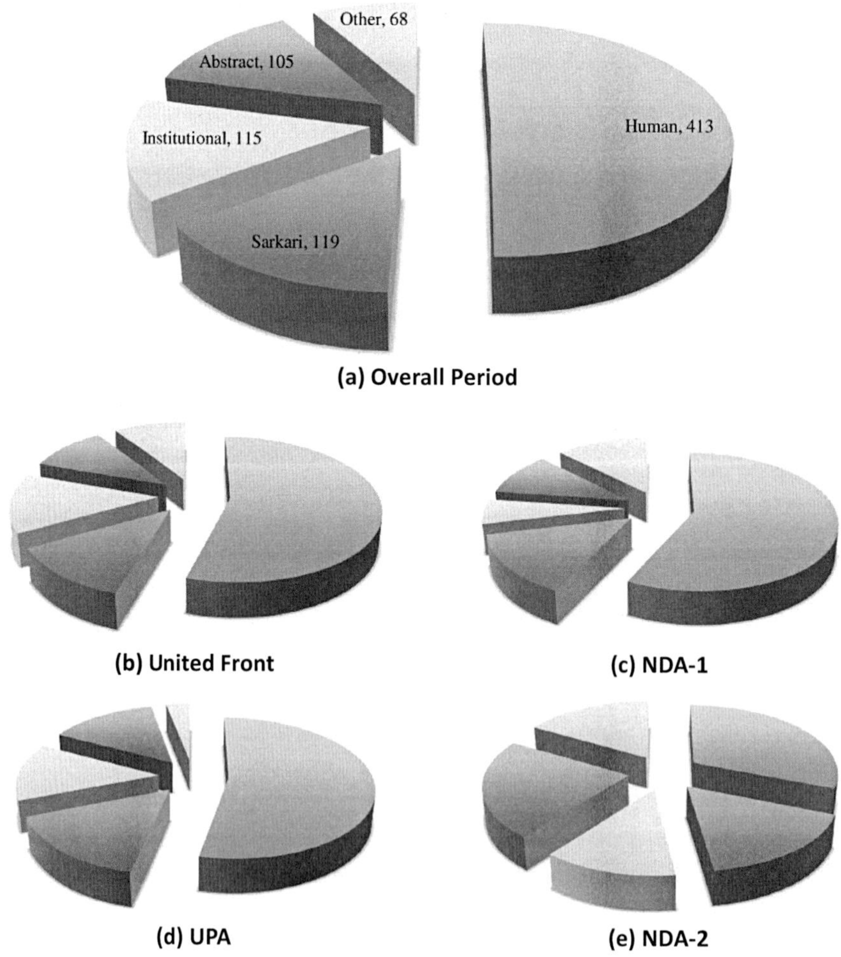

Fig.2: Icons by Category

Fully 26% of stamps are dedicated to commemorating establishments of the state and their anniversaries/jubilees, and also political icons, mostly from the ruling parties. *Read with the phenomenon of state institutions getting wider coverage at the cost of human icons, it seems evident that the state is increasingly comfortable celebrating itself, and is paying less attention to the people it rules.*

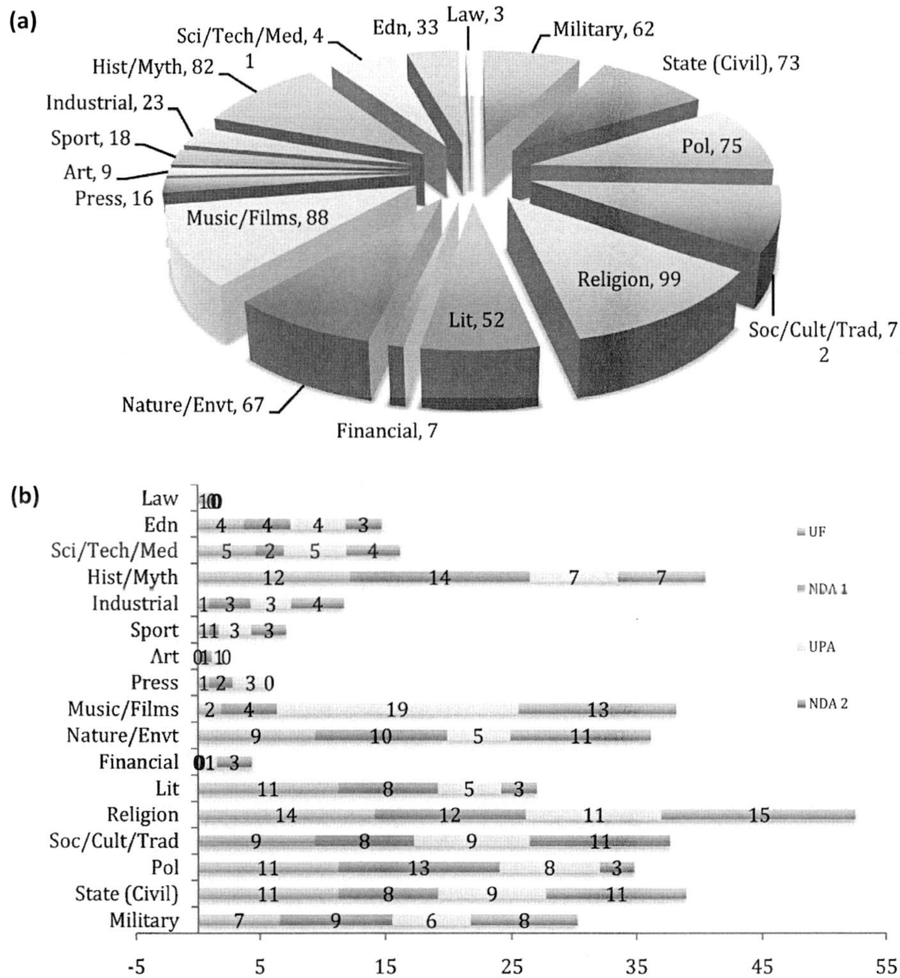

Fig.3 : Icons by Walks of Life
(a) Overall Period, (b) United Front, (c) NDA-1, (d) UPA, (e) NDA-2

Analysis 2: Military & Religious Icons

The military prowess of a country has been a great topic of its postal issueța way to reassure its citizenry and to frighten its enemies (among other methods). For example, as war with Nazi Germany became evident in 1938-39, the Soviet Union's stamps took on an increasingly militaristic tone [2]. Having fought three major wars and several smaller engagements, do the Indian Armed Forces get a prominent share?

Against this expectation, the share of military icons has nevertheless been low throughout, reaching a maximum of 9% under NDA-1 (early in whose tenure the Kargil War was fought). There appears to be a trend towards more equal representation of the forces, from a previously marked bias towards the army (Fig. 4). It is to be noted, however, that the Indian Army represents 86% of all defence personnel (1.18 million), so increasing

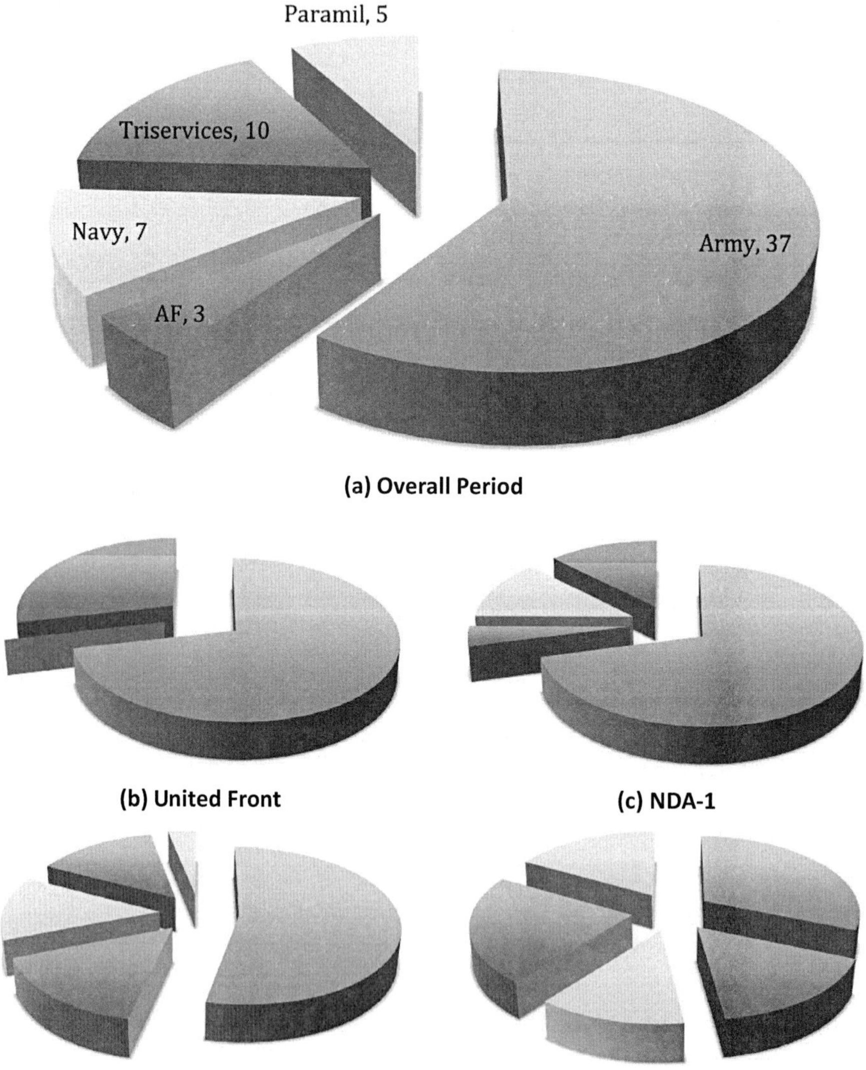

(a) Overall Period

(b) United Front **(c) NDA-1**

(d) UPA **(e) NDA-2**

Fig.4 : Military Icons

equality among the forces in terms of proportions of stamps issued, might actually appear unfair to the army. That said, the paramilitary forces, that number 1.08 million, have had scant representation throughout the period.

On the other hand, religious persons and institutions have had a good representation, taking up 12% of the total issue in the period of study. Between the prominent religious groups in India (Hindus, Muslims, Christians, Jains, Sikhs and Buddhists), the share of Hindu religious figures and institutions appearing on stamps tends to rise under the NDA-1 (69%) and NDA-2 (64%) governments (Fig. 5). However it is to be noted that Hindus constitute 80% of the Indian population (as per the 2001 census (9)). Muslims, who form the largest religious minority (14%) remain underrepresented under all regimes; with 3

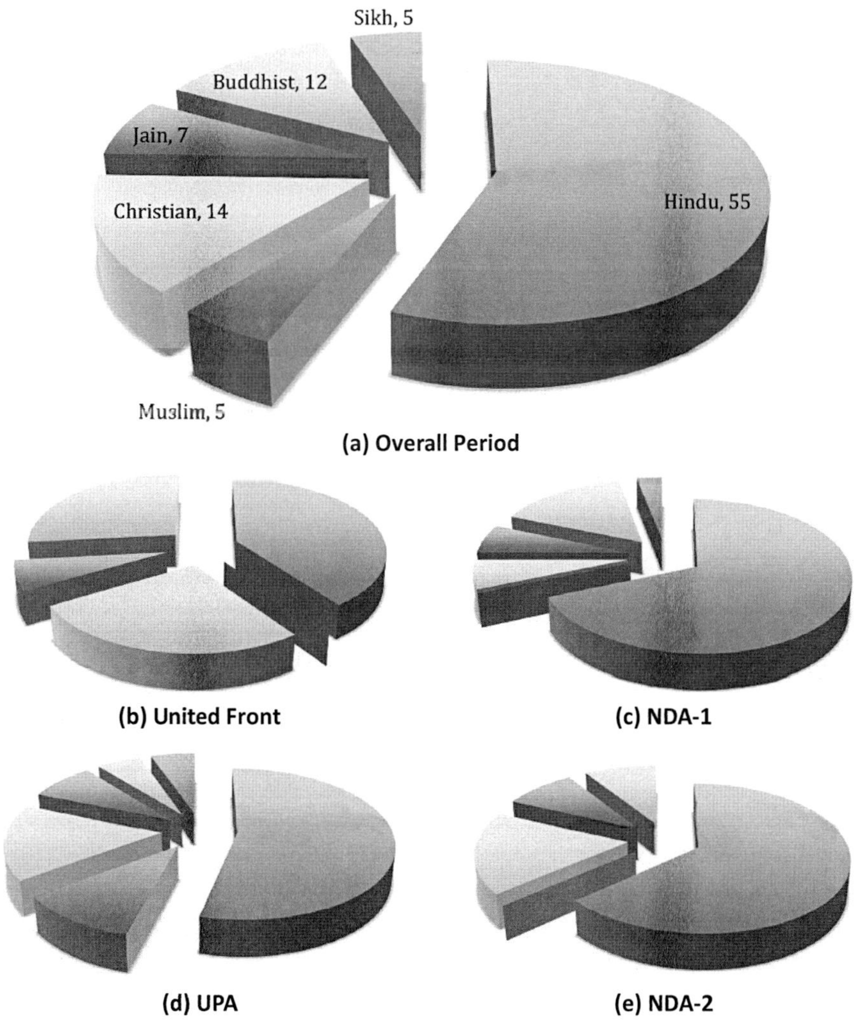

Fig.5 : Religious Icons

regimes completely ignoring them. The Jains (0.37% as per the 2001 census) punch well above their weight with upto 7% representation. Buddhism (0.7%) too is overrepresented in the stamps, peaking at 27% under the United Front Government.

Analysis 3: Internationalism and Regionalism

Regional icons occupy the lion's share of the stamps, though there has been a marked decline under NDA-2, as more stamps are issued featuring pan-Indian icons. Internationalism has been poorly represented in Indian stamps, with the share of foreign icons rarely exceeding 12% (Fig. 6). This stands in stark contrast to the internationalism of Independent India's initial decades, with India's championship of such entities as the Non-Aligned Movement (NAM) and G-77[10], and later India's membership of the World Trade Organisation, G-20 and pursuit of a permanent seat at the United Nations Security Council.

Figure 6: Regional, National and International Icons

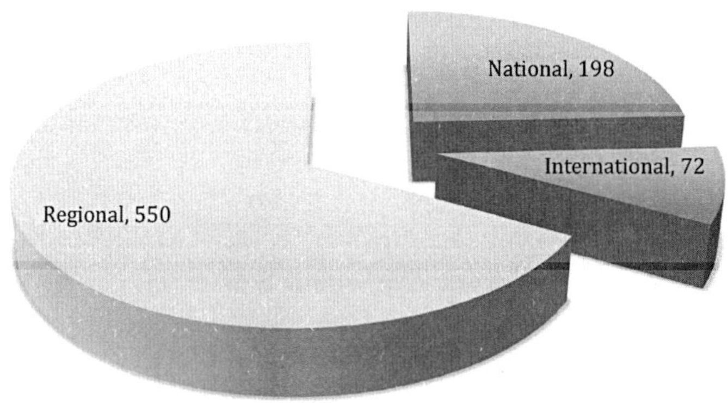

With so large a representation of regional icons, a detailed break-down was warranted. A state-by-state categorisation yielded a few surprises. Maharashtra (78), Tamil Nadu (70), Uttar Pradesh (58) and Punjab (42) take up a large proportion of the stamps (Fig. 7). Did this indicate a regional bias, or were the states getting their fair share of representation on India's 'little ambassadors'?

A reasonable metric was required to compare the stamps on regional themes. The number of Lok Sabha MPs from each state was found suitable for several reasons as enumerated below:

1. They are representative, in a political sense, of a state's population and political 'heft'
2. Their proportions between the states have not changed for the duration of the study.
3. At 543, the number of elected Lok Sabha MPs is comparable to the 550 stamps examined.

Table 2: States with the most positive and negative skews

State	% MPs	%Stamps	Skew
Maharashtra	8.84	14.18	+5.34
Tamil Nadu	7.18	12.73	+5.54
Punjab	2.39	7.64	+5.25
Uttar Pradesh	14.73	10.55	-4.19
Madhya Pradesh	5.34	2.91	-2.43
Telangana	3.13	0.73	-2.40

4. MPs can (and do) exert pressure to issue particular stamps.

For most states, I notice that the skews fluctuate. For example, Gujarat gets a positive skew (+3.78) under NDA-1, but a strong negative skew (-4.79) under NDA-2 (This might change as NDA-2 hasn't finished issuing stamps yet, and the issue of commemorative stamps follows a predetermined calendar). However, Maharashtra and Punjab have seen a positive skew throughout the period. We might attribute Maharashtra's outsized presence to the fact that many icons are related to Mumbai. *A separate analysis is warranted in the future.* It must also be noted that the Union Territories of the Andaman and Nicobar Islands, Lakshadweep, Daman and Diu and Dadra and Nagar Haveli remain unrepresented throughout the twenty-year period of study.

Tamil Nadu marks a pronounced skew (+5.54 for the entire period), exploding under the UPA government (+9.41). I decided to investigate this phenomenon further. The Ministry of Communications, which controls the Department of Posts, remained under the control of Shri Dayanidhi Maran and then Shri A. Raja, both ministers from the Dravida Munnetra Kazhagam (DMK), a regional party from Tamil Nadu and a member of the United Progressive Alliance[12]. In this six-year period within the ten-year rule of the UPA, the bias is even more pronounced, at 20.48. No other state comes close to this number, even though other states did see positive biases in this period (Table 3). A number of stamps depicting obscure historic figures and small-time politicians seem to be the hallmark of this period. I have taken the liberty to call this the DMK Effect or the Maran-Raja Effect.

I also investigated whether the DMK's other ideological leanings (atheism, rationalism) or its deep connection with films were reflected in the issue of stamps, but there is no major deviation from the overall proportions. Hence hyper-regionalism remains the singular bias. Other regional parties have also controlled the Ministry of Communications. Shri Ram Vilas Paswan of the Janata Dal (United) controlled the Ministry from 13/10/1999 to 1/9/2001 as part of the NDA-1 government, and earlier Shri Beni

Prasad Verma of the Samajwadi Party was Communications Minister in the United Front coalition government. *A study of biases under their control is also planned for the future.*

Table 2: Skew of all States through the study period

	STATE	OVERALL	UF	NDA1	UPA	DMK Control	NDA2
1	Andhra Pradesh	-0.24	-1.75	-1.50	1.78	2.84	-4.60
2	Arunachal Pradesh	0.00	1.06	-0.37	0.06	0.70	-0.37
3	Assam	-0.76	-1.15	0.53	-1.30	0.61	-2.58
4	Bihar	-2.46	-3.08	1.96	-5.66	-6.30	-1.48
5	Chandigarh	0.00	-0.18	-0.18	0.24	0.88	-0.18
6	Chhattisgarh	-1.66	-2.03	-1.51	-1.60	-0.96	-2.03
7	Delhi	0.89	0.14	0.78	0.84	0.84	1.65
8	Goa	0.36	2.49	0.15	0.06	-0.37	-0.37
9	Gujarat	-0.61	3.78	0.39	-2.66	-2.66	-4.79
10	Haryana	-1.11	-1.84	-0.29	-1.42	-0.78	-1.84
11	Himachal Pradesh	1.08	0.69	1.85	0.11	-0.74	2.20
12	Jharkhand	-1.67	-2.58	-0.51	-2.15	-1.51	-2.58
13	Jammu & Kashmir	0.17	0.32	0.45	0.17	-0.04	-1.10
14	Karnataka	-0.43	3.41	-2.05	-1.75	-0.90	12.49
15	Kerala	0.68	2.03	1.50	0.57	0.57	-3.68
16	Maharashtra	5.34	2.59	5.15	5.20	6.05	2.92
17	Manipur	0.36	-0.37	1.19	0.91	-0.37	2.57
18	Meghalaya	-0.19	-0.37	0.15	-0.37	-0.37	-0.37
19	Mizoram	0.00	-0.18	0.33	-0.18	-0.18	-0.18
20	Madhya Pradesh	-2.43	-1.05	-2.75	-3.21	-2.15	-2.40
21	Nagaland	0.36	1.24	0.33	0.24	-0.18	-0.18
22	Odisha	-2.23	-2.44	-1.28	-3.44	-2.80	-0.93
23	Pondicherry	0.00	-0.18	-0.18	0.24	-0.18	-0.18
24	Punjab	5.24	4.75	5.38	6.54	-2.39	-2.39
25	Rajasthan	0.12	-1.75	-3.05	3.48	0.72	-1.66
26	Sikkim	0.00	-0.18	-0.18	0.24	-0.18	-0.18

27	Sindhi	0.55	0.00	0.00	1.28	2.13	0.00
28	Telangana	-2.40	-3.13	-2.09	-2.71	-3.13	-0.19
29	Tamil Nadu	5.54	1.39	1.11	9.41	20.48	13.41
30	Tripura	0.36	-0.37	1.19	0.06	0.70	-0.37
31	Uttar Pradesh	-4.19	0.98	-7.48	-4.52	-8.35	2.91
32	Uttarakhand	0.72	0.51	1.15	0.36	2.27	2.02
33	West Bengal	-0.64	-2.02	0.56	-0.08	-3.48	-4.79
34	A&N Islands	-0.18	-0.18	-0.18	-0.18	-0.18	-0.18
35	Dadra & Nagar Haveli	-0.18	-0.18	-0.18	-0.18	-0.18	-0.18
36	Daman & Diu	-0.18	-0.18	-0.18	-0.18	-0.18	-0.18
37	Lakshadweep	-0.18	-0.18	-0.18	-0.18	-0.18	-0.18

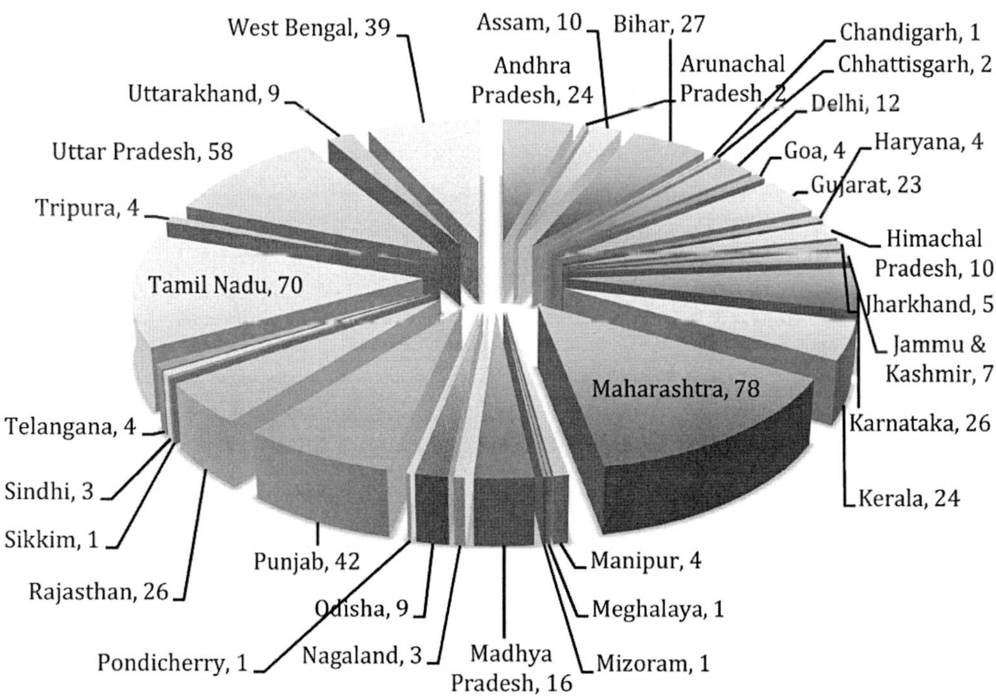

Fig.7 : Distribution Across States (1994-2016; % of Stamps Issued)

References

1. Stanley Gibbons, 2016. *GB Specialised Stamp Catalogue Queen Victoria, 16th Edition.* Stanley Gibbons, London.

2. Stoetzer, Carlos; 1953. *Postage Stamps as Propaganda*. Public Affairs Press, Washington, DC.
3. Cherrystone Philatelic Auctioneers, 2009. More lots within SOVIET UNION 1960-64 Issues. Accessed online: https://www.cherrystoneauctions.com/_auction/results.asp?auction=200909&searchtext=&country= SOVIET+UNION+1960-64+Issues.
4. Stanley Gibbons, 2013. *India & States Stamp Catalogue 4th Edition*. Stanley Gibbons, London.
5. Department of Posts, Ministry of Communications, Government of India. Accessed online: http://postagestamps.gov.in
6. Stamps of India: The Hub Site for Philately and Postal History of India. Accessed online: https://stampsofindia.com
7. India Picks: The pick of Indian topics. Accessed online: http://www.indiapicks.com
8. iStampGallery.Com: Stamp Collection Redefined. Accessed online: http://www.istampgallery.com
9. Registrar General & Census Commissioner, India, 2002. *14th Census of India*. Accessed online: http://www.censusindia.gov.in/Census_Data_2001/India_at_glance/religion.aspx
10. Kalyanaraman, S; November 19, 2010. *The Indian Advocacy of Internationalism in the Nehru Years*. IDSA Fellows' Seminar, New Delhi. Accessed online: http://www.idsa.in/event/TheIndianAdvocacyofInternationalis mintheNehruYears.
11. Raja Mohan, C; October 25, 2012. *Prospects for Indian Internationalism*. The Brookings Institution, Washington DC. Accessed online: (https://www.brookings.edu/events/prospects-for-indian-internationalism)
12. Department of Telecommunications, Ministry of Communications, Government of India. *List of Ministers of Communications*. Accessed online: http://www.dot.gov.in/minister/former-ministers.

Section - IV

Epigraphy

President's Address

Marathi Epigraphic Records:
A Rich Source of Regional History

Dr. Anuradha K. Ranade

An inscription means an old engraved record. It is also known as epigraph and therefore, the study of inscriptions is known as epigraphy. In other words **"Epigraphy is the study of inscriptions and inscriptions literallymeans any writing engraved on any hard substance".**

The objects which were used for engraving inscriptions in India were of various types such as lithic, metallic, earthen or wooden objects, pottery, bricks, shells, ivory plaques and other objects. The term inscription also includes in it - the writing in relief such as the legends on coins and seals which are usually produced out of moulds or dyes. Even the records painted on the walls or written in ink or on wooden tablets are regarded as inscriptions, although here the letter are not actually engraved, but painted.

Dr. B. N. Mukherjee has pointed out that writings on manuscripts of texts or document made of birch-bark, palm leaf paper etc. is generally excluded from the study of inscriptions or epigraphs. He opines that since these are also records marked with writings and hence should be included under the broad heading of ***Inscription***.[1]

Inscriptions are of immense value for the reconstruction of ancient Indian history for they provide authentic evidence based on actual finds of contemporary periods. They provide the information regarding contemporary political, social, economic, religious and cultural conditions and therefore, they are of utmostimportance for the study of ancient Indian history and culture. They also facilitate linguistic and paleographical research.

I take liberty of this platform to review in brief the significance of the Marathi inscriptions in the State of Maharashtra and other parts of the country.

Marathi is the spoken language of Maharashtra. It belongs to the family of languages derived from Sanskrit (Indo Aryan Group of Languages). Sanskrit ceased to be the spoken language by about 500 B.C. when Prakrit became the language of the people. One of the Prakrit dialects was 'Maharashtri Prakrit' which was in use since the time of the Satavahanas. By about 4th and 5th century A.D., Maharashtri Prakrit has changed to such an extent came to be known as 'Maharashtri Apabhransha' At the beginning of the 8th century A.D.. Marathi as a distinct language was already established. This form of Marathi till the mid of the fourteenth century is designated as Old Marathi.[2] The Scholars like S.G. Tulpule and Anne Feldhouse observes that the Marathi language of its early phase is to a great extent homogeneous in form and it is clearly distinguishable from ***Prakrit*** and ***Apabhramsha*** languages that preceded it as well as subsequent ***Middle Marathi*** (c.1350-1800)[3].

Since 11th century C.E., Marathi language seems to be much developed that it was used for writing inscriptions and thus we get Marathi epigraphic data for understanding historical facts. The Marathi epigraphical records are available from the 11th Century C.E. making its first appearance in an inscription from Akshi[4], dated 1012 C.E. Another inscription of Chamundraja, dated 1116 C.E. at Shravanbelgola[5], is an epigraph of two lines. Chamundraja was the prime minister of Rasmalla of Ganga dynasty, which is in Marathi, outside the region of Maharashtra[2.] The latest inscription in this early phase of Marathi language belongs to the Hindu dynasty is from Bandode in Goa dated 1413 C.E.

There are two distinct categories of stone inscriptions viz. those which are engraved on stone slab and the others which are carved out in relief[6]. All the Pre-Islamic stone inscriptions belong to the first type and majority of the later inscriptions belong to second variety.

These early Marathi Inscriptions belongs roughly to the old Marathi i.e., from 1000 to 1400 C.E. and figure in more than a hundred inscriptions in Maharashtra and adjoining regions. They are complete Marathi or semi Marathi i.e. some part in Sanskrit while some part in Marathi. They are the stone inscriptions and copper plates belonging to different dynasties namely, the Gangas and the Hoysalas of Mysore, the Shilaharas of North Konkan, the later Chalukyas of Kalyani, the Yadavas of Seunadesa and Devagiri, the Sangama dynasty of Vijaynagar Kingdom.

It has been observed that Marathi language underwent a great change during the 14th and 15th centuries, which is clearly visible from the inscriptions, and after 14th century, the Marathi inscriptions became rare and number of the Persian, Urdu and Arabic inscriptions increased under the Muslim rulers, such as the Bahamani and its succession states and the Farooqi rulers in this region. During this period, we get many bilingual inscriptions such as Persian and Marathi, Persian and local dialects, Persian and Sanskrit etc.

More than one hundred Marathi inscriptions of Early Marathi period are found from different regions of Maharashtra such as Konkan or coastal areas, western Maharashtra, Marathwada, Khandesh and Vidarbha areas. The find spots of these inscriptions help us in identifying the Marathi speaking area of this time. However, few Marathi inscriptions are from Shravanbelgola, Ranebennur, Bijapur and Bidar in present Karnataka State and also from some places in Goa. A map showing these places will be helpful in understanding the fact of cultural and lingual identity of Maharashtra during this period.

Marathi inscriptions of early phase mainly refer to the dynasties such as the Shilaharas, and the Yadavas and occasionally belong to the Gangas, Hoysalas of Mysore and the Vijayanagar Sangam dynasties. There are few Marathi inscriptions refer to the Muslim rulers such as Kutubuddin Khilji, Malik Bahadur and Bahamani Sultan Firozshah, which are important in understanding political influences and changes in Maharashtra during the period under study. They form the good nucleus for a historical study and are very useful for understanding socio-economic conditions of the period under study.

The Marathi inscriptions of the early phase are studied thoroughly and published in a Corpus by Shri S.G.Tulpule of Pune University in 1963 under the title of ***'Prachin Marathi Koriv Lekh'*** in the year 1963. About 76 dated and undated inscriptions of this period were published. After publication of this corpus, some other Marathi inscriptions were traced and are edited and published by various scholars viz. Anand Kumbhar, G.C.Shelke, Brahmananda Deshpande, G.H.Khare and S.V.Chitale, H.S.Thosar and Shantilal Puravar etc. in various Research Journals and Books like 'Shodhmudra', 'Marathwada Samshodhan Mandal Annual', 'Pratishthan' etc. The other scholars, who have contributed in the study of Marathi inscriptions are Shri M.G.Dixit, Shri V.B.Kolte, Shri V.V.Mirashi etc. have written their scholarly articles in various Research Journals like 'Bharat Itihas Samshodhan Mandal', 'Sanshodhan Muktavali' series, books like "Maharashtratil Kahi Tamrapat va Koriv Lekh" etc.

Geographical distribution of these Marathi inscription is all over Maharashtra i.e. in different regions of this Province, namely Konkan or the Coastline, Western Maharashtra, Marathwada, Kanhadesha (i.e. Khandesh) Vidarbha and Nagpur. The location of a few inscriptions e.g. Shravanbelgola, Ranebennur and Bijapur are beyond the present boundaries of Maharashtra. Though the numerous inscriptions are found in Marathi language, none of them are literary compositions. As a matter of fact, Marathi assumes literary form especially after the days of Seunas. The script used for majority of the Marathi inscriptions is Devanagari. However, rarely Kannada[7] (Khategram) and Modi (Wai copper plates, Barshi well Inscription, some of Jejuri inscriptions etc.)[8] scripts were used for Marathi inscriptions.

Marathi inscriptions of middle phase of Marathi Language (C.E.1350-1800) are available from the 16th Century till early decades of 19th century. Corpus of 152 inscriptions has been published by M. G. Dixit which are informative to some extent but need to be

Site of Old Marathi Inscriptions and Marathi Literary Activity (1100-1600 AD)

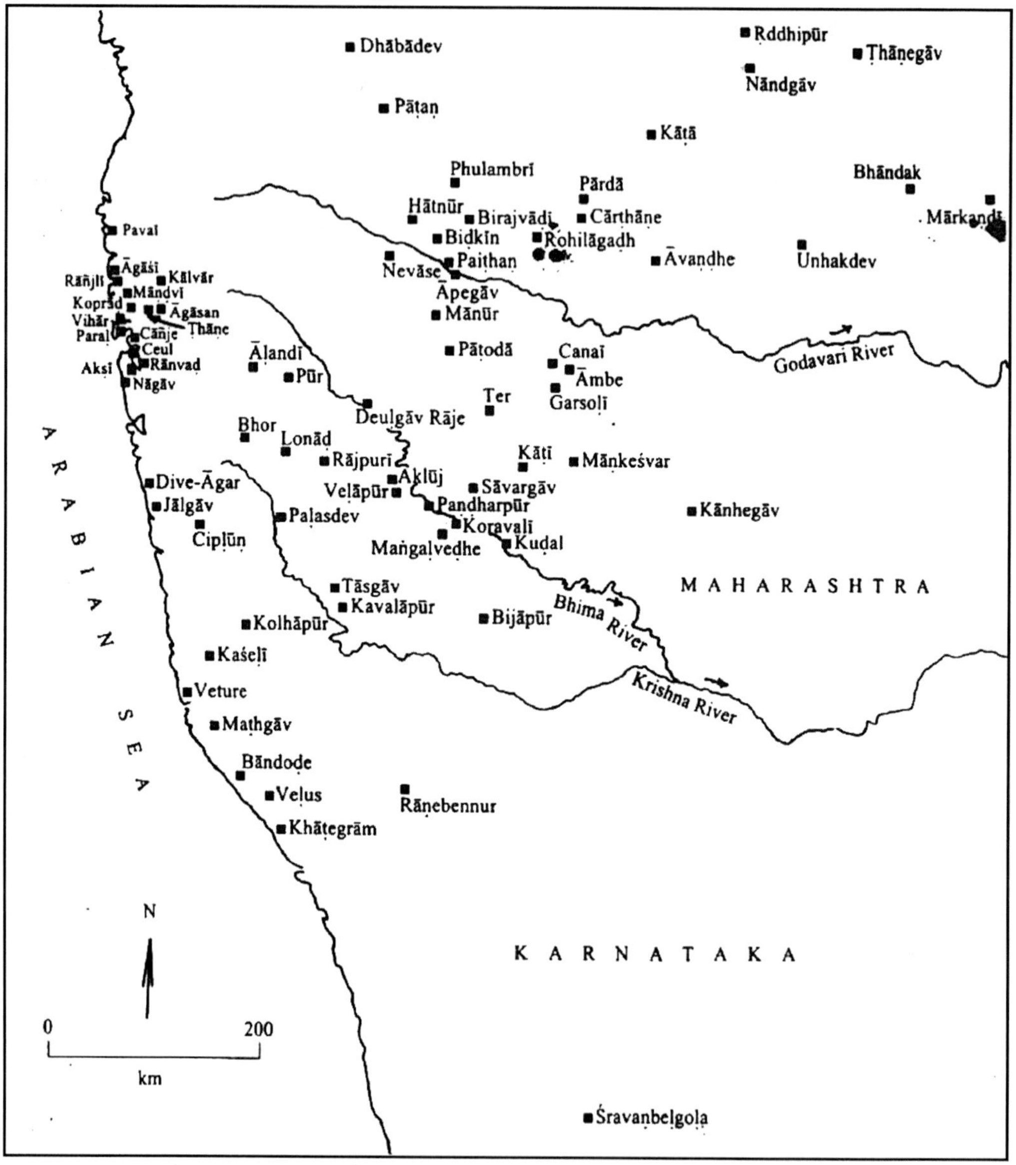

Sites of Old Marathi Inscriptions and Literary Activity

Source: A Dictionary of Old Marathi S.G. Tulpule and Anne Feldhouse

studied and explained thoroughly form historical perspective as the fresh data or the corroborative evidences to the established facts. Quite a considerable number epigraphs nave also been discovered outside present state of Maharashtra, both in North and South, where the Maratha dynasties rose to prominence.

Thus more than two hundred and fifty Marathi inscriptions of early and later phases engraved on stone and copper plates have so far been found and more than three fourth of these records are engraved on the stone and remaining are the copper Plates. Yet every year new discoveries and decipherment of epigraphs add to our knowledge. It must be noted that these inscriptions exhibit a mixture of Sanskrit and Marathi in the early phase which shows the recognition that Marathi had received in the official epigraphic records. They can be divided into three groups viz. those of the Yadavas and the Shilahara period (11th-14th century), The Period of the Bahamanis and Bahamani successor States (15th and 16th centuries) and the Maratha Period (17th and 18th Centuries).

These Marathi inscriptions are useful for understanding the contemporary socio-cultural, religious and economic life. Some data of the administrative system can be drawn from these inscriptions. They are useful for tracing the origin and development of the Marathi language. The earliest inscriptions are modeled upon preceding Sanskrit epigraphs.

The Marathi inscriptions are useful for tracing the origin and development of the Marathi language. They are important for reconstruction of political, administrative social and cultural history of this region.

An interesting fact may be noticed here. The early Marathi inscriptions refer to a number of coins particularly the amount donated to the individuals and the institutions. The gold coin that was in circulation was ***Gadyana*** or ***Gadyanaka***. Inscriptions from Pandharpur[9], Ambe[10] mention the word ***Gadyanaka*** while some other inscriptions record its abbreviated form as ***Ga***[11] ***coinage Suvarna Gadyanaka*** is also recorded in its abbreviated form as ***Su. Ga***[12] Silver Coins recorded in Marathi inscriptions are ***Tanka***[13]***(also mentioned as Tank, Tanka), Dramma***[14] **and Rukya.**[15] S.G. Tulpule, opines that though there are references of Tanka as a gold coin, the references to **Tanka** in Marathi seems to be the silver coin. **Dramma**[16]: A stone inscription from Nagaon dated 1367-68 gives some interesting information about purchase of land. Here, two 'Wadis' i.e. the orchard lands were purchased by one 'Sihipro' at the rate of 160 Drammas and 40 Drammas respectively.[17] Ruka too *appears to be a silver coin.*

It seems that there were copper coins and some other minor currency in circulation, The **Pana** and **Visova** were copper coins and records of Shilaharas mention both the coins. A Yadava inscription from Patan states that Patan town donated 20th part of Dama that it recovered against every Asu from purchasers.[18] **Kavada**[19] meaning a cowrie shell was used as a currency. Besides, the betel nuts also was used as a minor currency[20].

Acknowledgement

I feel extremely grateful to the office bearers of the Centre for History, Archaeology, Epigraphy and Numismatics (CHAEN) and Sathaye College for having conferred on me the honour of presiding over the section on Epigraphy being held at Parle Tilak Vidyalaya's Sathye College. I am highly thankful to the organizers who have given me this opportunity to preside over/ chair the session on Epigraphy.

I would like to express my appreciation to the Office bearers of CHAEN for their efforts in promoting research activities as well as providing a forum to the scholars from various related disciplines. I am sure, that many more annual conferences of the CHAEN in the coming years will provide a greater scope for the study of History, Archaeology, Epigraphy and Numismatics.

Friends, scholars and delegates, I once again express my gratitude to you for giving me this opportunity for addressing this august gathering. I am obliged to you for listening patiently and I thank the organizers and office bearers for giving me this opportunity. Thank you once again.

References

1. Mukherjee, B. N. Some Aspects of Hieratic, Hybrid and Mixed Scripts of Early India, XX Annual Congress of the Epigraphical Society of India, Bangalore, 1994.
2. *A Dictionary of Old Marathi*, S.G. Tulpule and Anne Feldhouse, Popular Prakashan, Mumbai, 1999, ISBN-81-7154-836-9.
3. *Ibid.*
4. *Prachin Marathi Koriv Lekha*, edited.by S.G. Tulpule, Pune University Publication, 1963, henceforth referred to as *PMKL.*
5. *PMKL* Insc. No. 01
6. Dhavalikar M. K., Marathi Epigraphy in *History of Medieval Deccan*, (1295-1724), Vol. II, Ed. Pro. H.K. Sherwani and Dr. P. M. Joshi, Govt of Andhra Pradesh, 1974.
7. *PMKL* Insc. No. 61.
8. *PMKL*, Introduction, p.52.
9. *PMKL*, Insc. No. 34.
10. *PMKL*, Insc. No 67.
11. *PMKL*, Insc. No. 29, 34, 41, 58 etc.
12. *PMKL*, Insc. No. 2.
13. *PMKL* Insc. No.56.
14. *PMKL*, Insc. No 58, 59.
15. *PMKL*, Insc. No. 34.
16. *PMKL*, Insc. No 3.
17. *PMKL*, Insc. No. 55.
18. *PMKL* Insc. No. 13, 21.
19. *PMKL*. Insc. No. 5, 23.
20. *PMKL* Insc. No. 23.

13

A Medieval Memorial Stone at Wagholi, District Pune: A Study

Dr. Manjiri Bhalerao

Wagholi, ($18^0 31'$ N, $73^0 51'$E), Dist. Pune, is a small town 17 KMs to the North East on the Pune-Ahmednagar high way. Today the town is famous for the Wagheshwar temple and some amusement park in the vicinity. This town is also famous for being the hometown of Sardar Pilajirao Jadhav. Sardar Pilajirao Jadhav was a very important personality during the rule of Chhatrapati Shahu in the early 18th century A.D. As he was the native of Wagholi, he constructed a Shiva temple at Wagholi. Later on after his death in 1751, his memorial temple was constructed in the campus of this temple[1]. This complex is located on near a lake. Over the period of time this became the cremation ground for the people living in Wagholi.

Some people could afford to have their memorial temples but the other people could not have one for them. Hence memorial stones were erected in their memory after their demise. Such memorial stones have been present in India since a long time i.e. since 3rd century A.D. The number of such memorial stones increased after the 12th-13th century CE. A large variety has been observed in these memorial stones in the early medieval period. The memorials tones in south India many a times carried the inscriptions informing the details of the person in whose memory the stone was erected. Such inscriptions are extremely rare in Maharashtra. These hero stones also depicted the events causing the death of the person in various panels, ultimately the hero was shown being taken to the heaven by the divine ladies and he was shown worshipping the Shivalinga. Thousands of such hero stones are found in Maharashtra and other parts of the country.

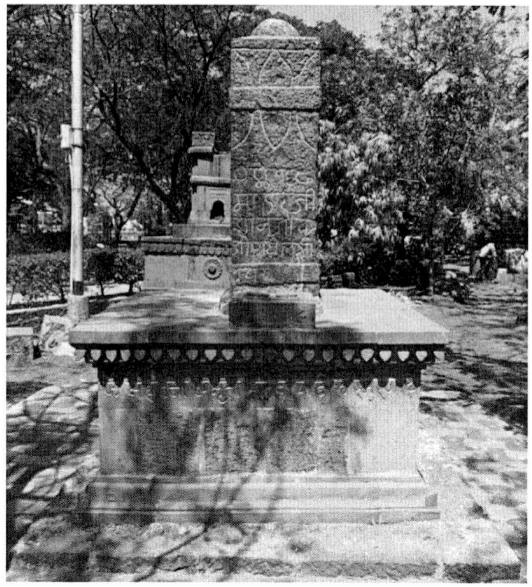

Pl.1: Memorial stone of Shri Mahadji Satav, Wagholi

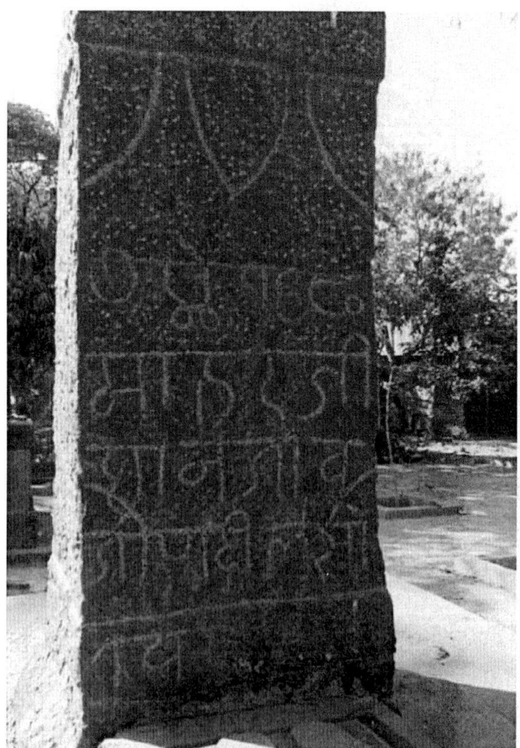

Pl.2: Inscription on the memorial stone

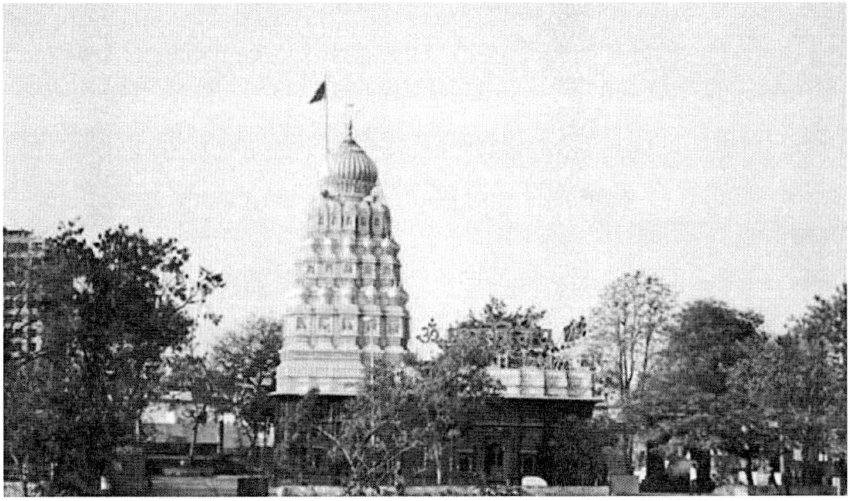

Pl.3: Wagheshwar Temple, Wagholi

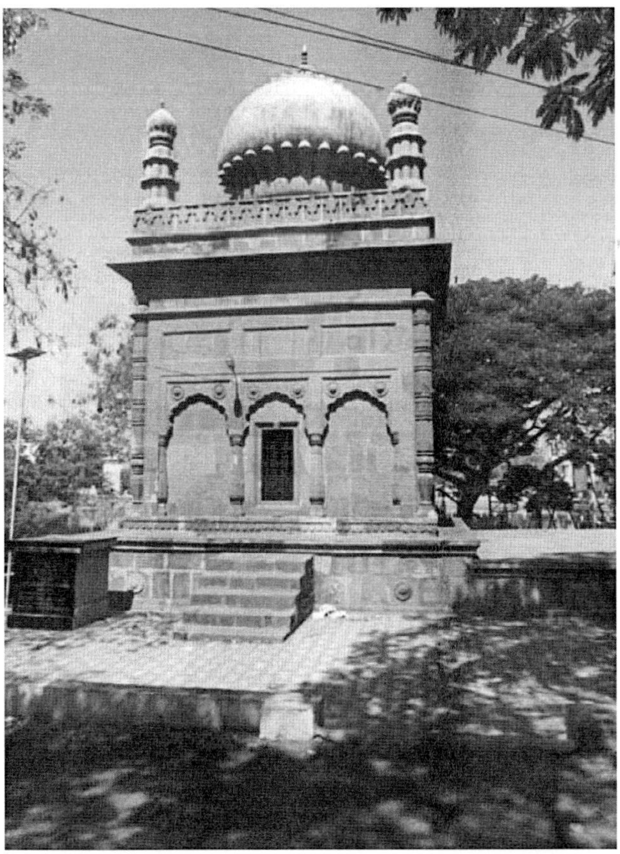

Pl.4: Memorial temple of Pilajirao Jadhav, Wagholi

In the case of Maharashtra the design and nature of the hero stones changed after 15th century A.D. The details carved on the hero stones were no longer seen on the hero stones. It became a rectangular stone with square base which tapered towards the top and was capped by a small domical projection. Very rare examples showed the image of only the person in whose memory the stone was erected. Sometimes they were monoliths looking like a pyramid of various levels. But there are hardly any inscriptions reported from these memorial stones.

The present memorial stone under study is a rectangular stone capped by a small domical projection. The stone is decorated with the bands of leaves at both the ends. It is placed in the abovementioned temple complex of Wagholi. This memorial stone has been fixed on a high platform by Manikrao Amrutrao Satav Patil in the memory of Mahadaji Amruta Satav Patil. The platform is inscribed with this information. However the memorial stone on top of this platform also bears an inscription giving the name of the person and the year of his death. The inscription is written in partially Modi and partially Devnagari script. It says, "Sake 1680 Maahadajee bin Jaavajee Paateel Saatava". It refers to Shaka 1680 and makes it to 1758 A.D. The name of the person is Mahadaji who was the son of Javaji and belonged to the Satav Patil family. Other than this there are numerous memorial structures and a few such memorial stones. However such an inscription is not seen on any of them. Hence this memorial stone becomes very important.

The Satav Patil family was also the native family of Wagholi they were the Patil of this place. Even though Pilaji Jadhavrao's memorial temple was constructed in this campus in 1751 A.D., the other memorial stones were also constructed in the same campus, indicates that this area was the traditionally a cremation ground and was on the southern boundary of the habitation. The situation has not changed till today. It is the official cremation ground for the inhabitants of the town.

The significance of this hero stone is in the uniqueness of the same. This is an extremely rare memorial stone of the medieval period which has an inscription engraved on it. The importance of the person is also suggested through this feature. Unfortunately, nothing else is known of this person Mahadji Satav Patil.

References

1. Jadhavrao, Suvarnalata Amarsinh, *Sardar Pilaji Jadhavrao : Vyakti ani Karya*, Avishkar Prakashan, Pune 2008:189

14

Raigad Plates of Vijayāditya: A Reappraisal

Dr. Ambarish Khare

Introduction

The Copper-plate grant of Cālukya king Vijayāditya under consideration in the present paper was originally published by K. B. Pathak[1] in which he refers to the find place as Rayagad. In the present paper, however, the place has been referred to as Raigad, following the prevalent practice of spelling the name of this place. Later, an attempt was made by Thosar[2], to identify the place names mentioned in this inscription. The aim of this paper is to reassess the identifications of Thosar.

Description

Pathak mentions that the said donative inscription has been carved on three copper plates, each measuring about 9.5 inches × 4.5 inches. The plates were in possession of Patil of the Raigad, situated in the then Mahad Taluka of the Kolaba District. The plates also had a ring with a seal having an emblem of a wild boar.

Contents of the Inscription

The plates begin with the benedictory word *svasti*, followed by verse praising the Varāha incarnation of Viṣṇu. Then follows the genealogical information of the Cālukyas, wherein they are mentioned as belonging to the Mānavya *gotra* and are called *hārītiputras* (sons of the goddess Hārīti). It further mentions that the Cālukyas were raised up by the seven mothers (*saptalokamātṛbhiḥ saptamātṛbhiḥ abhivardhita*) and they are the ones who have received the auspiciousness from the protection of Kārttikeya (*kārttikeya-parirakcaṇa-prāpta-kalyāṇa-paraṁpara*).

The inscription states that the Cālukyas reigned over all the other kings because they were under the auspicious surveillance of the Lord Varāha, the incarnation of Viṣṇu. The genealogy of the Cālukyas begins with the description of Pulakeśin (I) as usual. The inscription describes the king Pulakeśin (I) as performer of the Aśvemedha sacrifice and then describes his son Kīrtivarman followed by the description of the latter's son viz. Pulakeśin (II) as the one who has defeated the king Harṣavardhana, the lord of Uttarāpatha. Then his son Vikramāditya Satyāśraya-Śrīpṛthvīvallabha is mentioned as the one who has defeated the kings Pāṇḍya, Coḷa, Kerala, Kaḷabhra etc., and the one who has made Kāñcīpati to bow before him. His son Vinayāditya is then praised as "beloved son of his father", who, since his childhood, was a great warrior like Kārttikeya and acquired wealth from the whole of Uttarāpatha, Pārasīkadeśa and Siṁhaladvīpa. The donor of the present donation is his son Vijayāditya. The inscription states that the king Vijayāditya learned all the *śāstras* in his young age only, and increased the wealth of his family. Having the control over both the Southern and Northern regions (of India) like his grandfather, he is the real support of the whole world.

The copper plates further inform us that the king Vijayāditya, in his eighth regnal year (*vartamāna śaka* 625), while camping at the victorious camp (*vijayaskandhāvāra*) at Karahāma, donates the village Jallagrāma along with the village Nirūḷanagrāma situated in the Tālitaṭāhāra-viṣaya, to the Brahmin named Nāthera Caturvedin belonging to the Śāṇḍilya *gotra*, grandson of Annasvāmin and son of Devadīkṣita.

The donation ends with the usual verses beginning with the words *bahubhir vasudhā bhuktā*, *svāṁ dātuṁ sumahacchakyam* and *svadattāṁ paradattāṁ vā* respectively. At the end, the name Niravadya-Puṇyavallabha appears as the writer of the inscription.

Observations

Niravadya-puṇyavallabha, the writer of the present grant, was the successor of Śrīrāma-puṇyavallabha who wrote, in *śaka* 616, the Harihar Plates of Vinayāditya. One Niravadya-śrīmad-anivārita-puṇyavallabha was the writer of the Kāñcī inscription of Vikramāditya II. Dhanañjaya Puṇyavallabha, the writer of Kendur grant of *śaka* 672, speaks of himself as śrīmad-anivārita-dhanañjaya-puṇyavallabha in the Vakkaleri Plates of *śaka* 679.

Pathank opines that we have four generations of the writers mentioned in the Copper Plates of the Cālukyas, namely, Śrīrāma, Niravadya, Anivārita and Dhanañjaya. Their family name was Puṇyavallabha, according to Pathak.

About the identification of the geographical names mentioned in the inscription, the suggestions of Thosar are as follows:

Karahāmanagara is modern Karad. It is a known fact that this region was under the rule of Sendrakas and the father-in-law of Vijayāditya was the Sendraka chief Viṣṇurāja. This information is available in the Alampur eulogy of Vijayāditya. Tālitaṭāhāra-viṣaya has been identified by Thosar with Talawde region in the Taluka Rajapur of District

Ratnagiri. He identifies the donated village Jallagrāma with the modern village called Jalgaon in Taluka Dapoli of District Ratnagiri. However, he identifies another village mentioned in the inscription, i.e. Nirūḷaṇagrāma with the village Nerur in Taluka Kudal of District Sindhudurg.

These identifications can be doubted because of the far distances in all the three places. As per the description in the copper plates, both the villages Jallagrāma and Nirūḷaṇagrāma shall fall in the boundaries of the Tālitaṭāhāra Viṣaya. If we match the places identified by Thosar, we would see that all the three places fall in different Talukas and Districts in modern time. Tālitaṭāhāra falls in Taluka Rajapur and Jallagrāma in Taluka Dapoli, both from District Ratnagiri. Nirūḷaṇagrāma, according to Thosar, falls in Taluka Kudal of District Sindhudurg. One has to imagine that the Viṣaya called Tālitaṭ āhāra was so big, that is consisted of Talukas from modern Dapoli to Kudal. The distance between these Taluka places is about 250 to 300 kms. However, it is also possible to argue that the administrative units having large territories could have been present in ancient time. Thus, there is a want of another evidence to explicitly discard the earlier identification of place names.

This evidence comes from the Nerur Plates of Vijayāditya issued in *śaka* 622, i.e. three years before the Raigad Plates were issued. It was published by Fleet[3]. In the Nerur Plates, the king has donated a village named Nerur to a Brahmin called Dāsasvāmin belonging to Vatsa *gotra*. Thosar himself has identified the village Nerur of the Nerur copper plates with the village Nerur of Taluka Kudal, District Sindhudurg. That in just three years (from *śaka* 622 to 625) the name of the village changed from Nerur to Nirūḷaṇa and was also donated to a different Brahmin by taking back the earlier grant, is impossible believe. Therefore, on the basis of the evidence we get from the Nerur Plates, one of the two identifications shall stand discarded. Modern Nerur can either be Nerur of Nerur Plates or Nirūḷaṇa of Raigad Plates.

Conclusions

In the opinion of present researcher, the identification of Nerur of Nerur Copper Plates with Nerur in Taluka Kudal, District Sindhudurg is acceptable. But the village Nirūḷaṇa mentioned in the Raigad Copper Plates cannot be identified with Nerur mentioned above. This disapproval of Thosar's identifications comes from the far distance between the places as well as from the contradictory identifications that he has made.

The present researcher suggests that the village Nirūḷaṇa of the Raigad Copper Plates shall be identified with the village Nirul (or Nirool) in the Taluka Ratnagiri itself. Also, the village Tale from the same Taluka can be equated with the ancient Tālitaṭāhāra Viṣaya, instead of reaching to Rajapur Taluka and identifying the village Talawde with Tālitaṭāhāra Viṣaya. Two advantages that can be categorically noted because of the new identifications are as follows.

The first advantage is that the new identifications remove the contradiction between the identification of place names of the Nerur and Raigad Copper Plates. Second benefit is that the distances between all the places of which the names are appearing in the Raigad copper plates are reduced to such an extent that the identifications become more plausible. According to the new identifications, the distance between any of the two places is not more than roughly 150 kms. Although the identifications suggested in the present paper are acceptable on the basis of geographical position of the concerned villages as well as the linguistic similarity in their names, it is further necessary to see if any archaeological data helps to solidify these identifications. This work has been undertaken and would be published in future.

References

1. Pathak, K. B. 1910. "Rayagad Plates of Vijayaditya: Saka Samvat 625". Epigraphica Indica. Vol. X: 125-17.
2. Thosar, H. S., Historical Geography of Maharashtra and Goa. Mysore: Epigraphical Society of India, 2004, 546
3. Fleet, J. F., "W. Chalukya Grant of Vijayāditya, dated Ś. 622". *The Indian Antiquary*. Vol. IX: 1880,125-30.

15

Architecture of a Cave at Karle in the Light of its Donative Inscription

Anand Kanitkar

Introduction

Buddhist Rock cut caves of Karle are situated at a distance of around 60 kms from Pune. The cave group consists of 16 rock cut excavations. The great *Chaitya* cave at Karle is the largest in India of its kind. The cave group has an impressive repertoire of inscriptions which refer to donors from different strata of society, such as laymen, Buddhist monks and nuns, merchants and *Yavana*s. The inscriptions from the great *Chaitya* cave are of special interest to the researchers because of their significance in the history of the *Kṣatrapa*s and the *Sātavāhana*s.

This paper throws a fresh light on one of the caves and its donative inscription at Karle. All the scholars who have dealt either with the inscription or with the cave have not dealt with both of them together. This paper discusses the cave excavation process as well as some features of the rock cut cave which can be seen from the donative inscription and the cave architecture itself.

Buddhist Rock cut caves of Kãrle are situated at a distance of around 60 kms from Pune. The cave group consists of 16 cave excavations. The great Chaitya cave at Kãrle is the largest in India of its kind. The cave group has an impressive repertoire of donative inscriptions that refer to donators from different sections of society, such as laymen, Buddhist monks and nuns, merchants, Princes and Yavanas. The inscriptions from the great Chaitya cave are of special interest to researchers because of their importance in the history of the Kshatrapãs and the Sãtavãhanãs.

The cave no.15 at Karle is an interesting rock cut cave with an epigraphical record of private donation of the cave itself. Not much attention has been paid to this cave and inscription except for the personal names Harapharaṇa and Setapharaṇa which occur in this inscription and the regnal year 24 of Vāsiṣṭhīputra Śrī Puḷumāvi.[1]

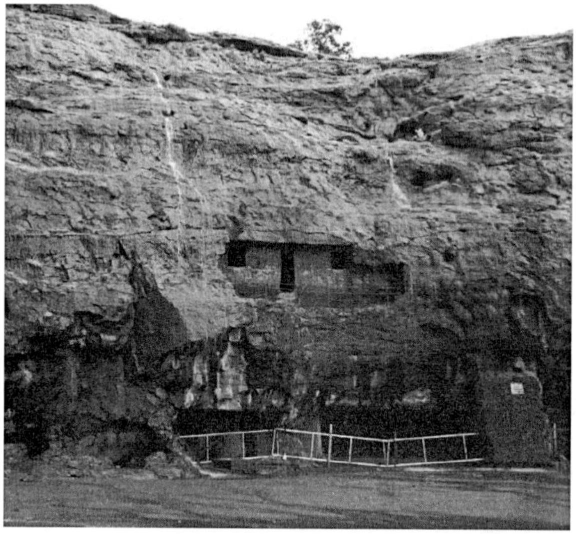

Fig.1 : Photo showing Cave no. 15 at Karle

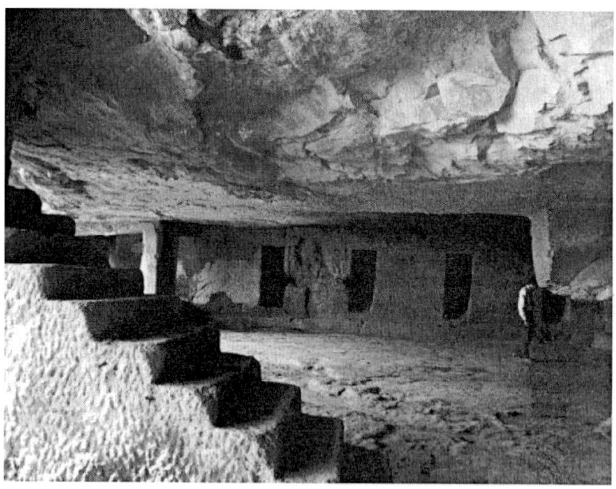

Fig.2 : Photo showing staircase to cave no 15

Cave no 15 is situated at the northernmost part of the Karle cave group. It is accessed by a staircase. One finds the inscription on the right wall of the cave.

The inscription mentions that Harapharana son of Setapharana has donated this nine-celled hall (Navagabha Matapa) in the 24th regnal year of Vāsiṣṭhīputra Śrī Puḷumāvi to *Mahasanghiyas* of all four quarters. And the last line of the inscription thus reads '*Sahet cha me puna Buddharakhitena matara chasya upasikaya Budharakhitasa matu (ya deya)dhamma patho ano'.*

This sentence has been translated as with me Buddharakhita and his mother have donated another pathway. Hence according to Indrajee it mentions that along with Harapharana who donated the nine celled hall, Buddharakhita and his mother donated a pathway, in this case might be a staircase.

Mirashi has taken the word patho as patho which means behind and thus he translates the sentence as 'another cave donated by Budharakhita and his mother is behind (this cave)'.

In the opposite wall of the inscription, there are two windows and a door is carved out. One can enter on the ledge path from the door. Thus, this cave has two doors. One which is accessible now with the excavated staircase and another in front of the inscription which is flanked by two windows.

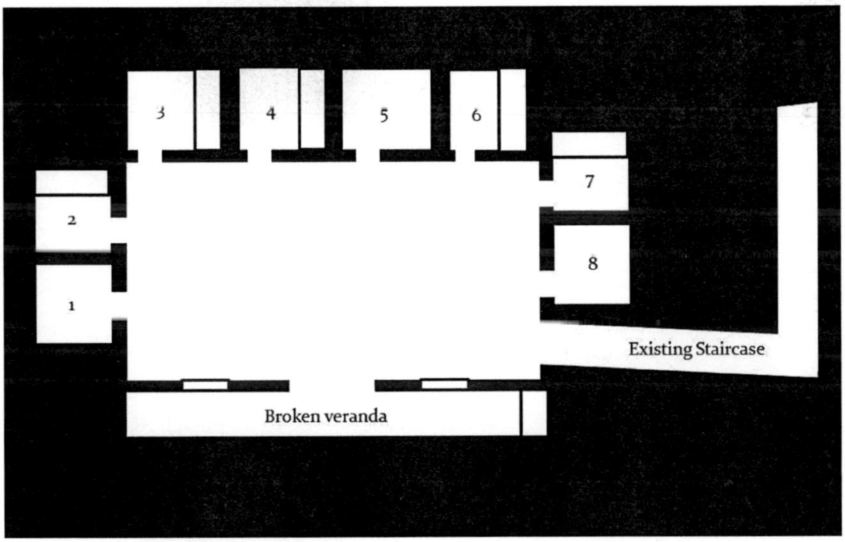

Fig.3 : Plan of the cave no 15 at Karle (after Fergusson 1860)

It is worth noticing that the plan provided by Fergusson shows only 8 cells in the hall whereas the inscription specifically mentions that the hall with nine cells was donated. None of the researchers mentioning the inscription noticed that the actual hall is with the 8 cells only. So did the hall had eight cells only and the ninth cell was did not take shape because of the staircase with which we access the cave no 15? Then what was the reason of excavating two doors for this particular cave.

If we observe carefully the ledge path, outside the door flanked with the windows, on the left side we can notice the remains of one cell and the carved bench in it. This must be the 9th cell mentioned in the inscription. Thus, we can conclude that it was actually a nine celled hall which was donated by Harapharana.

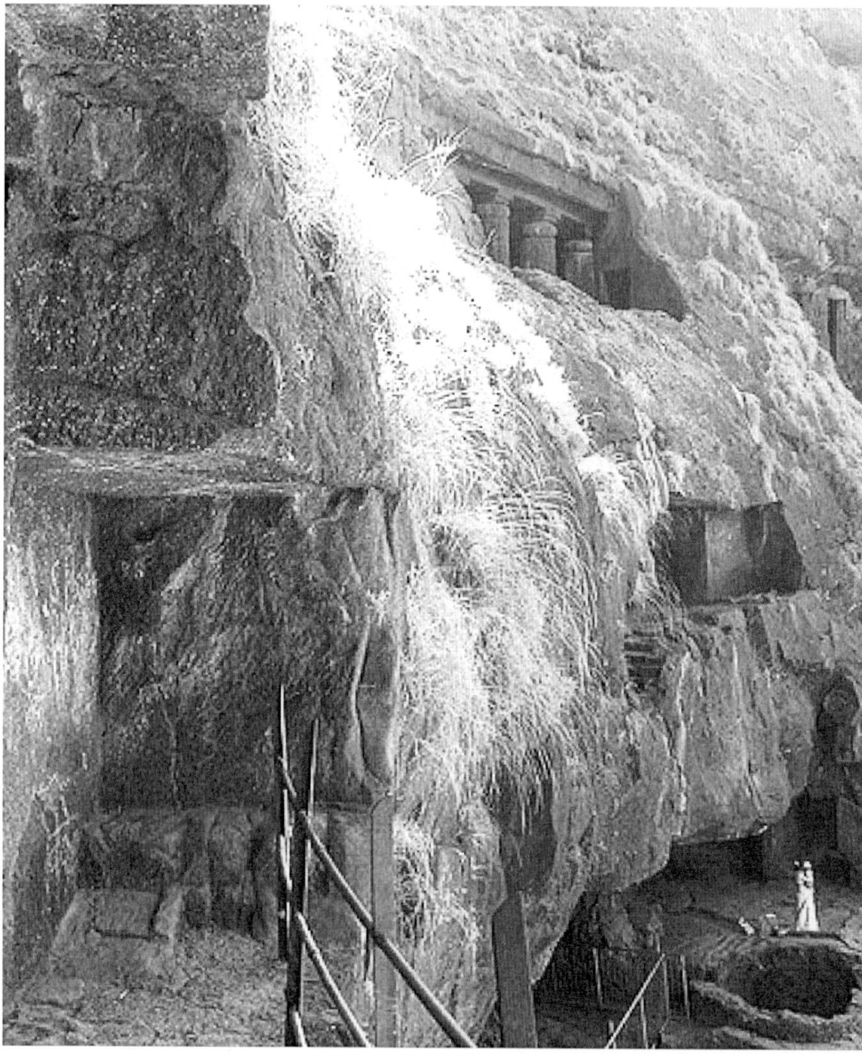

Fig.4 : Photo showing remains of the cell and the bench on the ledge

The last sentence of the inscription mentioned above needs to be put in the architectural context of the cave. Harapharana who has donated this cave in the regnal year 21 of Vāsiṣṭhīputra Śrī Puḷumāvi and it was completed in the year 24 of Vāsiṣṭhīputra Śrī Puḷumāvi. It might be possible that as is the case at Karle or Bhaje. The front part of the caves which has staircase or ledge path is many a time broken due to heavy rains and waterfalls. If we carefully look at the excavation work carried out at the cave no 15, we can deduce it to following stages:

1. Front part was the first part to excavate which had pillared veranda and a staircase for access.
2. In order to enter from the veranda a door was excavated and two windows which flanked it allowed more sunlight to enter.
3. While the workers were working to excavate the nine cells inside the hall, the staircase in front of the cave collapsed due to loose boulders falling from above.
4. Since there was no rock available in front of the veranda the excavators had to change their architectural plan.
5. Instead of the 9th cell on the right side of the hall, they excavated another staircase with which the cave could be accessed and is still accessed.
6. The architect must have made his observations and decided to excavate the ninth cell on the right side of the veranda itself where some more rock was available.

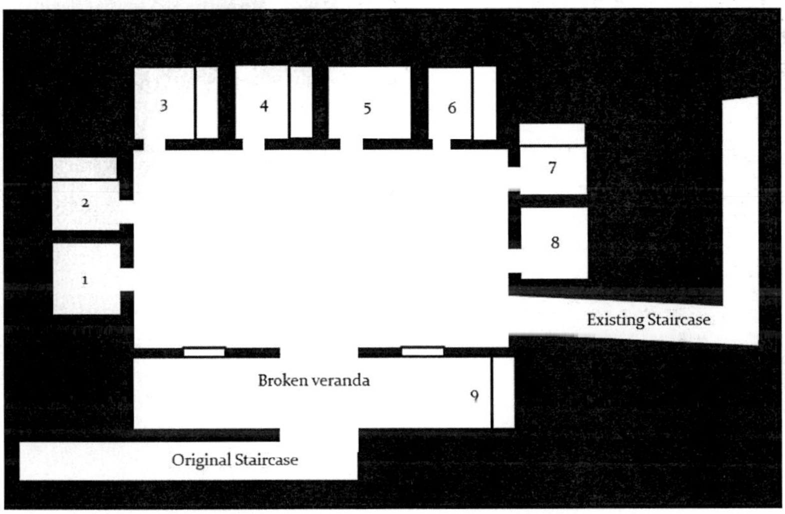

Fig.5 : Conjectural plan of cave no. 15
showing both the staircases and the 9th cell (by Author)

With the above conditions we see the 8 cells inside the hall and the 9th cell in the veranda. Thus the main donation of the nine celled hall with the staircase to access it on the first floor was given by Harapharana who records to have come in the 21st and 24th regnal year of Vāsiṣṭhīputra Śrī Puḷumāvi.

The excavation of another staircase needed some additional budget for the Sangha which was donated by Budharakshita and his mother in the absence of Harapharana who might not have paid visits so often to the Valuraka Sangha at Karle.

The last sentence of the inscription by Harapharana thus could be explained at the donation of another patha or staircase was given by Budharakshita and his mother. And it does not mention the donation of another rock cut cave donated by Buddharakshita and his mother. The word *Patha* or *Patho* has been used to denote pathway or staircase especially in the inscriptions at Kanheri and Kuda.

Many a times the researchers study the inscription apart from the architecture of the cave in which the inscription is found. This paper emphasizes that the donative inscriptions should be studied together with the architecture of the caves to better understand the excavation process and current condition of the caves.

References

1. H. Lüders, *Appendix to Epigraphia Indica and Record of the Archaeological Survey of India, Vol. X: A List of Brahmi Inscriptions from the Earliest Times to about A.D. 400 with the Exception of Those of Asoka.* Calcutta: Superintendent Government Printing, 1912. (Inscription Number 1106); ICK 20; D. C. Sircar, *Select Inscriptions.* 2nd ed. Calcutta: University of Calcutta, 1965. p.88; Mirashi V.V., *The History and Inscriptions of the Sātavāhanas and the Western Kshatrapas.* Bombay: Maharashtra State Board for Literature and Culture, 1981. p.20.

16

Devanagari Inscription from Mandapeshwar Cave

Shamika Sarvankar

The *Mandapeshwar* caves (18° 57' 47.7108'' N;72° 55' 53.1912'' E) are situated in Borivali – a suburb of Mumbai, Maharashtra. This cave temple achieved significant position in the history of Western Indian rock cut architecture; primarily it was *Shaiva* cave before the colonial (Portuguese) invasion, who transformed this cave temple into the church. After transition this church and surrounding area known as the *Montpezier* or *Monpacer*[1]. Even Today, area surrounded by cave is popularly known as Mount *Poinsor*.

Mandapeshwar Caves are considered as the one of the best place for understanding of Western Indian rock cut architecture.The site is located near to the Dahisar River and along with the river numerous archaeological remains were had been noticed. Mandapeshwar comprises of two caves, one is insignificant and unfinished and other evinces the religious history of 1400 years. Apart from these two caves on site, there is an attempt to excavate cave in the south of the smaller cave. Based on stylistic affiliation this cave has been dated to 2nd half of 6th century CE.[2] The ruins of an old Portuguese-built church stand on top of the caves. This cave temple play very important role in history starting from the 2nd century CE. to present day (Fig.1), even today also this is under worship.

Apart from the architecture part this cave temple produced the one important epigraph of late medieval period and which throw the light on cultural and religious activities of the same region. There was sufficient work has been done by Fergusson & Burgess[3], Sounder Rajan[4] on Mandapeshwar. All the scholars have been missed out one Devanagari inscription which is notice on the door jamb. For that present researcher documenting and deciphering this inscription.

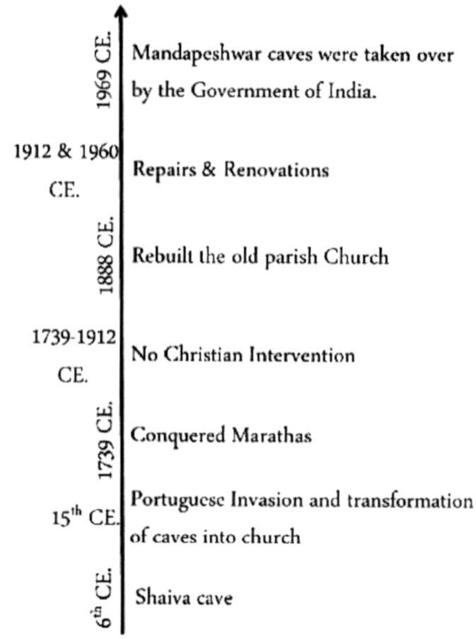

Fig.1 : Important Historical Events

Location:

The inscription is engraved on the door jamb of the sanctum of Mandapeshwar Cave. Inscription is not deeply engraved but apart from some of the letters other are clearly visible presently.

Language and Script:

The language used in the inscription is Marathi and Devanagari script used for engraving. There are total 11 lines written on the prepared surface.

Period:

In the first and second line of the inscription date has been mentioned, which refers the Samvatyear of 1911, month of the Chitra, on the six day of dark fortnight. The year 1911 which is corresponds to the 1854-55 CE.

Text of the Inscription: (Fig. 2)

Line 1 : samvate 1911 varshe

Line 2 : _ _ _ krushana shashte divase

Line 3 : _ _ _ chitre

Line 4 : _ _ _ nakshatra patrada

Line 5 : _ _ _ ma (?) nam o govinda shree

Line 6 : sta (?) na (?) koravasee nani?

Line 7 : bhakt pa dya dhyo shaktee

Line 8 : _ _ desha _ _ _ shree

Line 9 : Mandapeshwaren poo (pra) jaa

Line 10 : ka I sha ne karanda(?)ka

Line 11 : mathapeshwar do na(?) ha(?)

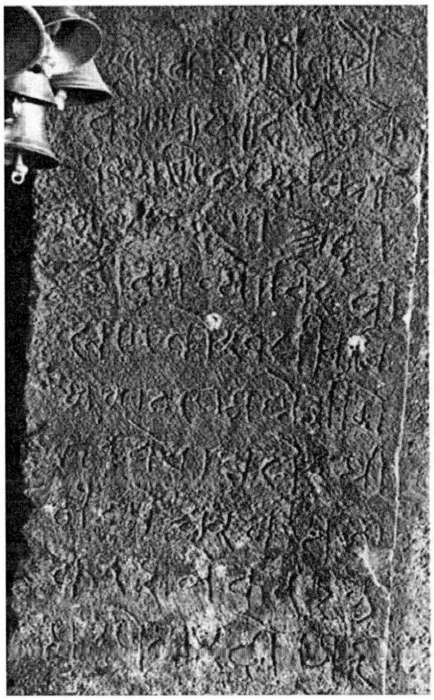

ओळ १ : संवते १९११ वर्षे

ओळ २ : ___ कृष्ण षष्ठे दिवसे

ओळ ३ : ___ चित्रे

ओळ ४ : __ नक्षत्र पात्रदा

ओळ ५ : म (?) नम ० गोविंद् श्री

ओळ ६ : स्त (?) ण (?) कोरक्सी नानि ?

ओळ ७ : भक्त प द्य द्यो शक्ती

ओळ ८ : __ दे् शा ___ श्री

ओळ ९ : मंडपेश्वरेन पू (प्र) जा

ओळ १० : क इ श ने क रं ड (?) क

ओळ ११ : मठपेश्वर दो ण ह

Fig.2 : Inscription and Reading

Remarks:

This inscription contends the date, palace and other relevant valuable information. Line 9 refers the location as *Mandapeshwar* mentioned in the line No. 9 as a *Mandapeshwaren* and line No.11 as a *Mathapeshvar*. The inscription refers *Govinda* has given the donation to the cave temple.

The inscription should in 1850's it is evident that the site was under worship as a *shaiva* shrine. After battle of Bassein in 1739 between Portuguese and Maratha, later took over the charge of this region. This was destruction to the Christian settlement and revival of *shaiva* tradition was initiated. This must be the popular *shaiva* tradition and not necessarily the older *pashupatashaiva* tradition which was revived. The inscription suggests that even after a century after revival of *shaiva* tradition, the cave temple under worship. Till the beginning of 20th century. The tradition continued and the Christianity was revived by initiative taken by Christians from Bandra and Thane. This inscription plays a significant role in the local history of Mumbai.

References

1. Campbell, J M, Gazetteer of the Bombay Presidency, Vol.XIV. Government Central Press, Bombay, 1882.
2. Soundara Rajan, K.V., Cave Temples of the Deccan, Archaeological Society of India, New Delhi, 1981.
3. Fergusson, James and Burgess, James, The Cave Temples of India, Munshiram Manoharlal, New Delhi, 1880.
4. *Op. Cit.*

17

The Sohgaura Bronze Plaque Inscription:
A Critical Appraisal

Soumya Ghosh

The well-known Sohgaura bronze plaque inscription was discovered from a village named Soghgaura in the Gorakhpur district of Uttar Pradesh. The plaque is 21/2 × 17/8 inches in size. Besides the Brāhmī inscription the epigraph also has a few symbols on the top. On the basis of its palaeography and also the content of the inscription is has been placed, almost certainly, in the 3rd- 2nd century BCE. The inscription has been edited and commented by stalwarts like Smith and Hoernle[1], Buhler[2], Fleet[3], Barua[4], Jayaswal[5], Chakravarti[6], and Sircar[7] and Ranjusri Ghosh.[8] This inscription is over discussed one yet there is scope for throwing fresh light or providing an interpretation afresh. I will make a humble attempt to look at the inscription co-relating it with the symbols above it and situate the above text in the Mauryan context.

Text: As read by Sircar:[9]

1. savatiyana mahamaga(ta)na [sa]sane manavasiti ka-
2. –da silimate vasagame va ete dave koṭhagalani
3. Tighavani māthula- ca[ca]- modama bhalakana cha-
4. –[la] kayiyati atiyāyikaya no gahiga(ta)vaya

Text: As read by J F Fleet:[10]

1. Savva-ti-yānamahāmaggānaṁ sāsane Manavasi-tikē
2. dasilimatē Usagāmē va ēte duve koṭṭhāgālāni
3. Tiyavani-Mathulā-Cham chu-medama-bhālakānaṁ vā-
4. lā kayyiyaṁti atiyāyikāya no gahitavvāya

Re-reading the Text: (Original)

LINE-1 : sava ti-yāna-mahamagana sasane [I] manavasi tike [I]

LINE-2 : dasilimāte usagame vā ēte duve Kohagalani

LINE-3 : tighavani mothula-cacu-medāma bhalakanaṁ [I] va-

LINE-4 : la kayiyati atiyāyikaya [I] no gahitavaya [II]

Text Sanskritized:

Sarvva triyānamahāmārgānāṁ śasanaḥ[I] Mānavasi trikaḥ [I] Dasrimātaḥ uṣṇagrāmaḥ ca ete dve koṣṭhāgārāni trigarbhāni mathurācañcumedāmabhārakānāṁ [I] Grahaṇam kāryīyantē / kārayiyati[11] atiyāyikāya [I] Nagrahitavyaṁ [I]

Grammatical and Orthographical Notes:

The inscription uses Māgadhī Prākrit and here we find that in case of the words *tike* and *sasane* i.e Sanskrit *trikaḥ* and *úāsanaḥ,* the visarga ending instead of 'o' becomes 'e' in Māgadhī Prākrit. In eastern Māgadhī often 'r' (as in *trika, trigarbhāni, grahitavya, sarvva, and uṣṇagrāmo, tri-yāna-mahāmārgānāṁ)* is dropped. Same in the case of ñ which also drops in the words cañcu, uṣñagrāma. In Māgadhī Prākrit ra becomes la and here the words *kothagarani* becomes *kothagalani*, *bhārakānā* becomes *bhalakana, Mathura becomes mathula, dasrimāte or dasirimāte becomes dasilimāte.* In Māgadhī Prākrit again all the tail m are dropped like in case of *bhalakana, gahitavaya* and *mahamagana*, this are actually bhārakānāṁ, grahitavyaṁ and mahāmārgānāṁ. The pāli word *kārayīyati*, probably becomes here kayiyati by assimilation of ra and shortening of ī & ā. But it also probable that, *kayiyati* actually comes from sanskṛt *kāryīyantē*, as būhler suggested.

It is worth mentioning here that though the inscription has been found in a non Māgadhī zone it is in Māgadhī Prākrit. Thus it seems that the inscription which was in the form of an order or notice was cast in a Māgadhī speaking/using zone i.e. metropolitan zone Pataliputra to the core area of Sravasti and thus there might had been probability of issueing the order by a central administrator.

The first line serves as an introductory note of the total context of the epigraph. Order or Notice (*sasane*) for all (sava) the vehicles (plying on) the three (*ti-yāna*) great roads (*mahāmagana*). Just after this the place name *Manavasi* is mentioned which is situated on a crossing/juntion of three roads (*tika* > *trika*). It should be noted that the last letter 'ke' of the first line has been squeezed to fit into the line, which in turn proves that it was important to fit this into it, to provide a complete meaning to this line and could not be a part of the second line. This also strengthens our argument in-keeping with Fleet's line of thought that it is a notice; we would like to further add to this that the first line itself is an introductory notification. We would like to therefore interpret the first line as: The order/notice for the vehicles (plying on) the three great roads (meeting at the) Manavasi junction. In other words we now would like to go with Fleet who had mentioned this for the first time that Manavasi was a junction where the three roads met.[12] It is further proved that this epigraph severed the above mentioned purpose of a 'notice' from the fact that there are four holes at the four corners to nail/hang/fix the notice on a specific surface. Sircar however takes the word s*avatiyāna* as Śrāvasti but we would like to differ from the above interpretation. This will be discussed in due course.

The syntax and tone of the inscription reflects that this was a common practice in early historic times in this region and the people were familiar with this kind of notices and therefore no detailing was required to understand the purport.

Second line reads *Dasilimate and Usagame ete duve komhagalani* of these the first two are place names *Dasilimate* and *Usagame* where the two (*duve*) storehouses (*koṭhagalani*)[13] were located. Here we would like to digress and bring in the symbols on the top of the inscription here as well two store houses have been depicted.

Line three begins with the word *tighvani* which has been interpreted as *trigarbhāni* by Sircar[14] and Buhler[15] which is in continuation of the second line and stands to mean that the two storehouses mentioned in line two were three tiered. After tighavani the line further reads: *Mathula, Cacu* and *Medama*. Again these three are place names *Mathula* has already been identified by scholars with Mathura,[16] *Cacu* has been identified by Fleet with cañcu[17] and *Medama* or *Modama* has been taken by Sircar as Mayudama without any satisfactory identification. We would also like to consider *Medama* as a place name and identify it with Mehndaval presently located in the Sant Kabir Nagar district of Uttar Pradesh. The place names are followed by the word *bhalakana* i.e. *bharakanaṁ* (Sanskrit) which is in genitive case ending and in Prākṛt there is a rule for the use of genitive for dative case endings i.e the words *bhalakana* may indicate either genitive or dative. The word *bhalakana* means load bearers or vendors i.e. for load bearers/vendors or of load bearers/vendors. This line means 'for the load bearers/ vendors (of) Mathura, Ca(ṁ)cu and Medama.

It might be again cited here that the symbolic representation of the store houses above are distinctly three tiered. There are two symbols representing two trees, one with leaves (to left) on the left of the storehouse and the other without leaves (to right), on the left of the store house. Probably the two palces were symbolically represented by the two trees here. In the centre there is a three-peaked hill with a crescent which is specifically a Mauryan symbol. To its right is the symbolic representation of sun and crescent (moon) placed one above the other respectively. To the left of the Mauryan symbol is a spear like object which again has a tiny three peaked hill within.

Last letter 'va' in line three is a continuation of line four it reads vala kayiyati. *Vala* means 'to take something'[18] and *kayiyati* (Sanskrit *kāryīyantē* or pāli *kārayiyati*) means a 'work to be done by many' or 'it is caused to be made'.[19] Followed by the word *atiyayikaya* (or atiyayikāya in Sanskrit) which means "for an emergency situation". These words has also been used in the same sense in Mahasthan inscription[20] which is also contemporary to our record. Arthasastra mentions three types of *atiyayika* viz. *suatiyayika* (drought), *udakatiyayika* (flood) and *devatiyayika* (fire). So *vala kayiyati atiyayikāya* in the record under discussion thus means to be taken by many in emergency situation. Again the tone here is also that of a notification or instruction that goods are to be taken from the storehouses mentioned above only in the emergency situation. Line 4 ends with a strong prohibitory note saying 'not to be taken' (no gahitavaya). This is imperative in nature and hence grammatically incomplete as it is indicative.[21]

Now in the light of the above analysis we would like to situate the present inscription in the Mauryan context. Before situating it, the purport of the inscription should be repeated again. Notification/Order for all the vehicles plying on the three great roads or highways. Notified or Displayed at the Manavasi juntion located on the crossroads of three highways connecting Manavasi with Mathurā, Camcu and Medāma. All the load bearers or vendors are instructed hereby to carry goods from the storehouses located at Dasilimata and Usagrama in conditions abnormal or in emergency situations. The two store houses were three tired. It is interesting to note that the symbols for these as discussed above have a tree with leaves and the other without leaves.

The first one stood for the symbolic representation of Dasilimata and the second without leaves for Usagrama. Another interpretation might also be put forth i.e. at the store house at Dasilimata the storehouse was a granary to store grains and hence a tree with leaves was used as its symbol. This might also include forest or tree products. At Usagrama all other products were stored which are not from trees hence the symbol, a tree without leaves. However, there is no corroborative evidence to prove this.

The notification was for specific vendors i.e. only those coming and going to Mathura, camcu and Medama from/to Manavasi. They could take the goods from the two storehouses mentioned in the inscription only in case of emergency. Secondly a prohibitory order has been proclaimed on taking anything from these store houses. This means that the prohibition was for not taking in normal conditions and also not to be taken by others other than those coming and going to Mathura, Camcu and Medama. Now the question that arises here is who issued this order or notice? The symbol on the cast bronze plaque may provide us with a clue. The use of Mauryan symbol in the centre, here indicates that it was an official order of the Mauryans. The symbol has been considered as Mauryan on the grounds that the punch marked coins of the Series VI which are beyond doubt Mauryan bear this as an official mark. Here it is almost an emblem of the Mauryans and is also found depicted on the spear like object besides the Mauryan symbol. The last prohibitory sentence in the inscription almost clearly shows that it can be none else other than the Mauryan official/ administrative authoritative tone. There is no direct mention of any ruler or any epithet which makes us infer that the record under discussion is issued from an administrative office. The officer who issued it had the right to use the official symbol but could not mention his name on the record.

We may assume that possibly minimum of three copies of this record were made. The bronze notice/ order displayed, was made by casting technique which indicates that its durability was kept in mind along with the fact that multiple copies were to be produced so a mould was prepared and the notification was finally cast. Two were probably for the display on the doors of the two storehouses i.e. at Dasilimata and Usagrama. One was probably retained at the administrative office. The size of the plaque was too small to be noticed if displayed at the highway or on a pillar, but if there was a fourth one then it could have been displayed at Manavasi junction.

The spear like object has a three peaked hill symbol within. It is clear that it is not a spear. Here a passage in the Arthaśāstra helps us to understand the context. The book mentions that, "the collector of customs and tolls should establish the custom house and a flag facing the east or the north in the vicinity of the big gates".[22] it further mentions that, "And for goods that have passed beyond the foot of the flag without the duty being payed, the fine is eight times the duty".[23] Thus the dhvaja or the pillar/post was closely related to custom or toll collection process of the state. If we suppose that there was such a mechanism of collecting toll tax and custom duties on certain points on the long distance trade routes then the spear like object was a pillar/post or dhvaja near the custom house. It functioned almost like modern check posts. Thus at Manavasi junction was located a similar toll collection unit and under the post/pillar goods were also exchanged or this was an exchange centre (In Arthaśāstra, how the traders used to sell or exchange their products, getting together at the foot of the post, that is described eloquently).[24] The nailing of the tiny bronze plaque bearing the epigraph could thus provide the pillar an official recognition. The traders were familiar with such custom posts which also might have helped them in locating places or finding directions.[25] This post might be a wooden post as no remains of stone pillar has been unearthed at Sohgaura. We would also like to propose that modern Sohgaura was the same as Manavasi.

At such centres there were two kinds of officials. One was sulkādhyakṣa (the director of custom) and the other was paṇyādhyakṣa (the director of trade). These two officers were under the samaharta, the collector general of the state.[26] But in Asokan inscriptions we do not get any equivalent officer but the system might more or less be the same and Manavasi junction was under one such officer.

Lastly we would like to discuss a little about the symbol on the flag/post. Here too the Arthasastra helps us to understand the context, "the receivers of the duty, four or five in number should record in writing (details about) traders who have arrived in a caravan, who they are, from what place, with how much merchandise and where the identity pass was issued or the stamping was made."[27] [*śulkadāyinaḥ catvāraḥ pañca vā sārthopayātan likheyuḥ - ke kutastyāḥ kiyatpanyāḥ? Kka cābhijñāmudrā*[28] *kṛtā*[29]] this *abhijñānamudrā* or the stamping/identity pass was probably issued to the traders against their payment of custom duties at each custom post and they had to carry this to the next post where this was required to prove themselves. The emblem marked high on the post (which is evident in the inscription) also leads us to think in the same line. Through this the Mauryan state probably intended to provide instructions to the traders/vendors to pay custom tax and collect the gate pass from the Manavasi toll collection unit.

Thus it mentions that such symbols or the emblem stamped on official document/ seals etc. provided easy passage to traders/vendors carrying goods for/on behalf of traders from one check post to the other. The vendors had to produce these to clear customs and if found without such official seals/sealing or documents then they had to pay a penalty.[30] These check marks or official symbols were also engraved or displayed on the posts.

According to Arthasastra Paṇyadhyak'a looked into the matter of trades in commodities. He used to control the prices by storing them during the time of abundance and releasing them during the time of scarcity.[31]

Our inscription only states that, during emergency or *atyayika* storied goods may be taken from those storages possibly by the official groups mentioned as the *vāhakas* of *Mathula, cacu* and *medama*.

In this inscription no *Adhyakṣa* or officer has been mentioned (like śulkādhyakṣa, paṇyadhyakṣa and mudrādhyakṣa), which leads us to assume that, this official order came from an administrative office or from an official under whom those Adhyakṣas were placed. This person may be an official like Sannidhāta.[32] However, in all probabilities the order came to Manavasi where the inscription was notified on the door where the pillar was stood and two official granaries were present. Thus, it might be an important centre of exchange. The order might have come from a superior office like Sravasti or any other city office.

References

1. Smith, V.A. and Hoernle, *Proceedings of the Ancient Society of Bengal*, 1894, pp.84-6.
2. Būhler, G., "The Sohgaura Copper Plate", *Indian Antiquary*, Vol.XXV, 1896, pp.265.
3. Fleet, J.F., "The Inscription on The Sohgaura Plate", *Journal of the Royal society, 1907*, pp.509-33.
4. Barua B.M., "The Sohgaura Copper Plate Inscription", *Annals of the Bhandarkar Oriental Research Institute,* Vol.11, No.1, 1930, *Bhandarkar Oriental Research Institute,* pp.32-48.
5. Jayaswal, K.P., "The Text of The Sohgaurah Plate", *Epigraphia Indica*, Vol.XXII, Archaeological Survey of India, pp.1-3.
6. Chakravarti, S.N., "The Sohgaurah Copper-Plate Inscription", *Journal Royal Asiatic society of Bengal. Letters*, Vol.VII, No.8, 1941, pp.203-205.

7. Sircar, D.C., "Notes on Some Inscriptions in the Collection of the Asiatic Society", *Journal of the Asiatic Society. Letters,* Vol.XLIX, No.4, 2007, pp.101-3; Vol.XVIII, No.1, 1952, pp.1-3.
8. Ghosh, Ranjusri, "Re-reading of the Sohgaurah Plaque Inscription by D.C. Sircar: A Note", *Journal of the Asiatic Society*, Vol.XLIX, No.4, 2007, pp.110-3.
9. Sircar, D.C., "Notes on Some Inscriptions in the Collection of the Asiatic Society", *Journal of the Asiatic Society,* Vol.XLIX, No.4, 2007, pp.101-3.
10. Fleet, J.F., "The Inscription on the Sohgaura Plate", *Journal of the Royal society*, 1907, pp.509-33.
11. *Ibid.*, p.519.
12. *Ibid.*, p.519.
13. Plural case ending has been used in this case instead of Dual as there is no dual in Prākṛt,
14. Sircar, D.C., "Notes on Some Inscriptions in The Collection of The Asiatic Society", *Journal of the Asiatic Society. Letters,* Vol.XLIX, No.4, 2007, pp.101-3; Vol.XVIII, No.1, 1952, pp.1-3.
15. Bühler, G., "The Sohgaura Copper Plate", *Indian Antiquary*, Vol.XXV, 1896, p.265.
16. Fleet, J.F., "The Inscription on The Sohgaura Plate", *Journal of the Royal society,* Kolkata, 1907, pp.509-33; Sircar, D.C., "Notes on Some Inscriptions in The Collection of The Asiatic Society", *Journal of the Asiatic Society. Letters,* Vol.XLIX, No.4, Kolkata, 2007, pp.101-3; Vol.XVIII, No.1, 1952, pp.1-3.
17. Fleet, J.F., "The Inscription on the Sohgaura Plate", *Journal of the Royal society*, 1907, pp.509-33. *cañcu* is identified with Kumāraviúya of Mahabharata i.e modern Vallia and Gazipur in Bihar by Moti Chandra in *Trade and trade routes in Ancient India,* New Delhi, 1977, Abhinav Publications, p.20.
18. Haragovind Das, Sheth Pandit T., *A Complete Prakṛt-Hindi Dictionary*, Delhi, Patna, Baranasi, Madras, 1963, Motilal Banarsidas, p.749. One of the meaning of the word 'vala' is *grahaṇ karna* or 'to take'. And there are also other meanings like *upar carna* or 'to load', *wapas ānā* or 'to toreturn' etc. but contextually we would like to consider 'to take'.
19. Fleet, J.F., "The Inscription on The Sohgaura Plate", *Journal of the Royal society, kolkata,* 1907, pp.519-20. Out of those two meanings The former and its correspondent sanskṛt word *kāryīyantē* is suggested by Bühler and the later with its correspondent Pāli alternative *kārayīyati* is suggested by Fleet. Both the meaning baer the almost same sense in respect to the context.
20. Krishnan, K.G., *Uttankita Vidyaranya Sanskrit Epigraph Series*, vol-2, Mysore, 1989, pp.104-5.
21. As we have in case of prohibitory orders like No Smoking which stands for the sentence No one is allowed to Smoke here by the order of the authority or Smoking here might lead to punitive measures.
22. Kangle, R.P., *The Kautīlya Arthaśāstra*, Part II, Bombay, 1963, University of Bombay, 2.21.1, p.141.
23. Ibid, 2.21.16, p.143.
24. Ibid, 2.21.7-9, p.142.

25. Contextually it may be cited here that Megasthenes' *Indica* refers to some royal officers called Agronomoy, and their duty was to maintain the roads and to establish plaques indicating the distance and directions. The two Laghman edicts of Aśoka were also issued and displayed on the roads with same purport. This trend actually reflected in symbolc representation of custom flag in Sohgaura inscription.
26. Choudhary Radhakrishna, *Kautilya's Political Ideas and Institutions,* Varanasi, 1971, Vidyavilas Press, pp.24, 86-92.
27. Kangle, R.P., *The Kautīlya Arthaśāstra*, Part II, Bombay, 1963, University of Bombay, 2.21.2, p.142.
28. *Abhijñana* and *mudrā* may also represent/reffer the two distinct things. *Abhijñana* was probably an official paper or the document on which the mudrā or the stamping was made.
29. Basak, R.G., *Kautilīya Arthaśāstra*, Kolkata, 1977, General Printers.
30. Kangle, R.P., *The Kautīlya Arthaśāstra*, Part II, Bombay, 1963, University of Bombay, 2.21.3, p.142. Here it is mentioned that, "For (goods) without the stamp the penalty double the dues."
31. Arthaśāstra mentions that, "in case of damage to the commodities (of traders) he (paṇyadhyakṣa) shuold show them favour from glut of commodities". See Kangle, R.P., *The Kautīlya Arthaśāstra*, Part II, Bombay, 1963, University of Bombay, 4.2.32, p.261.
32. In context of Mauryan administration, Sannidhata was the chief supervisor of the collection of revenue from the whole empire.

18

Padan Inscriptions:
Some New Observations

Dr. Suraj A. Pandit & Dr. Prachi Moghe

Padan is a lost site in Mumbai. The site was first reported by Pt. Bhagwanlal Indraji in his report on Sopara and Padan.[1] The site has been described by Pt. B. Indraji as follows,

"About eleven miles north of Bombay, and three miles north-east of Goregaon station on the Baroda railway, is a small range of hills whose northern extremity, jutting towards the deserted village of Akurli, goes by the name of PADAN. The Marathi word Padan corresponds to the Gujarati Padan and to the Hindi Padav, and means a place of encampment. The name Padan has been given to this hill, because during the rainy months the cattle from the neighbouring villages are taken to its dry flat top to save them from the mud and slime of the rice lands below. Many similar places are called Padan.

Padan Hill is from 180 to 200 feet above the level of the surrounding fields. It rises with an easy slope from the west, while on the east it is a sheer precipice. To the south it is connected with a range of small hills, and on the north it ends with a gradual slope. The surface of the top measures about 350 feet from north to south. It is somewhat broader in the south, narrowing northwards with a gradual downward slope. On the west much of the hill-top is on a higher level, like a raised platform. The hill lies five or six miles west of Kanheri, and the black cleft in which the Kanheri caves are cut can be clearly seen.

There is no building on the top of the hill. On the south appears something like the foundation of a wall, and on the north is a circular row of undressed stones. Neither of these are foundations of buildings; they are the sites of temporary huts erected during the rainy months by cattle-keepers. At the base of the hill to the west is a pond with a broken dam, which is almost dry in the fair season."

Present location of the site was difficult to identify due to change in landscape and rise in urban activities in Mumbai. Topo-sheet of 1942 does not give us any area call Padan in the map. Distance of the site given by Indraji is from Goregaon. An article by K.R.U. Todd has a map of microlith sites in Mumbai.[2] The map gives us the location of Padan hill where Todd had found some microlithic tools of the early period. Todds description of the site is interesting and give us some further clue in study. The description is as follows:

"On Padan hill at Kandivli, the microlithic horizon is overlaid by a sterile layer of black sand which, in its turn is capped by a pottery-layer of Early Buddhist Age. A small bas-relief of a deity was excavated from this layer." Todd dates these microliths to c. 500 BC.[3] This article help us to place the site of Padan in modern geographical context.

The survey of the region has proven that the site is located near Kandivli Western Express highway. It was in the vicinity of a deserted village 'Akurli'.[4] As authors understand that the present hill known as 'Bandongari' near 'Samata Nagar Police Station' is he Padan hill. The hill is covered today with large number of buildings and the northern side of the hill is occupied by 'Sports Authority of India'. It was supposed to be the large hill cut during the construction of Western Express Highway. Today Times of India press is located on the hill. The proximity to the 'Gorakshak Mandal' to the site confirms the location. It is also interesting to note that the part of the site of Padan was owned by the 'Gorakshak Mandal' till the recent past. Major portion of the site has been destroyed and now there are no traces of any of the inscriptions or symbols described by Indraji or microlith site reported by Todd. Thus we have to totally relay upon the description given by Pt. Bahagwanlal Indraji.

The report by Indraji talks about the total 12 symbols on this hill. 1. Gopadma, 2. Chakra, 3, 7 (a and b). Footprints, 4,5 and 6. Conch shell, 8. The Buddhist Trident, 9. Two Jugs (pots), 10. Jar, 11. Mirror with the round dick and handle, 12 Swastika.

Discussion on Symbols

These symbols are associated with some inscriptions. These are total 11 in numbers. The reading given by Indraji tally with the impressions published by him. The reading is as follows:

1. पवतस वासाअस आरोमो अपरिलो
2. कोसिकयस ऊदओ आरामो च
3. पवतो अभुंतो सिधवसति
4. बम्हचारि वि(म?)कराहि कुडबीका (णति?) दकातो
5. सधमुसल
6. मुसलदत्त

7. रामइकमो
8. नंदिपअं
9. मुसलदत्त
10. जिरासंघदत्त
11. ये धर्म्मा हेतुप्रभवा हेतुस्तेषां तथागतो ह्यवदत् तेषां च यो निरो(ध) एवं वादी महाश्रवण:

The first inscription is accompanied by swastika symbol. This symbol is seen in numerous Buddhist inscriptions. The inscription begins with this symbol. This is a left armed Swastik. There are no symbols associated with inscriptions 2, 3, and 4. Inscriptions 5, 6, 7 and 11 are engraved next to the footprints. Inscriptions 8, 9, 10 are engraved next to the Buddhist trident. Other symbols do not have any inscription associated with them.

Chronology:

There is no plan or any there details of the cave are available to us. Due to which it is very difficult to say anything about the date of this cave. Todd suggests this can be dated to 200 BC.[5] Though this is so there is no concrete evidence on the basis of which any date can be assigned. Inscriptions do not contain any date. Only paleographic dating o these inscriptions can help us to put these archaeological remains in chronological context.

Paleographically inscriptions 1 to 5 and 8 can be dated to 1st century CE. 6 and 7, 9 and 10 can be dated to 2nd-3rd century CE, and inscription 11 can be dated to 5th-6th century CE. It is difficult to assign any date to these symbols but they may be of the early date.

Discussion

Inscription shade some light on three phases in the development of local culture at Padan. Indraji summarizes his observations as follows:

"As the legend of Purna mentions a Brahmanical sage, and as there is a natural cave on the hill top fir for the residence of an ascetic, it may be inferred that the hill was once the residence of a Brahmanical sage; that some time later, about the first century after Christ, the footmarks and other symbols and six inscriptions, A, B, C, D, E and H were carved to connect the story of the sage with Buddha; that about a century later an attempt was made to connect the hill and its symbols with the Brahmanical story of Rama; and that in the sixth century Buddhist probably regarded the hill as holly, as some Buddhist of the Mahayana school carved on it the well-known Buddhist formula."

It is interesting to see that one of the inscriptions near a foot print make reference to 'Rama'. The creation myth of Konkan is associated with 'Bhargava Rama' which is also popularly kwon as Parshurama. One of the Nasik inscription give us the reference of Ramakunda at Sopara, the later legend confirms that this was associated with Parashurama and not the Dasharathi Rama. It is believed that Parashurama had created Konkan by pushing the sea behind. His arrow marked the boundary for the newly created land and seas had to give that land to Rama. There are numerous places shown from where this arrow was thrown. Though there is no evidence, this can be suggested that the footprint might have some with this legend, though not historically but culturally. Indraji suggests that the inscriptions referring to Musala and the symbols of footprints may have the early date than the inscription refereeing to Rama.[6] It is quite possible that this is a cultural memory which has been transformed in to the form of inscription in the later period. One cannot forget the present name of the hill i.e. '*Bandongari*' in this context.

It is interesting to note that one of the first five disciples Lakulisha, the founder of Pashupata school, is known to us as Kaushika. It is quite possible that the name mentioned of the ascetic in second inscription was a belonged to the school or tradition of Kaushika. This hypothesis suggests the early Pashupata affiliation of the site. Though this is so, there is no other historical evidence to suggest that the Pashupata Shaivism was popular in this region during this period.

These three phases, as suggested by Indraji indicate the transformation from Brahmanical to Buddhist. It is interesting to note that the authorship of 'Divyavadana' is assigned to Sarastivadin-s. Purna plays an important role even in the Mahasanghika Vinaya.[7] Sarvastvadin-á were supposed to be very influential in the region from 2nd to 6th century CE.[8] Thus one can say that the entire transition from Brahmanical to Buddhist must have taken place under the initiative of Sarvastivadin-s. Kanheri expanded at Magathane by having its own religious satellite settlement in second century CE.[9] The site of donated agricultural field in 2nd century CE and the later period monastery at Magathane is hardly 5 km away from the site.

There must have been the cult of Purna as suggested by literary and archaeological sources. It is interesting to note that there is a donation recorded at Kanheri in one of the inscriptions, given by Purnaka. He had given the donation of a Tadaga. Dr. Shobhana Gokhale suggests that he might have been from Sopara.[10] Though thre is no such reference seen in inscription, name of the donor is Purnaka and not Purna. It is not necessary that she should belong to Sopara, as his name suggests, he must have belong to the cult of 'Purna', which must be very popular in the region.

Observations:

1. Site initially was a Brahmanical site occupied by ascetics.
2. They probably belong to the Pashupata Sect.
3. The site was converted to Buddhism from Brahmanical affiliation after the conversion of masses in the region.
4. The process was initiated by most probably Sarvastivadin-s.

5. The cult of Purna which was popular in region must have been instrumental in the process of conversion of the site.
6. The story of Parashurama was probably associated with the hill as suggested by inscription as well as the modern name.

References

1. Indraji Bhagwanlal, 1882, *Antiquarian Remains at Sopara and Padan*, Education Society's Press, Mumbai.
2. 1984 (reprint), The Microlithic Industries of Mumbai, *Ancient India* number 6, 1950, ASI, Delhi. p.5.
3. *Ibid*, p.9.
4. Campbell J. M., 1882, Gazetteer of Bombay Presidency, Thana, Places of Interest. The village Akurli has been described under the description of the village Goregaon.
5. *Ibid*, p.9.
6. *Op. site*. pp.47-48.
7. Tatelman J., 2001, *The Glorious Deeds of Purna*, Motilal Banarasidas, Delhi.
8. Pandit S. A., 'Study of Architecture in the Light of Buddhist Nikayas: Kanheri a Case Study, *'A Bouquet of Indian Heritage Research and Management: Dr. Agam Prasad Felicitation'*, Agam Kala Prakashan, Delhi. 2015, pp.380-402.
9. Pandit S. A., 'Kanheri: the Sustain Patronage', '*Buddhism in Global Perspective, Vol. II*', Somaiya Publication, Mumbai. 2003, pp.465-480.
10. Gokhale S., 1991, *Kanheri Inscriptions*, DCPRI, Pune, p.86.

19

Numismatic Gleanings from the Corpus of Ass-curse Steles

Harshada Wirkud

Introduction

Ass-curse steles, a unique type of land or such grant or simply edicts, issued 10th - 11th century onwards, are inscription (inclusive of the Gaddhegaali i.e. the ass curse) bearing stones with a sculptural panel usually depicting copulation between a donkey and a woman. It is from this panel and the usually accompanied presence of a curse in the inscription which states that 'the miscreant's mother/wife will be copulated with a donkey as a punishment' is the reason that they are so termed. The Ass-curse Steles are thus extant proofs of corroborative cogent evidence in form of archaeological and epigraphical data. The coherent persistence of the nearly defined typology of these steles is probably only second to religious iconography. The depictive panel which pictorially represents the curse in toto, is perhaps a phenomena observed for the first time in case of direct correlation with the inscription.

These inscription-bearing steles are a veritable plethora of information of the period in which they were issued. They give us an enlightening insight with regards to the political, socio-religious as well as economic conditions of the times. This paper will deal with the numismatic evidence and it's analysis as obtained through these inscriptions.

Numismatics, simply defined is the study of or collection of currency which includes coins, paper money, tokens etc. However in a broader sense it also includes the economic and historical study of currency use and development over the period of time of its existence. One of the important sources of studying this history is inscriptions. Through epigraphs we come to know about the social, cultural, political as well as economical and such scenarios of the then contemporary world depending on the type of inscription. Economical aspect of the inscription may include information of the observed currency system and standards, tax system, changes in currency patterns, issues and such. This helps us rebuilt the economic history of the period on sound ground. Epigraphy and Numismatics thus are overlapping competences which if utilised diligently as tools of archaeology and even at an individual level can prove to be veritable mine of information.The corpus of Ass-curse steles is one such source of inscriptions which help us understand the economic aspect of the period in which they were issued as these are generally grant edicts.

Ass-Curse Steles (ACS)

Ass-curse steles, a unique type of land or such grant stones or simply edicts, issued 10th - 11th century onwards. They are inscription (inclusive of the Gaddhegaali i.e. the ass curse) bearing stones with a sculptural panel usually depicting copulation between a donkey and a woman. It is from this panel and the usually accompanied presence of a curse in the inscription which states that 'the miscreant's mother/wife will be copulated with a donkey as a punishment' is the reason that they are so termed. The Ass-curse Steles are extant proofs of corroborative cogent evidence in form of archaeological and epigraphical data. The coherent persistence of the nearly defined typology of these steles is probably only second to religious iconography. The depictive panel which pictorially represents the curse in toto, is perhaps a phenomena observed for the first time in case of direct correlation with the inscription.[1]

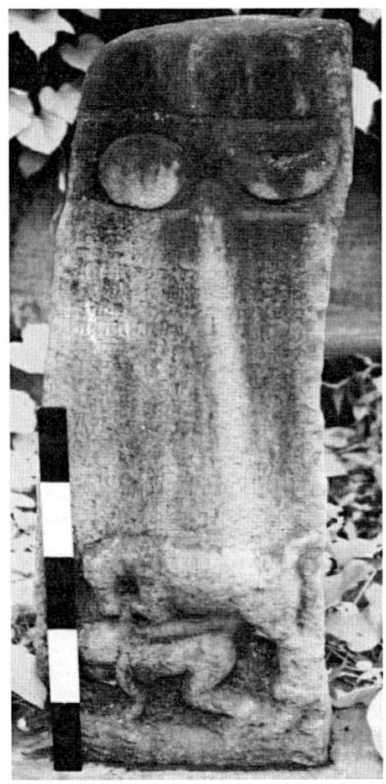

Fig.1. ACS from Akshi (©Harshada Wirkud/CEMS)

In case of these inscriptions the epigraphs have been deciphered; however no analysis or separate documentation alluding to the numismatic evidence was provided. It was simply stated.

Aim & Analysis

Thus, the main aim of this paper is to record and document separately the numismatic evidence as obtained from the ACS inscriptions. This paper is primarily a collated documentation of the numismatic data, in fact gleanings as gathered, with an elementary attempt to understand the terms and to evaluate theories that can help analyse the current data set and provide a base to elucidate further data. Advanced analysis will be the part of further studies and research and will include newly deciphered inscriptions and study of coins/coin hoards as obtained and attributed to the period and concerned issuing authorities.

Numismatics Gleanings based on issuances

Their first issuance is attributed to Shilaharas. There are approximately 17 known ACS of Shilaharas. Another 10 ACS's attributed to the Yadavas. There are 3-4 known ACS's of Vijayanagara Sangamas of which 3 from Goa and 1 from Maharashtra. We have one known each of Kadamba, Chalukya, Bahamani, Adil Shahi, and Alunayakaraya. Of these only 7 are monetary grants, around 16 are land grants, around 6 are edicts and rest deal with other donatory purposes like donation of an idol etc.[2]

Thus, based on the data obtained through the deciphered content following are few of the terms observed in the corpus of ACS. The weight of the currency mentioned, as per various texts, is added further[3]:

1. Drammas (as in cash, loosely equated): Gadhaiya Paisa type (53 grains)
2. Gadyanaka/Gadyana: 48 rattis/87.84 grains (Lilavati)
3. Dharana/Purana: 24 rattis (Lilavati) /32 rattis (Yajnyavalkyasmriti) /144 rattis / 320 rattis in case of gold (Kharepatan Plates)
4. Poruthi/Porutha drammas: equivalent to 8 ordinary drammas (Puratana Prabandha Sangraha)
5. Ratti: Abrus Precatorius seeds.

The coinage of Maharashtra in case of ACS thus varied from Dramma, Porutha Dramma, Dam, Gadyana, as well as Tanka (Vijayanagara-Goa).[4]

Discussion

The coinage as discussed above was quite a diverse one with Dramma being the most commonly used currency based on the inscriptional evidences followed by dam, tanka and Gadyana. Dam and Tanka are variants of Dramma. Thakkura Pheru in his Ganitasara equates 50 dramas with one tanka which when looking at the evidences seems silver issue.[5]

The term Dramma, abbreviated as 'dra' in many inscriptions (e.g. Shilahara Aparaditya II Lonad ACS uses the abbreviated 'dra') was based on the Roman weight standard derived from the Greek Drachma. These coins denoted the Indo-Sassanian or Gadhaiya type. They were supposedly issued in all three metals gold, silver and copper. However the term dramma was mostly used to denote silver coinage. In case of gold it was mentioned in the inscription by prefix 'Suvarna' but the gold coin issued was mostly Gadyana. Thus the use of the word dramma alluded to the adoption of the Drachm standard and its common usage to denote cash.

Another specific named coinage that we come across in the corpus is Porutha/ Poruthi Dramma. There are various theories with regards to this specific coin-term. Bhagwanlal Indraji connects these coins with Parthian Drachmas'. S.G Tulpule cautiously mentions that it may be related to a village called Poruth mentioned in Kharod Inscription of Kalchuri Ratnadev (III).[6]As per Deyell (1990: 113), the Poruthi drammas were issued from Gujarat Mint. "The Lekhapaddhati records that the paraupatha dramma or para patha dramma was stuck and thrice examined in Srimala/Bhillamala, modern Bhinmal, city north of Anhirwada Pattan." And which were then probably further circulated to the North Konkan region[7] from where we have many ACS documented.[8]

An almost blind numismatic continuity can be viewed here where the issues except for the Chhitaraja's coins that are found till date which bear his name. It also inadvertently suggests the projected - expected type of currency system for smooth running and stream lining of the kingdom in case of change of rulers. It helps us understand the process of assimilation and standardisation of different currencies over a spreading landscape not necessarily under one rule.The use of gadhaiya paisa, poruttha, dramma(if we take into consideration foreign origin theory too) points to the flourishing trade both with neighbouring regions as well as foreign and an almost standardised currency system facilitating trade as main source of revenue other than griha denaka or bhumi denaka tax.

Acknowledgements

I thank Dr. Mahesh Kalra, Convenor, CHAEN and Dr. Suraj Pandit, Parle Tilak Vidyalayas' Sathaye College for the opportunity. I also thank Dr. Shrikant Ganvir, Dr. Abhijit Dandekar, and Dr. Gopal Joge of Deccan College Post Graduate and Research Institute, Pune for the support and guidance. I thank Mrs. Mugdha Karnik, Mr. Samuel Nazareth and Dr. Kurush Dalal, from Centre of Extra-Mural Studies (CEMS), University of Mumbai, Kalina Campus for providing the opportunity of exploration. I thank the Ratan Tata trust for this study was part of the Project awarded by Ratan Tata Trust, titled, 'Documentation of Gadhegals from Maharashtra' under the aegis of CEMS.I am thankful to Archaeological Survey of India (ASI) and State Department of Archaeology and Museums and Directorate of Museums as well as Indian Railways, Mahalaxmi Office and various Museums that have been visited for this study. I thank all the individuals, family and friends for their help and support.

References

1. Wirkud Harshada, Public Perception of Ass-curse Steles and the Issue of Defacement Faced during Explorations in Maharashtra, *Heritage-Journal of Multidisciplinary Studies*, University of Kerala, 342.
2. Wirkud Harshada & Kurush Dalal, *Documentation of Gadhegals from Maharashtra*, (Unpublished Project Report), Centre for Archaeology, Centre of Extra-Mural Studies, Mumbai: University of Mumbai, 2016.
3. Ed. Mirashi V V, Corpus Inscriptionum Indicarum, Vol.VI, *Inscriptions of the Shilaharas*, DG ASI, Delhi, 1977, lxv.
4. Ed. Tulpule, S.G. *Pracheen Marathi Koriv Lekh* (In Marathi), Pune: Pune University, 1963, 101.

5. Habib Irfan, *Economic History of Medieval India*, 1200-1500, Pearson Education India, 2011, 22-24.
6. *Ibid.,* Tulpule, 101.
7. *Ibid.,* Habib, 22.
8. *Ibid.,* Wirkud & Dalal.

20

Epigraphs at Raigad Fort:
The Exceptional Ones..!

Dr. Milind Paradkar

Kautilya has stated that "A kingdom blessed with forts is invincible as the kingdom is able to defend itself and mount attacks on the enemy. A king who builds forts in naturally inaccessible regions of his kingdom at the minimum of costs truly makes his kingdom strong."

Chhatrapati Shivaji has proven Kautilya's words so right and that too after a period of 2000 years after being written. As a matter of fact, one can say that Chhatrapati Shivaji practiced the theory that Kautilya preached and thus set an example in India.

Chhatrapati Shivaji was coroneted as a sovereign king and ascended the throne in 1674. He built forts, floated a navy besides establishing war-ready armed forces and thus ensured the security and well-being of the region which was so far under the oppressive rule of the alien Muslim rulers. Within a short span of 30-35 years he brought under his control an area of approximately 100 miles width extending from Salher and Ahivantgad in northern Maharashtra to Karwar in the Konkan region in the south. With the help of the forts built on inaccessible, tall Sahyadri peaks covered by dense forests. Taking advantage of the very difficult geographical terrain under his command, he curbed the oppressive activities of the Muslim rulers like Aurangzeb and achieved results hitherto unknown. It was possible solely because of the support of the hill forts and sea forts that included impregnable forts built by him like Rajgad, Raigad, Pratapgad and Sindhudurg. Around 300-350 forts were proud witnesses of this era of planned freedom struggle and ultimately a just rule that changed the course of history in the long run.

His name and achievements are known to generations due to the forts, which still stand tall after centuries. His deeds have left an indelible mark on the history of the land

and a legacy that certainly will be remembered by generations and who will be proud about it for ages to come!

The mighty fort of Raigad, the capital of Chhatrapati Shivaji, is located at latitude 18 – 14' N and longitude 73 – 26' E. and is 2852ft above sea level. Based on the written sources, during the 12th century this fort was under the control of Vijaynagar empire. The 15th century saw Alauddin Shah 2nd brought the fort of Rairi under the Bahamani rule. The fort then moved under the rule of Nizamshah in 1479 and stayed with the Nizamshah until 1636 when it was taken over by Adilshah of Bijapur. During the Bijapur rule it was under the command of More-s of Javli region in Satara district. Chhatrapati Shivaji wrested this fort from More-s in 1656. Following this, other than the 44-year period from 1671 to 1733, the fort remained under the Maratha rule up until 1818 until the British arrived. This was almost 118 years. The 44-year period when Raigad was not under the Maratha rule, it was christened Islamgad when the forces of Mughal Emperor Aurangzeb took over this fort in 1689.

On the eastern side of the fort, approximately midway, lies a Shiva temple complex known by the name Jagadishwara. At the entrance of the temple complex is the Samadhi of Chhatrapati Shivaji, the spot where he was cremated. Historically speaking this is one of the most important places on Raigad due to the presence of the Samadhi.

The dimension of the temple area is around 120 ft long and 120 ft wide. Surrounding the entire temple on all sides are platforms 3ft tall and 10 ft wide. A wall of 6-7 ft in height protects the entire complex. Slit windows similar to the ones in the fortification walls surrounding the citadel are to be found here as well. The flooring of the entire complex is laid with basalt, the typical stone found in the Sahaydri. The complex has two entrances in the west as well as the east. The door on the eastern front is decorated. One may like to compare it with the entrance - Nagarkhana - of the King's court, as it looks like a small scaled replica of the court's entrance. There is a tiny staircase leading to the top of the temple nagarkhana from the inside. There are carvings of blooming lotuses on either side of the door on the outside. On the topmost corners of the nagarkhana carvings of Yaksha faces can be seen. Normally Yaksha faces adorn the doorframe of a Shiva temple. The nagarkhana has an arched doorway. There are remains of hinges, which were used to hold the wooden doors.

Just outside on the southern wall of the Nagarkhana is embedded the famous inscription on a 3' X 2' stone slab that reads as follows:

"प्रासादो जगदीश्वरस्य जगतामानन्दनोनुज्ञया।
श्रीमच्छत्रपतेः शिवस्य नृपतेःसिंहासने तिष्ठतः।।
शाके षण्नवबाणभूमिगणनादानन्दसंवत्सरे।
ज्यरेतिराजमुहूर्तकीर्तिमहिते शुक्लेशसार्पे तिथौ।।१।।

वापीकूपतडागराजिरूचिरैहर्म्यैवनैर्वीथिकैः।
स्तंभैःकुंभिगृहैर्नरेंद्रसदनैरभ्रंलिहैर्मीहिते।।
श्रीमद्रायगिरौ गिरामविषये हीराजिना निर्मितः।
यावच्चन्द्रदिवाकरौ विलसतस्तावत्समुज्जृंभते।।२।।"

This means that in the early morning of Jyeshta Shudha Trayodashi, Shalivahana year 1596, Chhatrapati Shivaji was coroneted and this is the day that he ascended the throne. This Shiva temple complex or the Prasada of Jagadishwara was built on that occasion. Hiroji Indulkar, the architect, built this beautiful fort which has wells, tanks, lakes, beautiful houses, streets, gardens, market place, decorative lofty pillars, elephant stables, and the king's palace that touches the clouds. It is wished that this magnificent fort would just remain so till the sun and the moon are adorning the skies.

There are only 3 locations in India where Chhatrapati Shivaji's name has been inscribed in stone. One is at the entrance of Shri Saptakoteshwar temple at Narve, in the state of Goa. it reads as:

श्रीसप्तकोटीश शके १५९०, किलकाब्दे कार्तिक कृष्ण पंचम्यां, सोमे श्रीशिवराज्ञा देवालयस्य प्रारम्भः

that the rebuilding of the temple of Shree Saptkoteshwara was initiated on the orders of Chhatrapati Shivaji and was started on kartika krushna panchami, Monday, Shake 1590. The second place his name is etched in stone is in Andhra Pradesh at the Jyotirlinga site of Shrishaila Mallikarjuna temple's southern Gopura, which is also known as Shivaji Gopuram ṣ saying that the Mallikarjuna temple was renovated at the behest of Chhatrapati Shivaji. The third location is at Raigad fort as has been described above.

This inscription at Raigad Fort is unique in many ways. As has been described earlier this is only the third instance of Chhatrapati Shivaji's name is found inscribed in a stone. Furthermore this is the one and only place in Maharashtra where the famous king finds a mention in an epigraph found so far. This epigraph is an only example where the occasion for building the fort, the name of the architect of the fort has been mentioned besides the specific date of the ceremony of coronation of Chhatrapati Shivaji. Archaeologically speaking, this is the only source of epigraphic information; to the existence of a king name Chhatrapati Shivaji, who was coroneted as a sovereign king on a particular day and at a particular fort called Raigad!

There are 3 steps to enter the Nagarkhana. On the centre of the middle step there is another epigraph that states:

सेवेचे ठायी तत्पर हिरोजी इंदुलकर.

Fort builder and architect Hiroji Indulkar's genius and the dedication to his master Chhatrapati Shivaji are worth sincere applause and so his humility and ability. This inscription is very similar to the seals of the ministers in the cabinet of Chhatrapati Shivaji, e.g.

श्री शिवचरणी तत्पर त्र्यंबकसुत मोरेश्वर निरंतर (seal of the Prime Minister)

or

श्री शिवचरणी तत्पर दत्तसुत अनाजी निरंतर (seal of the Secretary of State)

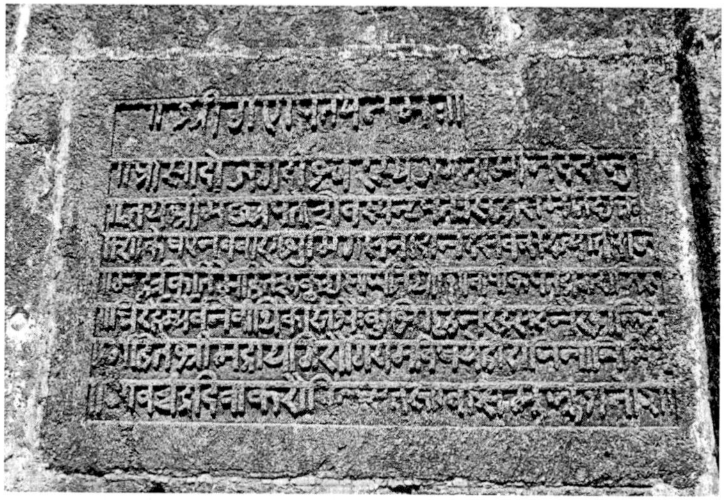

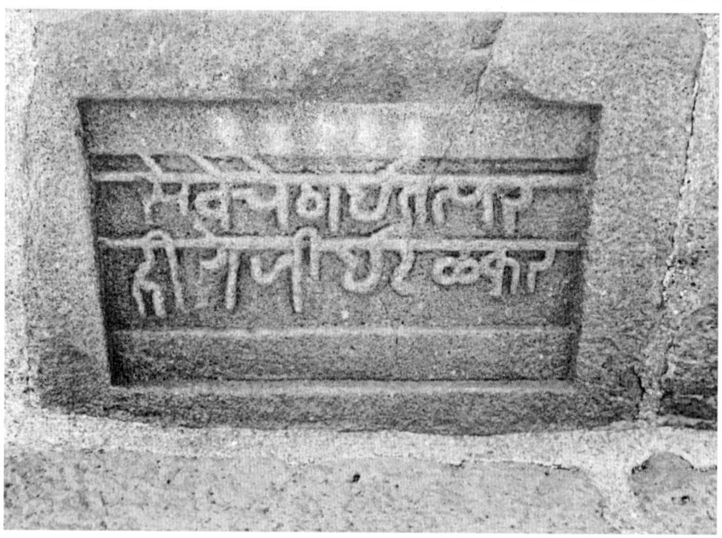

Based on the rhythm found in the wording of the three sentences, I strongly believe that this is surely the seal of the in-charge of the fort building department, architect Hiroji Indulkar, hitherto not found anywhere in the written records, and if so this is the only instance of a seal in the form of an epigraph..!

21

Comparing Nizam-ul-Mulk's Seals with Coins for the 'Independence' Debate

Dr. Mahesh A. Kalra

Introduction

Nizam-ul-Mulk Asaf Jah I (c. 1671-1748), born Mir Qamr-ud-din Khan and known as Chin Qulich Khan in the earlier part of his career, was a Mughal statesman of the highest pedigree also known as Khanazad in the later Mughal period. His family, beginning with his grandfather, Khwaja Abid (d. 1687), known as Qulich Khan and his father, Ghazi-ud-din Firuz Jang were important stakeholders in the Mughal 'Turani' establishment of Mughal Deccan right since the beginning of the reign of Emperor Aurangzeb in 1657-58.[1]

In the turmoil of the post-Aurangzeb era, the family of Ghazi-ud-din Firuz Jang fell upon hard times due to their policy of staying aloof in the two succession wars following the death of Aurangzeb and Shah Alam I within half a decade. However, the family emerged out of a self-imposed seclusion (much like Aurangzeb's in the second half of Shah Jahan's reign) in the era of Farrukhsiyar when the Sayyid brothers sought their support against other hostile factions of the Mughal nobility. This led to important postings for Chin Qulich Khan and other members of the family including his first cousin, Muhammad Amin Khan. In 1713, Chin Qulich Khan was appointed to the viceroyalty of Mughal Deccan by Farrukhsiyar on the recommendation of the Sayyid brothers with the title, Nizam-ul-Mulk Fateh Jang.[2]

In 1719, the Nizam-ul-Mulk's family and their followers colluded with a plot to execute the Sayyid brothers at the prompting of the new Emperor, Muhammad Shah and his mother, Qudasiya Begum. However, his cousin, Muhammad Amin Khan, an active colluderin the plot, emerged as the new Prime Minister of the Mughal Empire under the new dispensation.[3] However, Muhammad Amin Khan's sudden death at Agrawithin a year of his appointment propelled the Nizam-ul-Mulk to the vizierate of the Mughal Empire at Agra where he reached to assume office on 16 January 1722.[4]

However, the corrupt and debauched state of the Mughalcourt etiquette at Shahjahanabaddid not suit the dignified Nizam who had plans to revive the order and etiquette of Aurangzeb's era. Instead, the Nizam was mocked by Muhammad Shah's coterie as a 'Deccani monkey'.[5]

These circumstances forced the Nizam-ul-Mulk to turn back to Mughal Deccan to reclaim the viceroy's post after battling the Emperor's appointee, Mubariz Khan at the Battle of Shakharkheda on 11 October 1724. Post Mubariz Khan's defeat and death, the Nizam-ul-Mulk formally took over the administration of Mughal Deccan with only formal acknowledgement of suzerainty to the Mughal Emperor in form of Sikka and Khutba in the province. The Emperor on his part conferred the title 'Asaf Jah' on him with gifts and acceptance of his status as the Viceroy of Mughal Deccan. On his part, the Nizam-ul-Mulklargely stayed in Mughal Deccan improvising its administration and protecting it from the Marathas till the end of his life.[6]

Mughal and Maratha historians have long held that the Nizam-ul-Mulk declared himself 'independent' but the term 'independent' and labelling of the coinage of Mughal Deccan as 'Asaf Jahi' are terms to which the researcher strongly objects to in view of overwhelming evidence that the Nizam-ul-Mulk had not turned absolutely independent of the Mughal Empire but protected his and his domain's interests from the encroachment of Marathas and other players which might have undermined his authority in the region.

The third phase of the Nizam-ul-Mulk's career began with his victory over Mubariz Khan at Shakarkheda in October 1724 and Muhammad Shah was forced to bestow honours on the victor and recognize him as the Viceroy of Mughal Deccan. The period lasted till the end of the reign and has been termed as a period of independence by many historians and modern numismatists.[7] The period can be viewed more ambiguously as the Nizam-ul-Mulk strived to improve the conditions of Mughal Deccan by fending off Maratha rights on the region through both diplomatic as well as military actions. The Nizam-ul-Mulk's relations with the Marathas was complex at the best saw different phases in the period before Shakarkheda and after Shakarkheda quite well elaborated by his modern biographer, Yusuf Husain Khan on the basis of various contemporary correspondences of the Nizam-ul-Mulk with Maratha functionaries at both Satara and Kolhapur courts.[8]

Coming back to the Nizam's 'independence' from the Mughal centre, apart from coins and other literary/historical evidences, we come across the official seals of the Nizam-ul-Mulk Asaf Jah I which bear the epithet 'Fidwi-i-Muhammad Shah' (Servant of Muhammad Shah) which point to his continuance of the allegiance to the Emperor.[9] Prof.

M.A. Nayeem argues these as the proof of the Nizam's loyalty to the Mughal Emperor apart from historical sources quoted by Yusuf Khan.

Looking closely at the seals of the First Nizam, one sees the seal claim a military status for the Nizam (Seal 1) which claims the title Sipah Salar (Military commander) for the Nizam-ul-Mulk along with the title Asaf Jah conferred upon him by Muhammad Shah after the former's victory over the imperial appointee Mubariz Khan at Shakharkelda.[10] However, on closely examining Seal no. 2 which is of Inayat-ullah Beg, a sub-ordinate noble of the Nizam-ul-Mulk, we find the title, *Fidwi-i- Nizam-ul-Mulk Bahadur Asaf Jah* meaning 'Servant of the Nizam-ul-Mulk' with no reference to the Mughal Emperor. Additionally, the date on the seal is A. H. 1140 with the regnal year 15. Emperor Muhammad Shah's regnal year in A.H. 1140 would have been RY 10 but the seal has Regnal Year 15. This regnal year would have corresponded to A.H. 1125 which in turn corresponds to 1713-1714 C. E. Examininghistorical dates and events corresponding in Mughal Deccan to 1713-1714 C.E., we find the most prominent is the commencement of the Nizam-ul-Mulk's 'first viceroyalty', as his biographer Yusuf Khan calls it, in June 1713.[11] This matching of dates highlights the fact that the Nizam-ul-Mulk's coterie considered this date as the commencement of his 'reign' over Mughal Deccan, practically independent of the Mughal Emperor; though during that period, the Nizam was yet very susceptible to imperial interference due to the presence of the rival power of the Sayyid brothers. This seal seeks to thus build a myth of dating the Nizam's actual rule back by a decade or so before it began in 1724.

Official Seals of Nizam-ul-Mulk Asaf Jah I and his officers during Muhammad Shah's reign (1719-1748) (Courtesy: Dr. M. A. Nayeem, Hyderabad)

Legend B-T: SIPAH SALAR/ASAF JAH NIZAM-UL-MULK/ BAHADUR/FIDWI BADSHAH GHAZI/MUHAMMAD SHAH SANAH 10

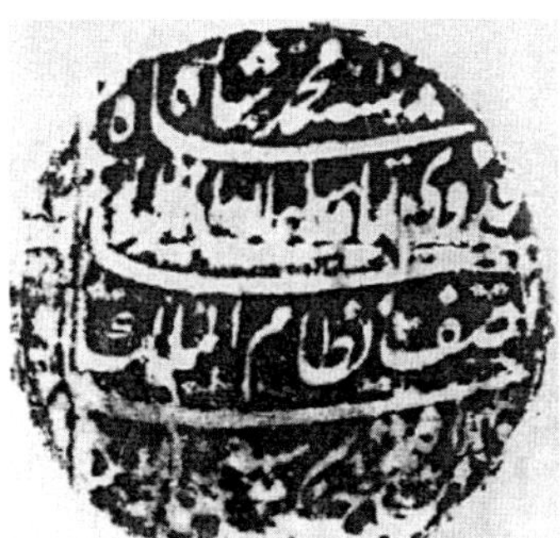

Seal # 1

Legend: INAYAT-ULLAH (Top line) BEG FIDWI/ NIZAM-UL-MULK BAHADUR 1140 AH RY 15/ASAF JAH

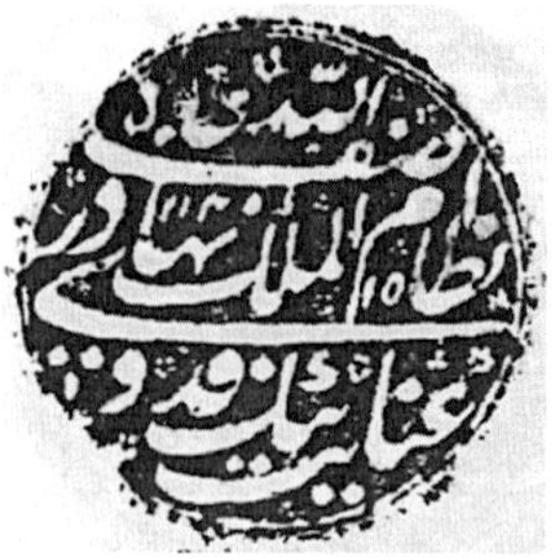

Seal # 2

Asaf Jahi Officer Murari Das A.H. 1142 Seal
Image Courtesy: Prof. M.A. Nayeem

Legend: Murari Daas/Fidwi/Asaf Jah AH 1142

Seal # 3

Yusuf Khan Asaf Jahi Officer? Seal AH (115)9/RY 29
Image Courtesy: Prof. M.A. Nayeem

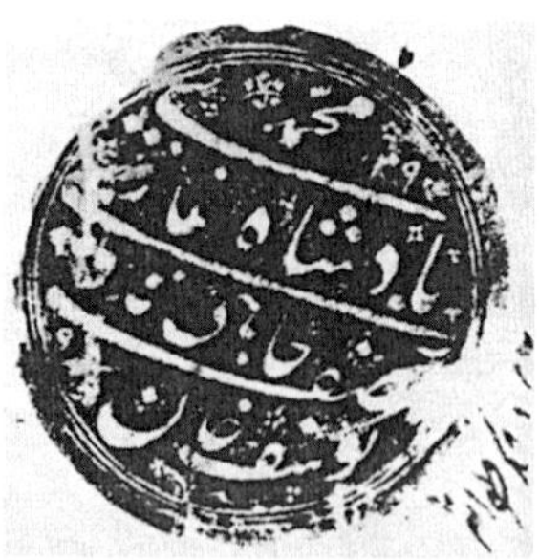

Legend T-B: Yusuf Khan/Asaf Jahi Fidawi/ Badshah Ghazi/Muhammad Shah RY 29

Seal# 4

However, the continued issuing of coins and reading of the Khutba in the name of the Mughal Emperor by the Nizam-ul-Mulk makes the claim of complete independence a little premature as the Nizam continued the outward charade of obedience for multiple reasons. The chief reason may be the fear of a reprisal under a stronger emperor after

Muhammad Shah. Other reasons include a genuine regard for the House of Timur as a loyal grandee of the Mughals as he was a Turani himself.[12]

Another reason for maintaining the 'façade' of Mughal Deccan (if the Nizam-ul-Mulk was capable of crystal gazing into the future) would be to appropriate the legitimacy of the Mughals long after the original branch in Delhi had withered away.[13] Hence, though he became autonomous in all administrative aspects from the imperial centre, he chose to demonstrate utmost loyalty to the Emperor. Ramusack argues for a different classification for the later established state of Haidarabad among other successor states.[14]

In the end, it may be concluded that though the Nizam-ul-Mulk did establish a proto-successor state by carving out of major areas of Mughal Deccan virtually free of central control by disabling the checks and balances by imperial officers, he continued to keep its institutions and traditions intact out of both traditional deference and pragmatic reasons.

References

1. Yusuf Hussain Khan, *Nizam-ul-Mulk Asaf Jah I - Founder of the Haidarabad State,* D. B. Taraporevala Sons & Co., Bombay, 1936, pp.1-41.
2. Ibid. p.65.
3. Ibid. p.136.
4. Ibid. p.142.
5. Uday S. Kulkarni Lecture on 'Bajirao Peshwa and Nizam-ul-Mulk' at Vasant Vykhanamala, Pune on 28/04/2016 on https://www.youtube.com/watch?v=1_Aq6pvhGAw. The Nizam was mocked as 'the old monkey from Deccan' for his archaic ways of dressing and adhering to the imperial court etiquette. Dr. Kulkarni attributes the quote to Khan Dauran, 'a close friend of Muhammad Shah' from a later Urdu source.
6. Munis D. Faruqui, 'At Empire's End: The Nizam, Hyderabad and Eighteenth-century India' in Richard Eaton et al eds *Expanding Frontiers in South Asian and World History ș Essays in Honour of John F. Richards,* Cambridge University Press, New Delhi, 2013, pp.1-38.
7. Discussions with Jan Lingen at the Oriental Numismatic Society Meeting in Tuebingen, Germany (3 May 2015) and Dr. K. K. Maheshwari, co-author, *Maratha Mints & Coinage* (September 2010).
8. Khan, *Nizam-ul-Mulk,* pp.180-194.
9. M. A. Nayeem, *Mughal Administration of Nizam-ul-Mulk Asaf Jah I (1720-1748),* Jaico Publishers, Bombay, 1985, pp.20-24.
10. Khan, *Nizam-ul-Mulk,* p.177.
11. Ibid. p.66.
12. Khan, *Nizam-ul-Mulk,* pp.157-58. A note in the Nizam's last advice to his successor, he stresses upon subservience to the House of Timur in various ways.
13. Munis D. Faruqui, 'At Empire's End', pp.28-30.
14. Barbara Ramusack, *The New Cambridge History of India III. 6 The Indian Princes and their States,* South Asian edition, 2008, pp.24-26.